T0221024

Digital Forensics and Internet of Things

Scrivener Publishing
100 Cummings Center, Suite 541J
Beverly, MA 01915-6106

Publishers at Scrivener
Martin Scrivener (martin@scrivenerpublishing.com)
Phillip Carmical (pcarmical@scrivenerpublishing.com)

This edition first published 2022 by John Wiley & Sons, Inc., 111 River Street, Hoboken, NJ 07030, USA
and Scrivener Publishing LLC, 100 Cummings Center, Suite 541J, Beverly, MA 01915, USA

For more information about Scrivener publications please visit www.scrivenerpublishing.com.

y Global Headquarters
River Street, Hoboken, NJ 07030, USA

tails of our global editorial offices, customer services, and more information about Wiley prodsit us at www.wiley.com.

ess Cataloging-in-Publication Data

76878-4

bay.Com
ssell Richardson

d Minion Pro by Manila Typesetting Company, Makati, Philippines

3 2 1

Digital Forensics and Internet of Things

Impact and Challenge

Edited by

Anita Gehlot
Uttaranchal Institute of Technology, Uttaranch

Rajesh Singh
Uttaranchal Institute of Technology, Uttara

Jaskaran Si
Forensic Sciences, Sharda U

and

Neeta Raj
Biotechnology & BioSciences, Lovel

A
tr
wi
is a

Wil
111

For d
ucts v

Limit
While t
resentati
specifica
ability or
tives, writ
website, o
tion does n
tion, websit
understandi
strategies co
where approp
commercial d
Further, reade
between when

Library of Cong

ISBN 978-1-119-

Cover image: Pixa
Cover design by R

Set in size of 11pt a

10 9 8 7 6 5 4

Contents

Preface

This book provides an opportunity to readers in the era of digitalization of forensic science and application of Internet of Things for the provision of technical benefits to the stakeholders. IoT forensics attempts to align its workflow to that of any forensics practice—investigators identify, interpret, preserve, analyse and present any relevant data. Like any investigation, a timeline is constructed, and, with the aid of smart devices providing data, investigators might be able to capture much more specific data points than in a traditional crime.

Currently, there exists no defined and accepted standard for IoT forensic investigations. This can be attributed in part to the heterogeneous nature of IoT.

Chapters 1-8 culminates in the amalgamation of Xilix FPGA and Xilix IP cores, VANET and IOT. The application of such tools in the forensic sciences is the gist of the book. However, Chapters 9-15 discuss the core aspects of machine learning in the areas of healthcare, criminal profiling and digital cyber investigation.

Cyber and digital frauds are the hallmark of today's era. There is an urgent need to produce knowledgeable resources for curbing such crimes; thus, this book will serve as a perfect instance for getting the best source of expertise. Additionally, it serves as a revolutionary merit for identification and apprehension of criminals in a smarter way.

Case studies related to digital and cyber forensics is a key feature of the book. The content of chapters serves as a jewel in the crown for law enforcement agencies, advocates, forensic experts and students. Hence, we hope the book is an asset for readers and users as they become aware of the ubiquitous societal issues of digital and cybercrimes. Finally, we owe a large debt of gratitude to Scrivener Publishing and Wiley and all authors of the book in particular, for their continued support and patience.

Prof. (Dr.) Anita Gehlot
Uttaranchal University, India

Prof. (Dr.) Rajesh Singh
Uttaranchal University, India

Dr. Jaskaran Singh
Sharda University, India

Dr. Neeta Raj Sharma
Lovely Professional University, India

The Editors
February 2022

1

Face Recognition–Based Surveillance System: A New Paradigm for Criminal Profiling

Payal Singh, Sneha Gupta, Vipul Gupta, Piyush Kuchhal and Arpit Jain*

Electrical and Electronics Engineering Department, UPES, Dehradun, India

Abstract

Security is the most important aspect in any spheres. We have to ensure these technologies evolve along with the advancement of various technology in the field of machine vision and artificial intelligence. The system of facial detection has become a topic of interest. It is widely used for human identification due to its capabilities that give accurate results. It is majorly used for security purposes. This manuscript provides method of face detection and its applications. Using this method, locking system will be designed to ensure safety and security in all types of places. Surveillance systems help in close observation and looking for improper behavior. Then, it performs actions on the data that has been provides to it.

Keywords: Face recognition, python, Raspberry Pi, deep learning, locking system, image processing, eigen faces, fisher faces

1.1 Introduction

Face detection is the method which is pre-owned to identify or verify an individual's identity using their face. There can also be image, video, audio, or audio-visual element given to the system. Generally, the data is used to access a system or service. This can be performed in two variations depending on its application. First is when the facial recognition system is taking the input (face) for the first time and registering it for analysis.

**Corresponding author*: arpit.eic@gmail.com

Anita Gehlot, Rajesh Singh, Jaskaran Singh and Neeta Raj Sharma (eds.) Digital Forensics and Internet of Things: Impact and Challenges, (1–18) © 2022 Scrivener Publishing LLC

Second is when the user is authenticated prior to being registered. In this, the incoming data is checked from the existing data in the database, and then, access or permission is granted.

The most important aspect of any security system is to properly identify individuals entering or taking an exit through the entrance. There are several systems that use passwords or pins for identification purposes. But these types of systems are not very effective as these pins and passwords can be stolen or copied easily. The best solution to this is using one's biometric trait. These are highly effective and useful. This system is designed for prevention of security threats in exceptionally secure regions with lesser power utilization and more dependable independent security gadget.

In this paper [1], the researcher has explained about the ongoing development in subject of facial acknowledgment, and executing features check along with acknowledgment proficiently at extent shows genuine difficulties at present methodologies. Here, we introduce a framework, called FaceNet, which straightforwardly takes in planning from facial pictures till the minimal Euclidean space which removes straightforwardly relate to the proportion of features likeness. When its area has been created, undertakings, like check with bunching, can handily executed apply quality strategies followed by FaceNet embeddings as peak vectors. In [2], the creators have expressed their technique using a significant convolutional network ready to directly smooth out the genuine introducing, rather than a moderate bottleneck layer as in past significant learning moves close. To get ready, we use triplets of by and large changed organizing/non-planning with face patches made using an original online threesome mining strategy. The benefit of our strategy is much more conspicuous real capability: We achieve top tier face affirmation execution using only 128-bytes per face. On the extensively used Named Countenances in the Wild (LFW) dataset, our structure achieves another record exactness of 99.63%. Our structure cuts the misstep rate conversely with the best dispersed result by 30% on both datasets. We likewise present the idea of consonant embedding, which portray various variants of face embedding (delivered by various organizations) that are viable to one another and consider direct correlation between one another. This paper [3] presents colossal extension face dataset named VGGFace2. The dataset contains 3.31 million pictures of 9,131 subjects, with a typical of 362.6 pictures for each subject. Pictures are downloaded from Google Picture Look and have colossal assortments in present, age, edification, identity, and calling (for instance, performers, contenders, and government authorities). The dataset was accumulated considering three goals: to have both incalculable characters and besides a gigantic number of pictures for each character; to cover a tremendous extent of stance, age, and personality; and to restrict the imprint upheaval. We depict how the dataset was assembled, explicitly the robotized and manual isolating stages to ensure a high accuracy for the photos of each character. To assess face affirmation execution using the new dataset, we train ResNet-50 (with and without Crush and-Excitation blocks) Convolutional Neural Organizations on VGGFace2, on MS-Celeb-1M, and on their affiliation and show that readiness on VGGFace2 prompts further developed affirmation execution over stance and age. Finally, using the models ready on these datasets, we display state of the art execution on all the IARPA Janus face affirmation benchmarks, for instance, IJB-A, IJB-B, and IJB-C, outperforming the previous top tier by an enormous edge. Datasets and models are straightforwardly open [4, 5] Late profound learning-based face detection strategies have accomplished extraordinary execution, yet it actually stays testing to perceive exceptionally low-goal question face like 28 × 28 pixels when CCTV camera is far from the gotten subject. Such face with especially low objective is completely out of detail information of the face character diverged from normal objective in a presentation and subtle relating faces in that. To this end, we propose a Goal Invariant Model (Edge) for having a tendency to such cross-objective face affirmation issues, with three indisputable interests.

In [6, 7] The ANN requires 960 inputs and 94 neurons to yield layer in order to recognize their countenances. This organization is two-layer log-sigmoid organization. This exchange work is taken on the grounds that its yield range (0 to 1) is ideal for figuring out how to yield Boolean qualities. In [8], face recognition utilizing profound learning strategy is utilized. Profound learning is a piece of the broader gathering of AI strategies dependent on learning information portrayals, instead of work oriented calculations. Training is overseen, semi-coordinated, and solo. Combining profound training, the framework has enhanced every now and then. A few pictures of approving client are utilized as the information base of framework [9]. Face recognition is perhaps the main uses of biometrics-based validation framework over the most recent couple of many years. Face recognition is somewhat recognition task design, where a face is ordered as either known or obscure after contrasting it and the pictures of a realized individual put away in the information base. Face recognition is a test, given the certain fluctuation in data in light of arbitrary variety across various individuals, including methodical varieties from different factors like easing up conditions and posture [10]. PCA, LDA, and Bayesian investigation are the three most agent subspace face recognition draws near. In this paper, we show that they can be bound together under a similar system. We first model face contrast with three segments: inborn distinction, change contrast, and commotion. A bound together structure is then built by utilizing this face contrast model and a definite subspace investigation on the three parts. We clarify the natural relationship among various subspace techniques and their exceptional commitments to the extraction of separating data from the face distinction. In view of the system, a bound together subspace examination strategy is created utilizing PCA, Bayes, and LDA as three stages. A 3D boundary space is built utilizing the three subspace measurements as tomahawks. Looking through this boundary space, we accomplish preferred recognition execution over standard subspace strategies. In this [11], face recognition frameworks have been commanding high notice from business market perspective, just, as example, recognition field. Face recognition has gotten significant consideration from explores in biometrics, design recognition field and PC vision networks. The face recognition frameworks can extricate the highlights of face and look at this with the current data set. The faces considered here for examination are still faces. Feature recognition of faces from still and clip pictures is arising as a functioning examination region. The present paper is figured dependent on still or video pictures caught by a web cam [12]. In this, they portray a multi-reason picture classifier and its application to a wide combination of picture gathering issues without the compensation of plan precision. Yet, the classifier was at first developed to address high substance screening; it was found incredibly effective in picture request tasks outside the degree of Cell Science [13]. Face acknowledgment is a specific and hardcase of article acknowledgment. Countenances are very sure things whose most normal appearance (forward looking countenances) by and large seems to be similar. Inconspicuous changes make the appearances remarkable. In this manner, in a customary incorporate space, forward looking appearances will outline a thick group, and standard model acknowledgment techniques will all things considered miss the mark to segregate between them. There are two essential sorts of the face acknowledgment systems. The first is to check if an individual excellent before a camera is a person from a bound social affair of people (20–500 individuals) or not. Generally, such structures are used to will control to structures, PCs, etc., the peculiarities of such systems are steady of response and little affectability to the checking singular position and appearance evolving. Frameworks of the resulting sort recognize a person by photo looking in a tremendous informational collection or insist its nonattendance. Such a structure should work with an informational index containing 1,000–1,000,000 pictures. It might work in detached manner. We endeavor to design a plan of the ensuing kind [14].

Face recognition has gotten significant consideration from scientists in biometrics, PC vision, design recognition, and psychological brain research networks due to the expanded consideration being given to security, man-machine correspondence, content-based picture recovery, and picture/video coding. We have proposed two mechanized recognition standards to propel face recognition innovation. Three significant assignments associated with face recognition frameworks are (i) face identification, (ii) face demonstrating, and (iii) face coordinating. We have built up a face recognition calculation for shading pictures within the sight of different lighting conditions just as unpredictable foundations [15]. Like a unique finger impression search framework, face acknowledgment innovation can help law authorization offices in recognizing suspects or finding missing people. To begin with, RIM is a novel and brought together profound design, containing a Face Hallucination sub-Net (FHN) and a Heterogeneous Acknowledgment sub-Net (HRN), which are commonly academic beginning to end. Second, FHN is an especially arranged tri-way generative quantitative and abstract assessments on a couple benchmarks show the power of the proposed model over the state of human articulations. Codes and models will be conveyed upon affirmation [16]. In this paper, as per the creator, the facial acknowledgment has become a central issue for a staggering number of subject matter experts. As of now, there are a phenomenal number of methodology for facial acknowledgment; anyway, in this investigation, we base on the use of significant learning. The issues with current facial acknowledgment convection structures are that they are made in non-mobile phones. This assessment intends to develop a facial acknowledgment structure completed in a computerized aeronautical vehicle of the quadcopter type. While it is legitimate, there are quadcopters prepared for recognizing faces just as shapes and following them; anyway, most are for no specific explanation and entertainment. This investigation bases on the facial acknowledgment of people with criminal records, for which a neural association is ready. The Caffe framework is used for the planning of a convolutional neural association. The system is made on the NVIDIA Jetson TX2 motherboard. The arrangement and improvement of the quadcopter are managed without any planning since we need the UAV for conforming to our requirements. This assessment hopes to decrease fierceness and bad behavior in Latin America [17]. The proposed method is coding and translating of face pictures, stressing the huge nearby and worldwide highlights. In the language of data hypothesis, the applicable data in a face picture is separated, encoded, and afterward contrasted and a data set of models. The proposed strategy is autonomous of any judgment of highlights (open/shut eyes, distinctive looks, and with and without glasses) [18]. This paper gives a short study of the basic concepts and calculations utilized for AI and its applications. We start with a more extensive meaning of machine learning and afterward present different learning modalities including supervised and solo techniques and profound learning paradigms. In the remainder of the paper, we examine applications of machine learning calculations in different fields including pattern recognition, sensor organizations, oddity location, Internet of Things (IoT), and well-being observing [19]. Future registering (FC) is an innovation of genuine Web of things on distributed computing concerning IT intermingling that has arisen quickly as an energizing new industry and life worldview. Future figuring is being utilized to incorporate the cloud, huge information, and cloud server farms that are the megatrends of the processing business. This innovation is making another future market that is unique in relation to the past and is developing toward continuously dissolving the current market. Web of things is a huge and dynamic region and is advancing at a quick speed. The acknowledgment of the Web of things vision brings ICT innovations nearer to numerous parts of genuine confronting major issues like a dangerous atmospheric deviation, climate security, and energy saving money on distributed computing. Cutting edge innovations in detecting, preparing, correspondence, and administrations are prompting IoT administration in our life like industry, armed force, and life ideal models on distributed computing climate [20]. At present, the quantity of robberies and character extortion has regularly been accounted for and has become huge issues. Customary ways for individual recognizable proof require outer component, like key, security secret word, RFID card, and ID card, to approach into a private resource or entering public space. Numerous cycles, for example, drawing out cash from banks requires secret word. Other such stopping in private space would likewise require stopping ticket. For certain houses, the house key is vital. Be that as it may, this strategy additionally has a few burdens, for example, losing key and failing to remember secret phrase. At the point when this occurs, it tends to be bothered to recuperate back.

1.2 Image Processing

Face recognition system is subcategorized in two segments. The primary includes processing of the image, and the secondary includes techniques for recognition.

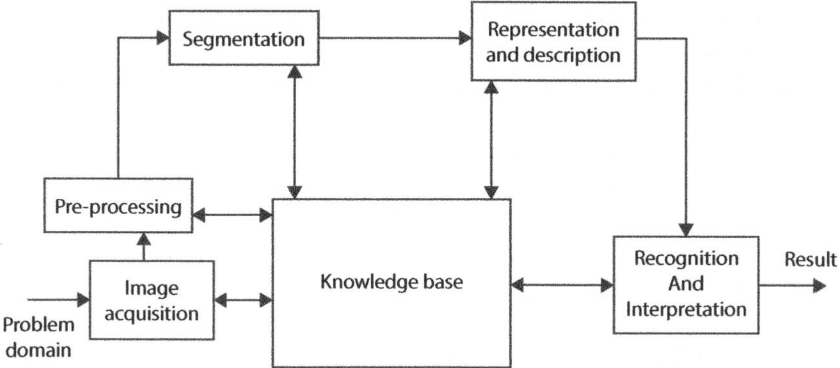

Figure 1.1 Fundamental steps of image processing in face recognition.

The processing of the image segment includes of image accession, image pre-processing, image segmentation, image description, and image recognition. The second part includes the use of artificial intelligence.

Fundamental steps in image processing are (as shown in Figure 1.1):

a. Image accession: to obtain an image digitally.
b. Image pre-processing: intensify the image in processes that increment the probability of advancement of the additional procedures.
c. Image segmentation: divide a given image in its elemental segment of parts.
d. Image representation: transform the given data into a suitable manner for the further procedure.
e. Image description: bring out the attribute which outcomes in some computable intelligence of interest of parts that are primary for distinguishing one class of parts from another.
f. Image recognition: allocate a tag to the parts based on the data delivered from its representation.

1.3 Deep Learning

It is a machine-based program which imitates the function of human intelligence. It can be considered as a subdivision of machine learning. As machine learning uses simpler concepts, and the deep learning makes used artificial neural networks in order to mimic how humans think and learn.

This learning is categorized into supervised, semi-supervised, or unsupervised.

Deep learning can be constructed with the help of connected layers:

- The foremost layer is known as the input layer.
- The bottom-most layer is known as the output layer.
- All the in between layers are known as the hidden layers. Here, the word deep indicates the connections between different the neurons.

Figure 1.2 depicts a neural network consisting of an input layer, a hidden layer, and an output layer. The hidden layers consist of neurons. Here, the neurons are interlinked with one another. The neurons help to proceed and transfer the given signal it accepts from the above layer. The stability of signal depends upon the factors of weight, bias, and the activation function.

A deep neural network produces accuracy in numerous tasks and might be from object detection to face recognition. This does not require any kind of predefined knowledge exclusively coded which indicates that it can learn automatically.

The Deep Learning process includes the following:

- Understanding the problem
- Identifying the data
- Selecting the Deep Learning algorithm
- Training the model
- Testing the model

Deep neural network is a very strong tool in order to construct and predict an attainable result. It is an expert in pattern discovery and prediction

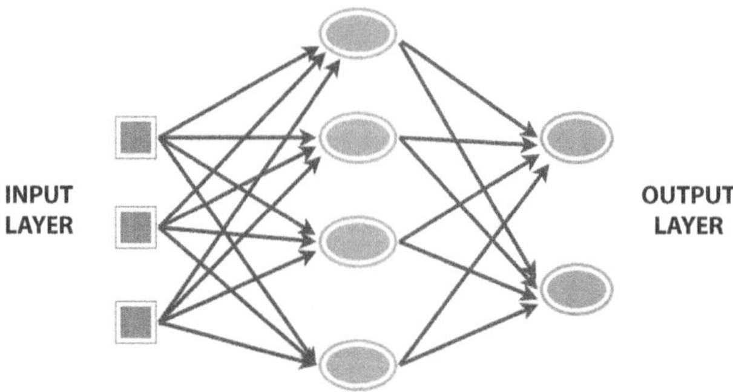

Figure 1.2 Layers of the model.

that is knowledge-based. Deep learning algorithms are keen to provide 41% more accurate results when compared to machine learning algorithm in case classification of image and 27% better fit in case of recognizing of face and 25% in recognizing of voice.

1.3.1 Neural Network

A neural network is an instrument that is designed to model in the similar way in which the brain responds or executes a task or function; it is usually simulated in digital computer-based software or carried out by using electronic components. It can resemble the brain in the following aspects:

- The knowledge is obtained by the network from its surrounding with the help of a learning procedure.
- Interneuron link strength, known as synaptic weight, is used to accumulate the obtained knowledge.
- The process that is operated to execute the learning procedure is known as the learning algorithm; the purpose of which is to reform the synaptic weights of the network in a well-organized mode to accomplish the desired layout objective.
- It is also possible to improve its own topology.
- Neural network is also mentioned in literature as neuro-computers, connectionist network, and parallel distributed processor.
- Neural network attains its computing power at the beginning from its power of computer at first from the massively side-by-side distributed arrangement and next from its potential to learn and then generalize.
- Generalization leads to the neural network constructing logical outputs for inputs not encountered throughout training (learning).

An ANN is specified by the following:

- Neuron model: Data processing component of the neural network.
- An architecture: A group of neurons along with connections connecting neurons.
- A training algorithm: It is used for instructing the Neural network by changing the weights to model a selected training task correctly on the instructing examples.

1.3.2 Application of Neural Network in Face Recognition

Face recognition implies comparing a face with the saved database of faces to recognize one in the given image. The associated process of face detecting is directly relevant to recognizing the face as the images of the face captured must be at first analyzed and then identified, before they get recognized. Face detection through an illustration assists to focus on the database of the system, improving the systems speed and performance.

Artificial Neural Network is used in face recognition because these models can imitate the neurons of the human brain work. This is one of the foremost reasons for its role in face recognition.

1.4 Methodology

1.4.1 Face Recognition

Face acknowledgment is subject to the numerical features of a face and is probably the most natural approach to manage face affirmation. It is one of the first robotized face affirmation structures. Marker centers (position of eyes, ears, and nose) were used to build a component vector (distance between the centers, point between them). The affirmation was performed by ascertaining the Euclidean distance between included vectors of a test and reference picture. Such a technique is vigorous against changes in enlightenment by its temperament; however, it has an immense disadvantage: The precise enlistment of the marker focuses is confounded, even with cutting edge calculations. Probably, the most recent work on mathematical face recognition was reported by Mulla M.R. [20]. A 22-dimensional component vector was utilized and it was investigated that huge datasets have appeared, that mathematical highlights alone may not convey sufficient

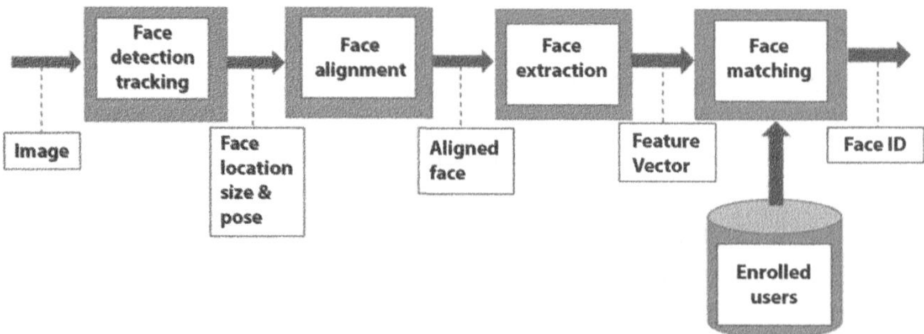

Figure 1.3 Structure of face recognition system.

data for face Recognition. Figure 1.3 depicts the detailed structure of face recognition system.

1.4.2 Open CV

OpenCV (Open-Source Computer Vision) is a famous library developed by Intel in 1999. This platform has various libraries. It helps in real-time image processing and includes various algorithms. It is equipped with programming interface to various languages like C++, C, and Python.

OpenCV 2.4 has a very useful new face recognizer class for face recognition. The currently available algorithms are as follows:

- Eigenfaces (**createEigenFaceRecognizer()**)
- Local Binary Patterns Histogram (**createLBPHFaceRecognizer()**)
- Fisher faces (**createFisherFaceRecognizer()**)

1.4.3 Block Diagram

This framework is controlled by Raspberry Pi circuit. Raspberry Pi electronic board is worked on battery power supply and remote web availability by utilizing USB modem; it incorporates camera, PIR movement sensor, LCD, and an entryway, as shown in Figure 1.4. At first approved

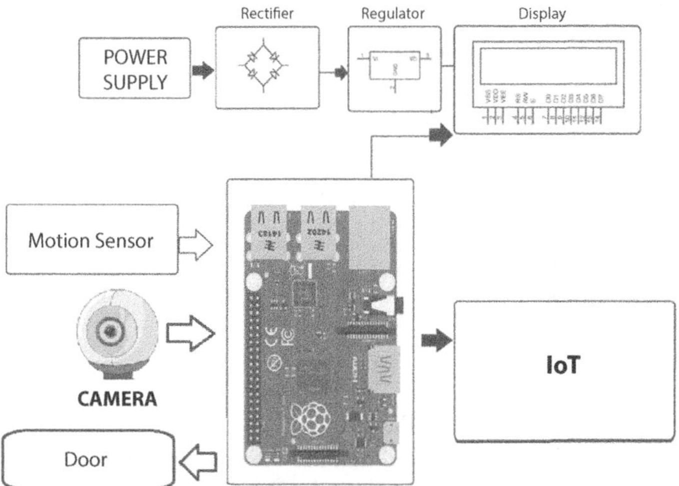

Figure 1.4 Block diagram of face recognition system.

countenances get enlisted in the camera. Then, at that point, the confirmation happens. At whatever point the individual comes before the entryway, PIR sensor will detect the movement; LCD screen shows the necessary brief and the camera begins perceiving the face; it perceives the face, and on the off chance that it is enrolled, it opens the entryway; if the face is not enlisted, then it will raise a caution and snaps an image and sends it on the qualifications. This is the means by which the framework works.

1.4.4 Essentials Needed

SD card with 16GB capacity preinstalled with NOOBS.
For display and connectivity:
Any HDMI/DVI monitor or TV can be used for pi Display. HDMI cables will also be needed.
Keyboard and mouse: wireless will also work if already paired.
Power supply: USB cables can be used for this. Approximately, 2 A at 5 V will be needed to power the Raspberry Pi.
Make an account on iotgecko.com for authentication check.

1.4.5 Website

If a person is unidentified, then a picture of is captured and sent to the website. All the monitoring data is sent over the website iotgecko.com so that the user can see the system status from anywhere and help boost the security.

1.4.6 Hardware

Figure 1.5 depicts the components used:

- Raspberry Pi 3 Model B+
- Camera
- Multimedia Mobile AUX System
- PCB
- 16X2 LCD Display
- DC Motor

1.4.7 Procedure

1. Set up the Raspberry Pi.
2. Format the SD Card and install NOOBS software in it.
3. Now, put the SD card chip in the Raspberry Pi slot and connect it to the facility supply using an adapter.

- Raspberry Pi 3 Model B+
- Camera
- Multimedia Mobile AUX System
- PCB
- 16X2 LCD Display
- DC Motor

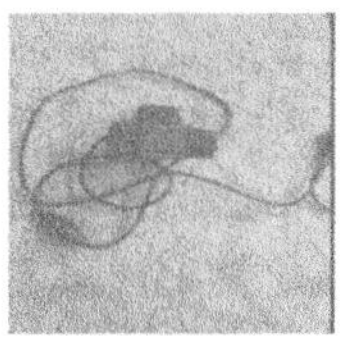
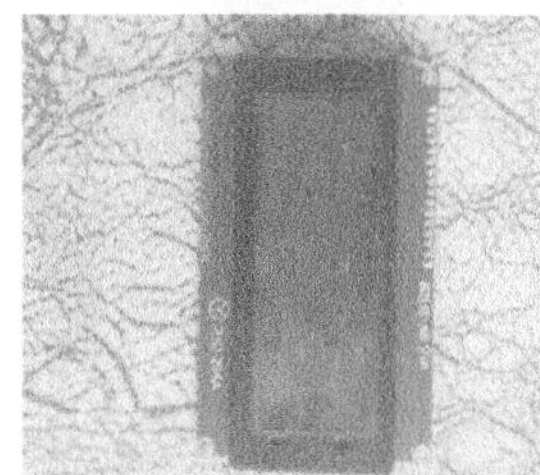
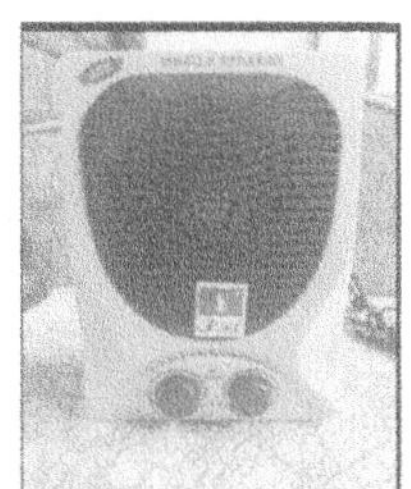

Figure 1.5 Components of the system.

4. Connect the monitor to the Pi using HDMI cable, and therefore, the mode of the monitor/TV should be in HDMI.
5. Within the display an option would come to put in the software package. Click on Raspbian, so it will get installed after some minutes.
6. Perform all the language and display setting consistent with your preferences.
7. Now, we will start working with the software (Figure 1.6 Raspberry Pi).

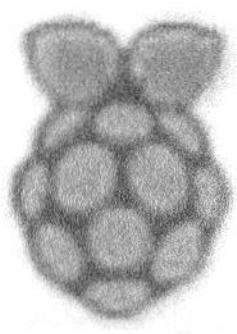

Figure 1.6 Welcome to the Raspberry Pi desktop.

Figure 1.7 Setup.

8. Write the code on the Python3 IDE and upload it on to the Pi.
9. Now, make all the connections as per the circuit diagram.
10. Connect the full setup as per Figure 1.7.
11. Now, place on the whole system again and connect the chip with the code to the Pi.
12. In the beginning, connect your system to the net. All the prompts also will be heard and seen as we have got connected it to the Buzzer.
13. First, registration process will occur and that we register the authorized faces by clicking on the register option on the LCD with the assistance of keyboard as depicted in Figure 1.8.
14. In the display, the face registration process will be seen and therefore the images will get captured. We will also be able to input the name of the person here as depicted in Figure 1.9.
15. Click on start option, the method of door lock system will begin as depicted in Figure 1.10.

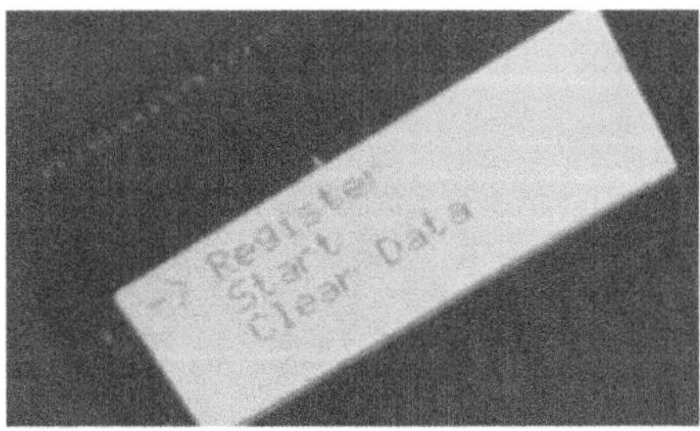

Figure 1.8 Options on display.

Figure 1.9 Image of registration.

Figure 1.10 LCD displaying door lock system.

16. For verification, when someone is available in front of the camera, the image gets captured.
17. If the person is registered, then the door opens, and it says welcome.
18. If the person is unknown, then the door remains closed, and it says invalid, gives a beep, and displays unknown face message as depicted in Figure 1.11.

Figure 1.11 Unknown face recognized.

19. All of these prompts are visible on the screen and the LCD display.
20. In case of an invalid entry the image of the individual is caught and given to the IoT geeks website for security purposes.

1.5 Conclusion

The face recognition technique possesses both demanding and significant technique of recognition. Among each biometrics methodology, face detection has some of the great advantages, i.e., it is totally user-friendly. In this research, all of us tried to give an introduction part for face detecting technology. We have covered the basics of this technology, the subparts of the machine learning need to be studied, the block diagram of this system, and the hardware components needed to be accumulated.

The computational models, which were executed in this undertaking, were taken after broad examination, and the fruitful testing results affirm that the decisions made by the researcher were reliable. This framework was tried under sturdy conditions in this exploratory study. The completely robotized front facing view face recognition framework showed basically wonderful precision.

The face recognition system with the latest technology is now cost effective, providing high percentage of accuracy and much more reliable system. This system possesses a high immense scope in India. This technique could be efficiently utilized in banks, universities, verification of driving license or visa and passport, in defense, and also in government as well as private sectors.

As an end, security system by using face acknowledgment got together with IoT is adequately done. The face acknowledgment can see the face and prepared to send notice to a customer when a dark being has been recognized through IoT. Of course, this endeavor is that this undertaking really has a significant room of progress to be done, especially in the viability of the image taking care of part. Due to the module used which is Raspberry Pi 3, taking care of period of the coding took a long time to measure the image taken and take an action. By using another better module, this endeavor can be improved remarkably.

We conviction that this paper gives the perusers a vastly improved agreement and information about the face acknowledgment framework, and we might likewise want to spur the perusers who are intrigued to find out about this theme to go to the references for the further point by point study.

References

1. Schroff, F., Kalenichenko, D., Philbin, J., FaceNet: A Unified Embedding for Face Recognition and clustering, in: *Publised in 2015 IEEE Conference on Computer Vision and Pattern Recognition (CVPR)*, IEEE, Boston, MA, USA.
2. Datta, A.K., Datta, M., Banerjee, P.K., *Face Detection and Recognition: Theory and Practice*, p. 352 Pages, Chapman and Hall/CRC CRC Press, Florida, 2016, 2019.
3. Qiong, C., Li, S., Weidi, X., Parkhi, O.M., Zisserman, A., VGGFace 2: A dataset for recognising faces across pose and age. *IEEE Conference on Automatic Face and Gesture Recognition*, 2018. *Int. J. Res. Appl. Sci. Eng. Technol. (IJRASET)*, 9, VI, June 2021.
4. Tian, J., Xie, H., Hu, S., Liu, J., Multidimensional face representation in deep convolutional neural network reveals the mechanism underlying AI racism. *Front. Comput. Neurosci.*, 10 March 2021, https://doi.org/10.3389/fncom.2021.620281.
5. Kamencay, P., Benco, M., Mizdos, T., Radil, R., A new method for face recognition using convolutional neural network face recognition system - state of the art. *Adv. Electr. Electron. Eng.*, 15, 4, 663–672, 2017.
6. Gutta, S. and Wechsler, H., Face recognition using hybrid classifiers // Pattern Recognition. *IJCNN'99. International Joint Conference on Neural Networks. Proceedings (Cat. No.99CH36339)*, vol. 30, IEEE, Washington, DC, USA, pp. 539 –553, 1997.
7. Chollet., F., *Keras: The Python Deep Learning library*. Keras.Io, 2015, Astrophysics Source Code Library, record ascl:1806.022, Pub Date: June 2018.
8. Januzaj, Y., Luma, A., Januzaj, Y., Ramaj., V., Real time access control based on face recognition, in: *International Conference on Network security & Computer Science (ICNSCS-15)*, pp. 7–12, 2015.
9. Barnouti, N.H., Al-Dabbagh, S.S.M., Matti, W.E., Face recognition: A literature review. *Int. J. Appl. Inf. Syst.*, 11, 4, 21–31, Sep. 2016.
10. Xiaogang, W. and Xiaoou, T., A unified frame work for subspace face recognition. *IEEE Trans. Pattern Anal. Mach. Intell.*, 26, 9, 1222–1228, 2004.
11. Patil, Prof. B.S. and Yardi, Prof. A.R., Real Time Face Recognition System using Eigen Faces. *Int. J. Electron. Commun. Eng. Technol. (IJECET)*, 4, 2, 72–79, 2013.
12. Jing, X.-Y., Wong, H.-S., Zhang, D., Face recognition based on discriminant fractional Fourier feature extraction. *Pattern Recogn. Lett.*, 27, 1465–1471, 2006.
13. Starovoitov, V., Samal, D., Votsis, G., Kollias, S., Face recognition by geometric features. *Proceedings of 5-th Pattern Recognition and Information Analysis Conference*, Minsk, May 1999.
14. Rein-Lien, H., *Face Detection and Modeling for Recognition*, PhD thesis, Department of Computer Science & Engineering, Michigan State University, USA, 2002.

15. Sajjad, M. *et al.*, Raspberry pi assisted face recognition framework for enhanced law-enforcement services in smart cities. *Future Gener. Comp. Sy.*, 108, 4, 995–1007, November 2017. Project: Facial Expression Analysis for Law-enforcement Services.
16. Rizon, M. *et al.*, Face recognition using eigenfaces and neural networks. *Am. J. Appl. Sci.*, 2, 6, 1872–1875, 2006.
17. Agarwal, M., Jain, N., Kumar, M.M., Agrawal, H., Face Recognition Using Eigen Faces and Artificial Neural Network. *Int. J. Comput. Theory Eng.*, 2, 4, 624–629, 2010.
18. Shanthamallu, U.S., Spanias, A., Tepedelenlioglu, C., Stanley., M., A brief survey of machine learning methods and their sensor and IoT applications. *2017 8th Int. Conf. Information, Intell. Syst. Appl. IISA 2017*, vol. 2018-January, pp. 1–8, 2018.
19. Oh, S.H., Kim, G.W., Lim., K.S., Compact deep learned feature-based face recognition, for Visual Internet of Things *J. Supercomput.*, 74, 6729–6741 (2018), Published: 28 November 2017.
20. Mulla., M.R., Facial image-based security system using PCA. *Int. J. Power Electron. Drive Syst. (IJPEDS)*, 11, 1, 417–424, March 2020.

2

Smart Healthcare Monitoring System: An IoT-Based Approach

Paranjeet Kaur

Department of Pharmaceutical Chemistry, School of Pharmaceutical Sciences, Lovely Professional University, Jalandhar, Delhi G.T. Road, Phagwara, Punjab, India

Abstract

Healthcare services are looping over its economic affairs. Overgrowing elderly age of people as well as non-resistible rapid increase of complex diseases seeks the demands for the emergence of internets or digital services to revolutionize all commercial healthcare treatments. Day by day, the world is approaching out of reach healthcare services, where large proportion of people are getting unproductive due to old age and getting exposed to deadly diseases and ultimately can lead to end of the world. Fortunately, artificial intelligence has led the command over these commercialized services to make healthcare reliable in terms of cost and accessibility. "A new model known as the Internet of Things (IoT) provides a diverse applicability, including healthcare." IoT is a network which consists as inter-related and inter-connected devices or things that are able to communication and computation over the internet. Over these years, a number of advanced application based on IoT have been proposed for convenience of patients, doctors, and caregivers. The revolution of IoT is revamping modern healthcare with social and economic prospects and also with promising technologies.

Keywords: Internet, healthcare, sensor, hospital, patient

2.1 Introduction

The internetwork of corporeal articles or items, implanted by programming and sensors to obtain and send information among them and focal

Email: paranjeet.25047@lpu.co.in

Anita Gehlot, Rajesh Singh, Jaskaran Singh and Neeta Raj Sharma (eds.) Digital Forensics and Internet of Things: Impact and Challenges, (19–36) © 2022 Scrivener Publishing LLC

servers with no or least human remedies, is referred to as Internet of Things (IoT). IoT helps in remotely controlling and getting to these things along with a current framework. "This makes an open door for joining of physical world and PC-based framework, which brings about improved effectiveness, precision, and monetary advantage [1–5]."

In 1999, Kevin Ashton introduced IoT; Kevin Ashton interfaces such various sensors to the corporeal item and transfers this data over the web. This IoT mechanical ability is nowadays served under express domains of presence along with computerized oilfield, living arrangement, and erection mechanization, grid, advanced clinical cure, insightful haulage, etc. [6, 7].

Thing could be anything which has physical presence, going from an extremely little item like nanochip to enormous estimated assembling. These things are implanted with sensors, actuators, and complex programming which empower them to send and get information. In the following 5 years, IoT will be field of innovation where most speculation will be done as a result of its progressive development rate. There are distinctive versatile applications and wearable gadgets which drove patients to catch their well-being information. Emergency clinics additionally use IoT to give ongoing human services offices and to monitor their patients and work force. A portion of the IoT medicinal services applications used to screen diverse well-being angles including pulse observing, blood glucose checking, heart working, and observing physical wellness [8–12].

Among the list of use empowered by IoT, brilliant and associated social insurance is of specific significant one. Arranged sensors, either to be put on the body or to be utilized in the live condition facilitate the possibility of gathering of our physical and psychological wellness [13]. The internet and the web have developed over the years to reach their current date structure. The development can be broadly arrayed into five stages.

Stage 1: Advanced Research Project Agency Network. This task was fundamentally utilized for examination of research purposes by academicians as well as exploration foundations.
Stage 2: HTML was developed during this interval and groups started to rush for name of their spaces.
Stage 3: This stage includes value-based trade framework.
Stage 4: The social sites: These sites have now gotten a mechanism of social communication such as Facebook, Twitter, and Groupon.
Stage 5: "The Internet of Things (IoT)".

It is a massive significant advancement that can effectively alter the manner in which individuals work, learn, and live [14], for example, "advanced mobile phones, internet TVs, sensors, and actuators to the internet" [15]. Web of Things works sustainably and mainly focuses on early therapeutic investigation of diseases, its mechanism status, and patient care at home [16].

2.2 Healthcare at Clinics

Web of things tends to develop frameworks that observe patients admitted in hospitals whose health conditions seeks immediate and close checkup. These systems comprising of checking frameworks employ different sensors to use all health status data which is separated and send to portals and the cloud. For additional investigation, this data is then sent to parent sources via remote, audit is carried out subsequently, and patient health signs are monitored. Rather, it provides a determined computerized current of knowledge. In this way, the nature of care got improved by consistent consideration tending to reduce care expenditure moreover dispenses with the need for a guardian to take part in information assortment and investigation [17].

2.3 Remote Healthcare

Lack of prepared access to viable well-being checking frameworks may prompt numerous untreated or undertreated well-being, which has been confronted common issue everywhere all over the globe. Be that as it may, little, ground-breaking obscure arrangements correlated with means of the IoT make it effectively working from observation to visiting patients. Information regarding patient's well-being can be efficiently collected by employing these arrangements. This information is then taken over by sensors, which further break down the information by using complex calculations and afterward share it through remote availability. The clinical experts would then be able to make fitting well-being suggestions remotely.

2.4 Technological Framework

In healthcare observation, various applications have been emerged, which are as follows.

Wireless Sensor Networks (WSNs) are a significant empowering innovation of IoT. It interconnects different actuator center points and sensors within a system by distant correspondence. This joins the system into an increasingly raised level structure through a framework entryway [18, 19]. General Sensor Network (USN) is a development of the WSN fused among the software plan of the IoT. Entryways comprise server farm focuses that assemble sensor data, inspect it, and confer it to the cloud through wide-area mastermind (WAN) propels over a short time. Doors can be planned for home or clinical settings. In-home settings may be a bit of greater system resource that furthermore manages imperatives, beguilement, and various structures. Sensors measure corporeal data of the limit to be checked. Sensor centers are customarily lightweight, prudent, and simple to send and keep up. A disadvantage is that the capacity and convenience are confined via sources like sensor precision, processors, memories, imperatives resources, etc. As remote sensor center points are ordinarily very minimal electric contraptions, they should be structured with a confined power wellspring of under 0.5–2 ampere-hour and 1.2–3.7 volts. Interfacing WSNs to the internet is feasible in three standard moves close as shown in Figure 2.1. The first composed strategy is consists of the association of both autonomous WSN and the internet through a solitary portal. This philosophy is starting at now grasped by far most of the WSNs getting to the internet and presents the most raised pondering between frameworks.

The subsequent methodology frames a half-breed arrange which shows an expanding reconciliation degree. It is made out of both, a considered

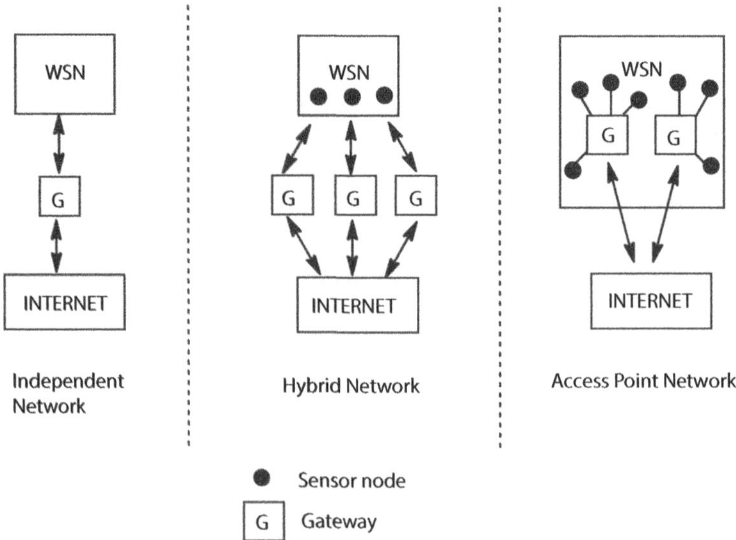

Figure 2.1 WSNs connection to the internet.

system structure that stays autonomous and a couple of double sensor hubs that can get to the web.

In the latest methodology, the Internet can be joined by various sensor hubs in one bounce [20].

2.5 Standard UIs, Shows, and User Requirements

Usability is enhanced by enabling show gadgets to convey a lot of data with the assistance of "graphic user interfaces" (GUIs). This data can be readable easily through vivid descriptions made by the GUIs. Processors with high designs seek the advancement in developing a more improved version of GUI.

The full use of this worldview in human services zone is both medical clinic—focused and home-focused which will prompt diminish the need of hospitalization. Parallelly, it benefits quality and effectiveness of treatment and at last prompts improve strength of patients.

2.5.1 Advantages

- Simultaneous detailing and checking
- End-to-end network and reasonableness
- Data grouping and examination
- Tracking and alarms
- Remote clinical help
- Research
- Integration: various gadgets and conventions
- Data over-burden and precision
- Cost
- Long stays at hospitals can be reduced
- Visiting hospital for regular checkup is also limited

2.5.2 Application

These applications can be further subdivided into different zones: personal and medicinal services, undertaking, utilities, and portable. This includes personal and healthcare IoT at an individual level, undertaking IoT at the extent of a network or portable, the utility of information and technology at a nationwide or local scale, and manageable IoT which is generally scattered across distinctive fields because of the idea concerning connectivity and scale.

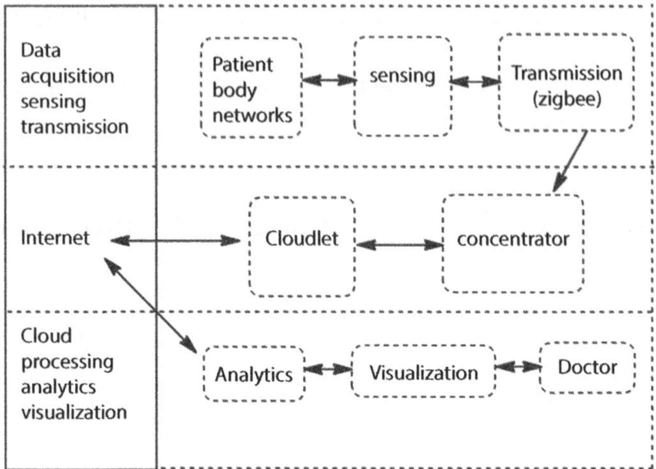

Figure 2.2 IoT-cloud-based remote health monitoring.

2.6 Cloud-Based Health Monitoring Using IoT

A device utilizing the IoT division is astoundingly led to and conspicuous at whatever point and wherever over the Internet. Devices that are based on IoT in remote prosperity checking systems are suited for the ordinary recognizing endeavors just as transfer of information with each other, thus interface with and transfer the information to prosperity foundations through the Internet, on a very basic level unraveling set up and association assignments. As exemplified in Figure 2.2, such structures can offer sorts of help, for instance, customized alert to the nearest human administrations establishment if there should arise an occurrence of an essential disaster for a directed patient [21].

2.7 Information Acquisition

This is demonstrated by different sensors that are wearable and measure the physiological biomarkers, "for example, ECG, skin temperature, respiratory rate, EMG muscle movement, and stride (pose)". These sensors interface with the operation, however, an intermediate data aggregator or concentrator, which is constantly an advanced cell situated in the region of the patient. "The data being part of the framework are liable for passing information from the patient's home to the server farm of the Healthcare Organization

(HCO) with guaranteed security, in a perfect world in close to constant." With a short range radio, the tactile securing stage is regularly furnished, for example, "Zigbee or low-power Bluetooth" is utilized to transfer sensor information to the concentrator [22, 23]. Regularly, a capacity/preparing gadget in region of a portable customer is often alluded to as a cloudlet and is utilized to increase its stockpiling/handling ability at whatever point the neighborhood versatile assets do not satisfy the application's prerequisites [24]. The cloudlet can be a nearby handling unit (for example, a work station) which is straightforwardly available by the concentrator through Wi-Fi organization. Notwithstanding giving brief stockpiling before correspondence of information to the cloud, the cloudlet can likewise be utilized for running time basic errands on the patient's accumulated information. "In addition, the device called cloudlet would be utilized to transfer the accumulated information to the cloud" if there should be an happening of restrictions on the cell phone, for example, brief absence of network or vitality.

2.8 The Processing of Cloud

It has three different divisions: examination, stockpiling, and perception. These systems are intended for storing patient's biomedical data for longer duration and also helping experts of healthcare with analytic data. Based on the cloud, clinical information storage and the forthright hurdles have been noted down onto the paper [25, 26]. "Sensor assessment alongside e-health records that help with conclusions and guesses for various well-being conditions and sicknesses. Also, visualization is a key necessity for any such framework since it is unreasonable to request that doctors pore over the voluminous information or investigations from wearable sensors". Perception methods that build data and investigations open to them in promptly edible management are fundamental if the wearable sensors are to affect clinical work.

2.9 IoT-Based Health Monitoring Using Raspberry Pi

The mixture of Raspberry Pi and IoT turns into another development innovation in human services framework. "Raspberry Pi in itself acts as small clinic in the wake of interfacing these (temperature, respiration, accelerometer, and heartbeat) sensors." This Pi functions as little center in numerous spots. It gathers information obtained via sensors which are afterward moved remotely to the site IoT as illustrated in Figure 2.3. Raspberry Pi board is associated with the web; the board of MAC address is placed onto

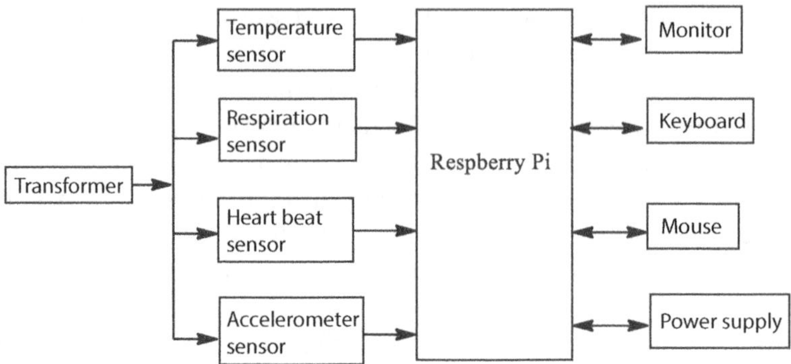

Figure 2.3 Health monitoring using IoT-based Raspberry Pi.

the web. After that, in IoT site, it includes MAC address of this board. At that point, the sensors yield is associated with the IoT site.

Sensors signals like interior warmth level, breath, heartbeat, and patient's turns of events assessed are watched. "These transducing signals transmits to the Raspberry Pi by methods for enhancer circuit and signal conditioning unit (scu), considering the way that the extent of signs are less (gain), so intensifier circuit is used to get the banner and transfer the signals to the Raspberry Pi." The Raspberry Pi acts as small PC processor system which is linux-based. Here, patients' interior warmth level, body advancements, breath, and heartbeat are assessed using separate sensors and it might be seen in screen of PC using Raspberry Pi similarly as checking through wherever on the planet using web source.

2.10 IoT-Based Health Monitoring Using RFID

RFIDs work the radio recurrence labels, learning genuine counters, and sensor of RFID that passes information among a peruser and an item besides is recognize, follow, and group [27]. In these electronic medicinal services, the protection of the patient is not thought about yet it is fundamental if there should arise an occurrence of healthcare seekers and this is the significant burden of this framework. To stay away from this disservice, the RFID innovation is utilized. It deals with the healthcare seekers reports with its versatility and ease of use. Likewise, the fundamental preferred position of RFID is that it opposes a wide range of assaults and dangers so less commotion are available in signal. In this framework, to make sure about the careful valuation return, regulating and looking at the wellness state of and to expand the intensity of loT, the combination of microcontroller with sensors is available.

The various sensors are utilized to quantify the various boundaries. These sensors are "ECG [28] sensor, blood pressure sensor, temperature sensor, motion sensor, EEG sensor, and blood glucose sensor". To get the effective yield, the mix of shrewd sensors with microcontroller parts is mulled over on the grounds that it has bunches of focal points like as mean force work out, joined exactitude-simple capabilities, and neighborly UI.

In the smart medicinal service framework, the loT and RFID assume a significant job. "In this framework, the various transducers are installed in the body of healthcare seekers and as indicated by the signs from the sensors, RFID, and loT the patient can be screen. The RFID labels submit element acknowledgment automatically through assessment the tag, that connected to objects [29]. Two kinds of RFID labels are available, *viz.*, dynamic RFID and passive RFID."

In these electronic signal structures, the "ADC are sent to RFID/Bluetooth gadget through microcontrollers". RFID/B1uetooth gadgets remotely pass these signs to the phones for the transfer of information via assistant to the desired destiny. Internet either employs the web services or the base station for the transmission reason. Each tasks should be possible into four various sections and offering various types of assistance to one another for joined working.

2.10.1 Sensor Layer

It is first layer of the framework comprised of fundamental piece of the composed framework. As appeared in Figure 2.4, there are various sensors

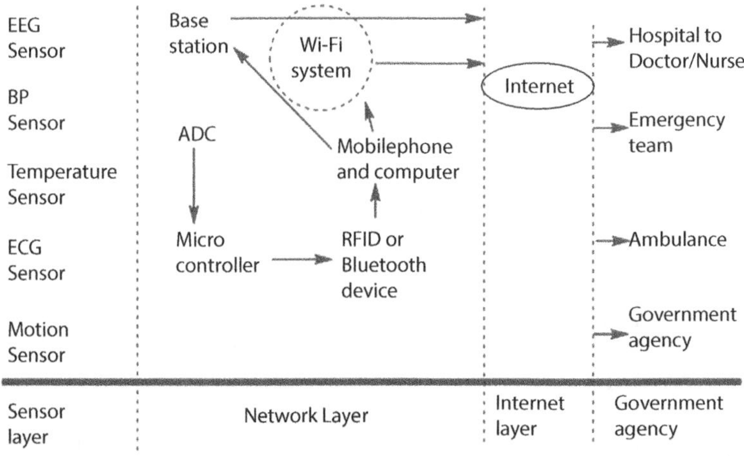

Figure 2.4 Healthcare monitoring model using RFID.

are available, for example, "temperature sensor, blood glucose, EEG sensor, blood pressure sensor, motion sensor, and ECG sensor." All of these sensors investigates and gathers individual data and moves it to the following layer, for example, organize layer.

2.10.2 Network Layer

This level plays out a highly important job in interaction which can be employed for connecting apparatuses to organize by systems for unique conventions like as "2G, 3G, 4G, with Routers". Network level even supports the promotion of mismatching messages traversing standard convention suite, for example, "WAN for 3G, MAN for 4G IEEE 802.20, ITU G.992. I-ITU G.992.5". The Bluetooth connects the two gadgets. At the moment when these two objects tend to be similar, they really seems to send information among these connected devices [30]. The data transferred and received at that moment is around 720 Kilo bytes at each interval. The Wi-Fi was created by "NCR organization/AT&T in Netherlands in 1991". With the help of this innovation, we can trade the data at least between two objects. Wi-Fi has been produced for portable registering gadgets, such as workstations; however, currently, it is widely employed for variety of different significant purposes and purchaser hardware like TVs, DVD players, and advanced cameras [31]. Simple to advanced adaption is an electronic course where interminably fanciful wave is refonned, aside from correcting its essential substance, through a staggered wave.

2.10.3 Service Layer

In this layer, information straightforwardly perceived from the online is legitimately gotten to by the "specialists/nurses, crisis group, emergency vehicle, and government organization". As indicated by this information, the above bodies can oversee the cases very easily; furnish central helps the need of necessity and checkout prescription details. By utilizing web for conveying data to the devices, diverse conventions and proficiencies can be helped by system layer.

2.11 Arduino and IoT-Based Health Monitoring System

This particular segment is done for checking the variation of limits of an individual seeking health nourishing utilizing the web of things. In this such individuals checking framework subject to the IoT adventure, the steady limits of a healthcare seeker's prosperity are being passed on to the cloud using web organize. These limits are sent to a remote internet region with the objective that customer can see these nuances from wherever on the planet. IoT industrious checking has three sensors for monitoring temperature, heartbeat sensor, and moistness. Such endeavor is significant since the specialist could screen health seeker's well-being just by surfing a site or URL. Moreover, nowadays, various IoT applications are furthermore being made. So now, the health of the patients can be assessed or monitored by using the Android applications. To work IoT-based prosperity watching structure adventure, Wi-Fi affiliation is needed. The Wi-Fi composes getting interfaced by microcontroller or the Arduino board while using an "internet-module". Otherwise, such endeavor does not perform any function without internet. Wi-Fi zones can be created by employing a Wi-Fi module or using Hotspot via mobile phone. The Arduino UNO board constantly examines commitment from these three sensors. "By then, it transmits this information to the cloud by transmitting this signal to a particular URL/IP address. By then, this movement of sending data to IP is reiterated after a specific timeframe."

2.12 IoT-Based Health Monitoring System Using ECG Signal

An IoT is about human services framework usage conspiration utilizing "Hidden Markov Model (HMM) chain and Electrocardiogram (ECG)" sensors inside the setting of e-health. The purpose of the plan is to ensure

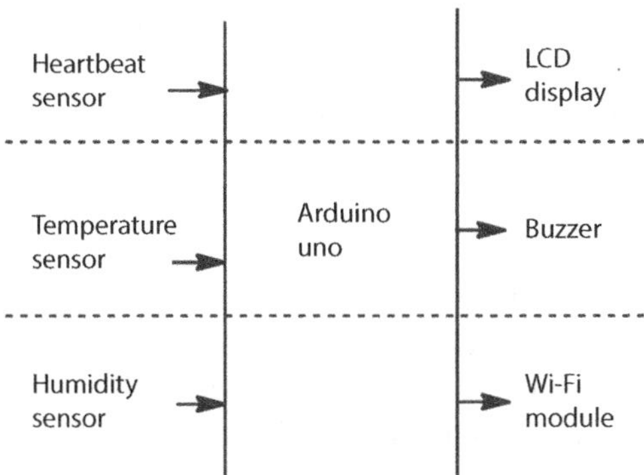

Figure 2.5 Arduino-based health monitoring system.

that proper checking is encouraged, therefore facilitating convenient mediation for patients with cardiovascular disorders (CVD) and subsequently upgrading clinical administrations for such patients. As constant checking of patients from various areas stays a basic test for IoT-based social insurance frameworks, this usage utilizes tolerant way estimator, persistent table, and ready administration plans inside the medical clinic to encourage the localization and ideal mediation for the regimen for patients with CVDs as depicted in Figure 2.5.

2.12.1 System Model

This particular division will demonstrate the proposed engineering as shown in Figure 2.6. They are made out of "heterogeneous gadgets [i.e., sensors, user equipment (UE), fringe gadgets, and so on)", which interface with the nearest "Base Stations (BSs) and Access Points (APs)" to trade information, therefore yielding data in the actual real time. Clients (that is, the patients) are regarded as either inactive or versatile in IoT conditions. These clinical sensors, for example, the lightweight three-appendage, lead to remote ECG gadget associated with every patient's body to transfer moment information to the patient's cell phone, at that point advances progressive information at spans to the BS or AP [32]. On the patient's body, the heartbeat is gathered from the clinical sensors to pass the ECG signal onto the mobile phone. Such sensors pass at low force since they set near the patient's heart, "assisted with accelerating their battery life and to diminish risks of improper expression to electromagnetic emission on the subject" [33]. All information is transferred through Bluetooth to the UE. In wards, the UE transfers all approaching data and localization to the nearest AP or BS; further, this medical clinic database is sent to the healthcare clinics or hospitals where the controllers can monitor or record every patient's sign, and afterward collect it in the patient table. The clinical team oversees all the refreshed tables, and on account of any urgency, the controllers produce alarm, enabling the clinical team to intercede in an opportune way.

2.12.2 Framework

It comprises of four head parts, to be specific: tolerant way "estimator, ECG signal sensors, persistent table director, and medical clinic ready framework/database controller" as shown in Figure 2.7. In this system, ECG signs and the patients' areas are sent to the APs and BSs and afterward sent to the medical clinic data in the system to refresh every patient's table with new approaching information. For the situation where an anomalous pulse

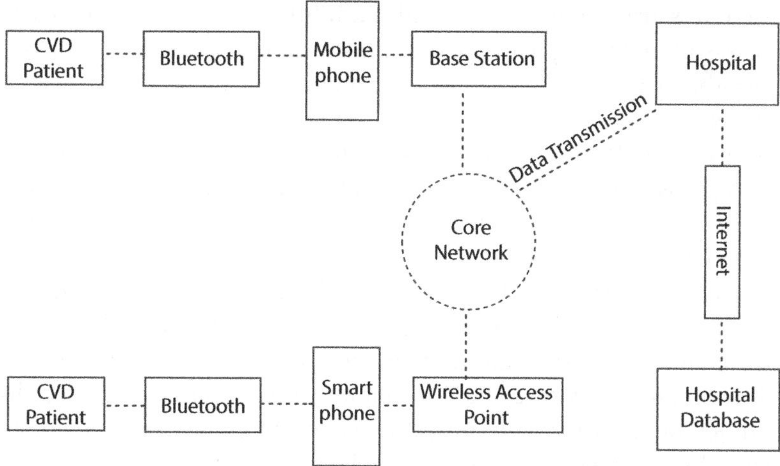

Figure 2.6 Healthcare system via IOT.

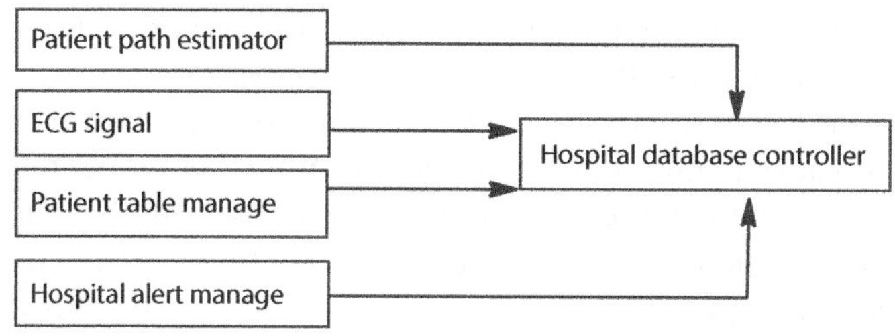

Figure 2.7 Systemic model of health monitoring using ECG signal.

movement is identified, the controller creates new principles to produce an alert/caution to the clinical faculty and gives the faculty all the important data about the patient's past interview and localization, which helps in the conclusion and following of cardiovascular mood issue. These segment portions of the framework are portrayed advertisement their activity itemized as follows.

2.13 IoT-Based Health Monitoring System Using Android App

In healthcare applications, the sensor comprising network would enable patients overviewing their health conditions easily. Body Sensor Network (BSN) are being employed for developing Android-based advanced applications related to health management system. The hubs of BSN incorporate "pulse rate sensor, temperature, and humidity". The established structure is successful in dealing with the concerns went up against by people seeking healthcare and specialist by watching human activities as per everyday environment.

Body essentials (pulse\temperature\humidity) are imperative factors in deciding prosperity of and help checking the technique of intervention just as an evidence for that particular remedy. While it tends to be feverish and dreary to go for bigger populace of patients to gather the substantial data on a severe daily practice, the exactness and the delay just as the alignment of instrumentation indicates the negative outcomes. To tackle this issue, we offer a carefully adjusted and ongoing crucial estimation gadget that can work continuously, record the information, and pass onto the specialists. It additionally informs with a caution when these body parameters need noteworthy consideration. While it ameliorates the proficiency of well-being following records, the information created by estimation can likewise be utilized for factual reason. Target of this gadget is to refine the efficiency and productivity of social insurance. The structure and working of the gadget is as per the following:

In the model, there are two essential body parameters that we have decided to gauge real-time pulse and temperature. Let us assume by estimating one of the parameters of first individual seeking healthcare certainly body temperature named ABC and continuous beat of second individual seeking healthcare named DEF, and separated from these, we are likewise observing gradually the status of the ward where various such healthcare candidates are available. There are such a significant number of pulse sensors accessible in the commercial however we have utilized Pulse Rate Sensor SEN-11574. We can gauge our heartbeat whenever by placing the sensor. This is a simple sensor, yet we need to peruse it by Raspberry Pi which takes just computerized inputs, that is the reason we have utilized ADC (ADS1115). We have utilized advanced GPIO ports on Raspberry Pi to interface the ADC at that point associated the beat sensor to the ADC on channel A0. So as to quantify temperature and stickiness, we have utilized DHT11. DHT11 functions as a temperature and stickiness sensor in which temperature goes is from 0°C to 500°C with precision of ±20°C and dampness extend is from 20% to 80% with ±5% exactness. The examining pace of DHT11 is 1-Hz methods; it will peruse one perusing each second. It comprises a NTC thermistor, a mugginess detecting segment, and an IC. NTC thermistor is a huge obstruction which changes its opposition as the temperature varies, and as a result of NTC (Negative Temperature Coefficient), the obstruction diminishes as the temperature increments. This transducer is developed by sintering of semiconductor type materials like pottery or polymers to furnish greater changes in the obstruction with only a little change in temperature. After this, the following steps needs to be followed [34–36].

2.13.1 Transferring the Information to the Cloud

After we have effectively followed the above data, it should be sent to cloud where it very well may be put away and showed and moved to the application. Raspberry Pi utilizes internet to pass on information to the cloud and create data from concomitant databases.

2.13.2 Application Controls

From the cloud, when the application has the imperative information, it speaks and classifies to the body vitals of every patient. It, at that point, shows the important organization in an intuitive user interface where specialists can undoubtedly find the state of alluding patients. It has isolated login certifications for specialists and victims. Specialists can screen the well-being status of the considerable number of patients appointed to them while patients can just see their well-being status by signing in utilizing their particular login qualifications, while dampness status is available to the two specialists just as patients.

2.14 Conclusion and Future Perspectives

IoT has revolutionized the way of utilizing work premises conveying to human care services. These advances improve the item, causing a bigger impact by uniting minor changes. Headways in IoT are for the most part utilized for associating the various gadgets like as sensors, apparatuses, vehicles, and different items. Every one of these gadgets may furnish with "radio-recurrence ID (RFID) tag, sensors, actuators, cell phones, and numerous other". By utilizing loT, every one of these gadgets is associated with building up the correspondence among them and proficiently gets to the data. With health IoT, medicinal service experts might have the option to receive persistent data, store it, and investigate it in a continuous way to test and track the patient. In any case, interconnected wearable patient devices and therapeutic administrations data (for instance, ECG signals) are reliant upon security breaks. To this end, this paper portrays a cloud-consolidated health IoT checking structure, where before sending to the cloud for "secure, safe, and first class prosperity watching", human administrations data are being watermarked. Future work will incorporate testing the proposed health IoT checking framework for data security and notice limits, similarly as completing a test primer with real-world healthcare seekers and prosperity specialists.

References

1. Kortuem, G., Kawsar, F., Sundramoorthy, V., Fitton, D., "Smart objects as building blocks for the internet of things". *IEEE Internet Comput.*, 14, 1, 44–51, Jan–Feb. 2010.
2. Zanella, A., Bui, N., Castellani, A., Vangelista, L., Zorzi, M., "Internet of things for smart cities". *IEEE Internet Things J.*, 1, 1, 22–32, Feb. 2014.
3. Kamilaris, A. and Pitsillides, A., "Mobile phone computing and internet of things: A survey". *IEEE Internet Things J.*, 3, 6, 885–898, Dec. 2016.
4. Laplante, P.A. and Laplante, N., "The internet of things in healthcare: Potential applications and challenges". *IT Prof.*, 18, 3, 2–4, May–June 2016.
5. Laplante, P.A. and Laplante, N., "A structured approach for describing healthcare applications for the internet of things". *2015 IEEE 2nd World Forum on internet of things (WF -IOT)*, Milan, pp. 621–625, 2015.
6. Niranjana, S. and Balamurugan, A., "Intelligent E-Health Gateway Based Ubiquitous Healthcare Systems in Internet of Things". *Int. J. Sci. Eng. Appl. Sci. (IJSEAS)*, 1, 9, December 2015.
7. Ullah, K., Shah, M.A., Zhang, S., "Effective ways to use Internet of Things in the field of medical and smart healthcare". *2016 International Conference on Intelligent systems Engineering (ICISE)*, 2016.
8. Catarinucci, L. *et al.*, "An IOT- aware Architecture for smart healthcare systems.". *IEEE Internet Things J.*, 2, 6, 515–526, Dec. 2015.
9. Dohr, A., Modre-opsrian, R., Drobies, M., Hayn, D., Schreier, G., "The internet of things for Ambient Assisted Living". *2010 seventh International Conference on Information Technology: New Generation*, Las vegas, NV, pp. 804–809, 2010.
10. Corno, F., De Rubbis, L., Rofarello, A.M., "A Healthcare support system for assisted Living facilities: An IOT solution", in: *Proceedings of 2016 IEEE 40th Annual Computer Software and Applications Conference (COMPSAC)*, Atlanta, GA, pp. 344–352, 2016.
11. Ali, N.A. and Abu-Elkheir, M., "Internet of nano-things healthcare applications: Requirements, opportunities and challenges". *2015 IEEE 11th International conference on wireless and mobile computing, Networking and Communications (WiMob)*, Abu Dhabi, pp. 9–14, 2015.
12. Ma, Y., Wang, Y., Yang, J., Miao, Y., Li, W., "Big Health Application system based on health internet of things and Big data". *IEEE Access*, 99, 1–1, 2017.
13. https://ieeexplore.ieee.org/abstract/document/7207365

14. Evans, D., *The Internet of Things:How the Next Evolution of the Internet Is Changing Everything*, Cisco, USA, April 2011.
15. Kortuem, G., Kawsar, F., Fitton, D., Sundramoorthy, V., "Smart objects as building blocks for the internet of things". *Internet Comput.*, 14, 44–51, 2010.
16. Simonov, M., Zich, R., Mazzitelli, F., Personalised Healthcare Communication in Internet of Things, *In Proc. of URSI GA08*, 2008.
17. Niewolny, D., *How the Internet of Things Is Revolutionizing Healthcare*, Freescale Semiconductors, USA, 18 Oct 2013.
18. Vermesan, O. and Friess, P., "Internet of Things Strategic Research and Innovation Agenda", in: *Internet of Things- Converging technologies for smart environment and Integrated Ecosystems*, p. 54, River Publishers, Denmark, 2013.
19. Pang, Z., "Technologies and Architectures of the Internet-of-Things (IoT) for Health and Well-being", in: *Doctoral Thesis*, KTH Royal Institute of Technology Stockholm, Sweden, January 2013.
20. Christin, D. *et al.*, "Wireless sensor networks and the internet of things: selected challenges". *Proceedings of the 8th GI/ITG KuVSFachgesprächDrahtlosesensornetze*, pp. 31–34, 2009.
21. Chen, M. *et al.*, "EMC: Emotion-aware mobile cloud computing in 5G". *IEEE Netw.*, 29, 2, 32–38, 2015.
22. Chen, M. *et al.*, "AIWAC: Affective interaction through wearable computing and cloud technology". *IEEE Wirel. Commun.*, 22, 1, 20–27, 2015.
23. Chen, M., "NDNC-BAN: Supporting Rich Media Healthcare Services via Named Data Networking in Cloud-assisted Wireless Body Area Networks". *Inf. Sci.*, 284, 10, 142–156, Nov. 2014.
24. Chen, M. *et al.*, "A survey of recent developments in home M2M networks". *IEEE Commun. Surv. Tut.*, 16, 1, 98–114, 2013.
25. Niewolny, D., *"How the Internet of Things Is Revolutionizing Healthcare"*, White paper, Available: cache.freescale.com/files/corporate/doc/../IOTREV HEALCARWP.pdf, Accessed 31st July, *Freescale semiconductor*, US, 2013.
26. Pandeya, S., Voorsluys, W., Niua, S., Khandoker, A., Buyyaa, R., "An autonomic cloud environment for hosting ECG Ecosystem analysis in the design of open platform-based in-home healthcare terminals towards the Internet-of-Things data analysis services". *Future Gener. Comp. Sy.*, 28, 147–154, 2012.
27. Jin, J., Gubbi, J., Marusic, S., Palaniswami, M., "An information framework for creating a smart city through Internet of Things". *IEEE Internet Things J.*, 1, 112–121, 2014.
28. Jara, A.J., Zamora-Izquierdo, M.A., Skarmeta, A.F., "Interconnection Framework for mHealth and Remote Monitoring Based on the Internet of Things". *IEEE J. Sel. Areas Commun.*, 31, 47–65, 2013.
29. Lee, K., Gelogo, Y.E., Lee, S., "Mobile gateway System for Ubiquitous system and Internet of Things, Application". *Int. J. Smart Home*, 8, 5, 279–286, 2014.

30. Gelogo, Y.E., "Internet of Things (loT) for U-healthcare". *Adv. Sci. Technol. Lett.*, 120, 717–720, 2015.
31. Gelogo, Y.E., Hwang, H.J., Haeng-Kon, K., "Internet of Things (IoT) framework for u-healthcare system". *Int. J. Smart Home*, 9, 11, 323–330, 2015.
32. Qi, N. *et al.*, "Energy-efficient cooperative network coding with joint relay scheduling and power allocation". *IEEE Trans. Commun.*, 64, 11, 4506–4519, 2016.
33. Atat, R., Lingjia, L., Yang, Y., "Privacy protection scheme for ehealth systems: A stochastic geometry approach". *2016 IEEE Global Communications Conference (GLOBECOM)*, IEEE, 2016.
34. Kumar, R. and Pallikond Rajasekaran, M., "An IoT based patient monitoring system using raspberry Pi". *2016 International Conference on Computing Technologies and Intelligent Data Engineering (ICCTIDE'16)*, IEEE, 2016.
35. Gope, P. and Hwang, T., "Untraceable sensor movement in distributed IoT infrastructure". *IEEE Sens. J.*, 15, 9, 5340–5348, 2015.
36. Lin, Y. *et al.*, "A home mobile healthcare system for wheelchair users". *Proceedings of the 2014 IEEE 18th international conference on computer supported cooperative work in design (CSCWD)*, IEEE, 2014.

3

Design of Gesture-Based Hand Gloves Using Arduino UNO: A Grace to Abled Mankind

Harpreet Singh Bedi*, Dekkapati Vinit Raju, Nandyala Meghanath Reddy C. Partha Sai Kumar and Mandla Ravi Varma

SEEE, Lovely Professional University, Punjab, India

Abstract

Nowadays, technology and science are advancing at a rapid pace. The advancing or smart technology is "augmenting" the way of living in society. People need "smart" solutions to their problems. So, in this chapter, we would like to introduce a paradigm of smart technology, gesture-based wheelchair using Arduino UNO. The ideology is to introduce a wheelchair where physically challenged, deaf and mute or elderly people, can control the wheelchair and send an emergency message or SOS using GSM module, and a nearby person can see the emergency message on the LCD. The abovementioned tasks can be performed using hand gestures. This enables the disabled person to drive the wheelchair and move from one place to another with more efficiency. The proposed idea is to be comprised with comfort and mobility to the person in the wheelchair. Arduino UNO is the microcontroller which interfaces the components and performs tasks; flux sensors detect the hand gestures; MEMS sensor is used to convert digital signals into mechanical tasks; motor IC drives the motors; and GSM module sends the message to the responsible person. This makes our idea to be cost efficient compared to the joystick-controlled or voice-controlled wheelchair.

***Keywords*:** Arduino, hand gloves, wheel chair, drives, motors

**Corresponding author:* harpreet.17377@lpu.co.in

Anita Gehlot, Rajesh Singh, Jaskaran Singh and Neeta Raj Sharma (eds.) Digital Forensics and Internet of Things: Impact and Challenges, (37–44) © 2022 Scrivener Publishing LLC

3.1 Introduction

The age of modern science has brought massive technological changes by utilizing modern electrical, electronic, and mechanical systems. In recent time, approximately 2.78% of the population require a wheelchair especially for elderly and disabled people. Embedded systems and digital information technology are becoming more relevant in our daily lives [1].

A special purpose system in which the computer is fully embedded to the unit or system it controls is known as an embedded system. These automated systems have made our lives much more convenient and relaxed. Traditional wheelchairs, as we all know, have several drawbacks in terms of versatility, bulkiness, and functionality. Here, we are developing a clever approach to allowing users to use hand motions and sync them with the movement of the wheelchair [2]. The idea is to provide a wheelchair which provides more mobility, and it will make people familiar with the machine, in the future. We can improve the mobility and usability of wheelchair with high accuracy [3].

A gesture-driven hand glove is a device that can be controlled using hand movements rather than the traditional keypad system [4]. Humans are frantically trying to come up with new ways to communicate with computers. In real life, it is a debilitating issue for a paralyzed person [5]. So, these types of systems are getting better and better with time. When movements were used for this interaction in this implementation, it resulted in a significant breakthrough. We present a method for controlling a mechanized wheelchair using only finger movements [6, 7]. This article aims to develop a prototype for a smart wheelchair-using idea from embedded systems to control it which is very useful for physically handicapped people [8].

3.1.1 Block Diagram

Arduino UNO: It is an open-source electronic device and has an onboard 8-bit ATmega328p, where it allows anyone to perform their own projects. It comprises a crystal oscillator, serial communication, voltage regulator, etc., to support Arduino UNO. Arduino IDE is a platform where one can program the Arduino UNO for the desired outcomes.

Flex Sensors: A flex sensor is a low-cost, simple-to-use sensor that measures the amount of bending or variations in resistance caused by bending.

MEMS Sensors: These are low-cost inertial sensors with high precision that are used in a wide variety of industrial applications. These sensors sense external stimuli and carry out mechanical tasks.

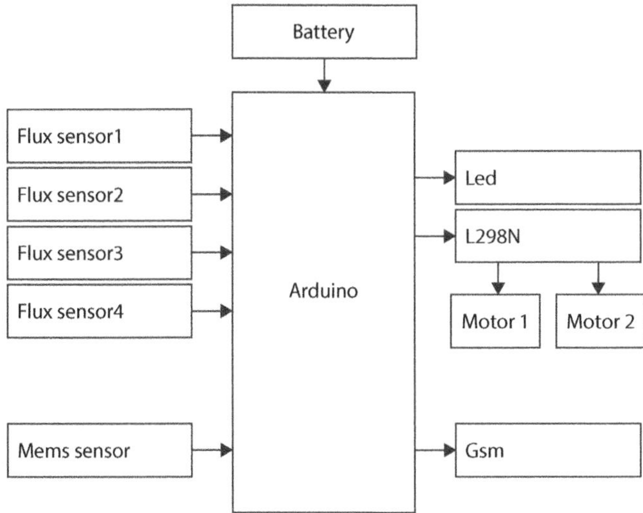

Figure 3.1 Block diagram of gesture-based hand gloves using Arduino UNO.

DC Motors: Compared to stepping motors, DC motors are faster, cost efficient, and compact in size.

GSM module: This module is widely used in Internet of Things (IoT) and embedded systems projects. Using AT commands, one can read, write, or delete SMS messages.

LCD Display: It is low cost and easy to program. It is an alphanumeric display which can print both alphabet and numbers.

3.1.2 The Proposed New Design

The new design was implemented for a variety of reasons, including both functional and ethical concerns. A simple and proven technology, as well as corresponding precision control, are integrated into the practical consideration of the equipment. The equipment is easier to manage and operate with because of the more efficient, easy-to-understand implementation [9]. The approach is also cost-effective, user-friendly, and simple to explain to people who are engineers. This design aims to solve the issue by creating a smart wheelchair that is different and special to disabled people, allowing them to travel around their neighborhood, workplaces, and markets without feeling any less important than other people due to their disability [10].

3.1.3 Circuit Diagram

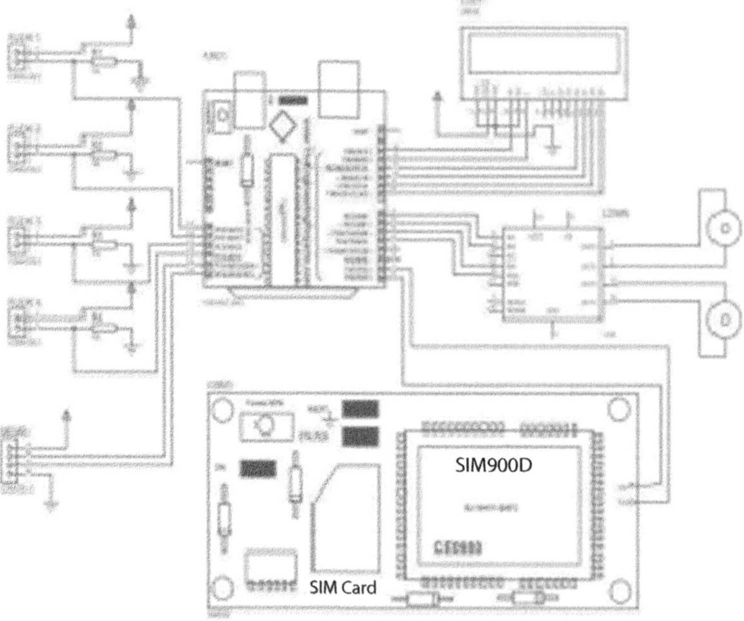

Figure 3.2 Circuit diagram of gesture-based hand gloves using Arduino UNO.

3.2 Result and Discussion

The complete hardware and the components required are mentioned along with the circuit diagram. We used the Arduino IDE for programming for the desired outcomes.

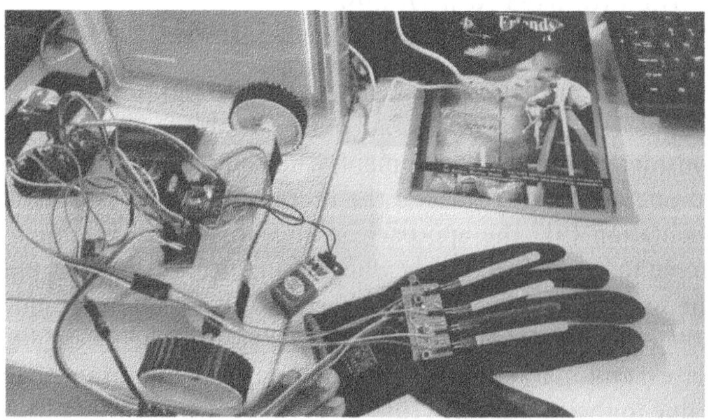

The proposed implementation is affordable and reliable as far as utilization is concerned. This gesture-based hand gloves to drive the wheelchair have many merits over the conventional wheelchair or SOS facility.

3.2.1 Data Analysis

The aim of this effort is to evaluate the efficiency of the finger's motion and to use the accelerometer to adjust the wheelchair's direction based on its finger. During the experiment, if the finger moves to the correct right hand, the wheelchair will move right, while if the finger moves to the wrong side, the wheelchair will move left. As shown in Table 3.1, wheelchair inventions can be operated in four directions: forward, reverse, left, and right.

Table 3.1 shows how we use an algorithm to regulate the motion of a wheelchair. The method is very simple, as previously mentioned, for a wheelchair whose motion is controlled with your index finger. The system was carried out with the same finger posture for the purpose of referring to it as the stable movement or "neutral position". The wheelchair is propelled by electric motors that are operated by hand gloves that have a movement sensing system attached to them and are set to start mode.

3.3 Conclusion

The plan sets out to design and build a simple sensor microcontroller-based technology that had never been used in a wheelchair environment before. The aim of this work is to create an easily controllable, low-cost, and low-power wheelchair to bridge the communication gap between physically

Table 3.1 Algorithm setting for wheelchair direction.

Index finger	Input from Arduino				Directions
	D1	D2	D3	D4	
Stable 0°	0	0	0	0	No movement
Bend to Right 45°	0	0	0	1	Right movement
Bend to Left 45°	0	0	1	0	Left movement
Bend to Backward 45°	1	0	0	0	Reverse movement
Bend to Forward 45°	0	1	0	0	Forward movement

disabled, deaf, and mute people and the public. A wheelchair offers a disabled person fresh hope for living a full life. It instills in them the courage to function independently. This proposed work helps such communities to regain their confidence and makes them to do some tasks independently. It also acts as a personal assistant as well as SOS. Since the wheelchair is fully automated, it reduces the effort and physical strength of the disabled person. It can carry the load up to 100 kg.

3.4 Future Scope

The future scope of this work is to use this gesture-based wheelchair in old age homes where the implementation will be useful for the people who find difficulty in their movements. This can be improved by many advancements such as, for physically challenged people who are unable to move their hands, they may have a wheelchair developed with a tongue motion driver to drive the wheelchair's motors. It is also possible to have a speed control feature. For safety measures, we can implement high-power sensor like ultrasonic sensor for object detection. Self-power generation from the rotation of the wheel could be possible in the future, with the device being charged by solar power. Therefore, the stress associated with charging the battery may be alleviated. Artificial Intelligence can also be included to make wheelchair more technically advance.

References

1. Pande, Prof. V. V., Ubale, N.S., Masurkar, D.P., Ingole, N.R., Mane, P.P., Yaman, F., Lin, Q., Agrawal, G.P., Hand Gesture Based Wheelchair Movement

Control for Disabled Person Using MEMS. *Int. J. Eng. Res. Appl.*, Vol. 4, 4(Version4), 152–158, April 2014. Available: www.ijera.com (Accessed, Nov. 10, 2014) (13).

2. Kazerooni, H., Fairbanks, D., Chen, A., Shin, G., *The Magic Glove*, University of California Berkeley, Berkeley, California, 2006.
3. Zimmerman, T.G. *et al.*, A Hand Gesture Interface Device. *II Proc. Human Facttors in Computing System and Graphics Interface*, ACM Press, New York, April 1987.
4. Anoop, K.J., Ezhilan, I., Raj, S., Seenivasan, R., Pandian, C., Designing and modeling of controlled wheel chair incorporated with home automation. *Int. J. Adv. Res. Electr. Electron. Instrum. Eng.*, AnISO 3297:2007 Certified Organization). 3, 2, 2014.
5. S. Interactive Glove - International Journal of Industrial Electronics and Electrical Engineering,
6. International Journal of Engineering and Computer Science, 4, 9, pp. 14439–14442, Sep 2015.
7. World Health Organization, *World report on disability*, 2011.
8. Chowdhury, SM Mazharul Hoque, *Smart wheelchair for disabled people*, Diss. Jahangirnagar University, 2019.
9. Warad, S., Hiremath, V., Dhandargi, P., Bharath, V., Bhagavati, P.B., Speech and flex sensor-controlled wheelchair for physically disabled people. *Proceedings of 10th IRF International Conference*, Pune, India, 01st June-2014.
10. Shayban, N. and Muhammad, A.G.K., Wireless Head Gesture Controlled Wheelchair for Disable Persons presented by Shayban Nasif & Muhammad Abdul Goffar Khan (EEE Department Rajshahi University).

4

Playing With Genes: A Pragmatic Approach in Genetic Engineering

Prerna Singh* **and Dolly Sharma**†

Department of Computer Science and Engineering, Amity School of Engineering and Technology, Amity University, Noida, Uttar Pradesh, India

Abstract

Genetic engineering, otherwise, recombinant technology, implies the bunch of competencies acquainted with incising and linking along with genetic material, specifically DNA from various other species, and to incorporate the derived hybrid DNA into an organism to derive novel blend of heritable genetic material. Three main methods concerning genetic engineering are plasmid, vector, and biolistic methods. Derived crossbreed DNA is incorporated within an organism to shape a novel blend of heritable genetic material.

This can result in the production of a genetically modified organism (GMO) that will possess enriched or enhanced characteristics or traits or produce desirable bioactive compounds for being used in several fields such as research, industries, medicine, healthcare, pharmaceuticals, and agriculture and for developing the human life experience, in general.

Approaches in the present methods comprise the specific rearing of creatures and plants, hybridization, and recombinant deoxyribonucleic acid (rDNA). With the headway of genetic engineering, researchers would now be successful in modifying the pattern of genomes to eliminate various diseases that occur due to hereditary mutation. In this work, we will lighten up genetically engineered food crops and its advancements which lead to curing deadly diseases.

Keywords: Genetic engineering, DNA, RNA, genetically modified organism, therapeutics

**Corresponding author*: prernasingh21nove@gmail.com

†*Corresponding author*: dolly.azure@gmail.com

Anita Gehlot, Rajesh Singh, Jaskaran Singh and Neeta Raj Sharma (eds.) Digital Forensics and Internet of Things: Impact and Challenges, (45–58) © 2022 Scrivener Publishing LLC

4.1 Introduction

The plain handling of genes of an organism using biotechnology is recognized as genetic engineering. It is a group of advancements adjusted to proceed with the genetic structure of cells, along with the moving of genes in and through the species boundaries to derive novel organisms. Cloning is the process of taking genetic data from one living organism and constructing exact replicas of it.

Since decades, the title genetic engineering has been used not merely in science as well as in other fields. The promotion of genetic engineering is the effect of its major use in labs across the globe and, modernization. Genetic engineering involves citified techniques of gene manipulation, alteration and, cloning.

Genetically modified organisms (GMOs) are the organisms examined with the recombinant DNA. Its construction can be simplified in the following steps:

1. Isolation of interested gene
2. Gene duplication
3. Gene pattern
4. Transition
5. Selection
6. Inclusion and manifestation of recombinant DNA

Alignment of all the genetic evidence is in the form of genes developed by DNA which through several biotechnologies can be handled to be utilized in various fields of science.

At present, genetic engineering is broadly utilized at different parts of medication to deliver immunizations, antibodies, and animals that can be utilized as examples for diseases (most basic model mice) or to be utilized as organ donors (for example, pigs) or for interbreeding or crossbreeding, for example, chimeras alike the blotched mouse are designed through gene targeting as shown in Figure 4.1.

Alternate action of genetic engineering is gene therapy which concentrates to compensate abnormal genes and restore correct gene expression in cells. Whereas in agriculture, GM foods resistant to certain pests, diseases, herbicides, and environmental conditions are being ministered by genetic engineering.

Digital forensics is a way toward utilizing scientific methods and processes to determine electronically saved data and decide the occurrence of a sequence of events in which a specific incident is prompted. Various

Figure 4.1 Chimeras designed through gene targeting (source: https://en.wikipedia.org/wiki/File:ChimericMouseWithPups.jpg).

methods have been evolved to embed data into a DNA sequence for the purpose of data storage, watermarking, or communication of secret messages. The power to recognize, separate, and decode messages from DNA is significant for forensic data collection and data security.

Advances in DNA (deoxyribonucleic acid) innovation in recent years have led to infamously explicit forensic identification techniques.

4.2 Literature Review

The thoughts and findings of researchers which will be further analyzed throughout this section of the research paper will help answer the following question: What are the benefits of these technologies in society today and what could transpire in terms of gene modification within our world in the future primarily in food agriculture and curing deadly diseases? [1]. In the market, GM crops have been for over a decade. These technologies are favorable and can be consumed due to insect resistance and herbicide-tolerant benefits and positively influence humans and nature [2]. It has granted an approach to remove restrictions and make the Integrated Pest Management part of host plant resistance. It has minimized reliance on chemical pesticides improving food quality, yield increase, and examining its safety [4] GM crops cures hunger issues malnutrition in the world as they ensure a high quantity of vitamins and proteins [5]. To quicken the pace of basic research, agricultural breakthroughs, and medical advancements, RNA-guided [6, 7] Cas compound CRISPR technology is used as an instrument [8]. It has modified human genes and cure genetic diseases. It has advanced in germline gene modifications.

4.3 Methodology

In regular livestock production, farming, and even animal reproduction, selective breeding training has been working out for individuals to derive offsprings having appealing characters. In genetic alteration, notwithstanding, recombinant hereditary advancements are utilized to create life forms whose genetic information has been accurately modified, for the most part by the consideration of qualities from irrelevant types of living beings that code for characteristics that would not be acquired effectively through traditional selective breeding. GMOs are delivered utilizing logical strategies that incorporate recombinant DNA innovation and reproductive cloning.

From the cell of the cloning individual, the nucleus is extricated and embedded in the host cell with enucleated cytoplasm as in regenerative cloning. The procedure brings about the generation of an offspring that is hereditarily indistinguishable from the benefactor person.

The first-ever organism, a sheep called Dolly, was formed in 1996 through the mentioned cloning strategy. Afterward, organisms, including pigs, horses, and canines, were produced by the reproductive cloning technique.

Agribusiness, medication, research, environmental administration, and several other fields have become a part of hereditary enhancements. It primarily focuses on the extraction of fragments of an alien DNA and transferring it into the genome of suitably selected species having modified function.

4.3.1 Plasmid Method

It is the most generally used procedure. It utilizes plasmid, i.e., a tiny extrachromosomal DNA particle within a cell as shown in Figure 4.2 (source: https://en.m.wikipedia.org/wiki/File:Hartsock_Genetic_Engineering_Bacteria_Cell_Division.png).

Plasmid is included in a holder carrying restriction enzymes and afterward chops down into little pieces. A clingy sticky end is created which determines the cutting of the DNA by the restriction enzyme. A ring is formed by the consolidation of sticky clingy ends of DNA and

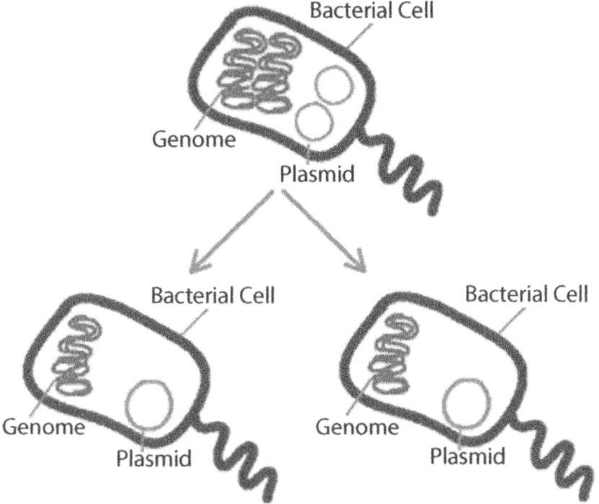

Figure 4.2 Plasmid method in a bacterial cell.

the DNA of the plasmid. They are made to stabilize. The formed plasmids are placed with a culture of live bacteria after which it will start expressing itself.

4.3.2 The Vector Method

This method uses vectors that are small DNA molecule used as a vehicle to carry foreign genes into another cell as shown in Figure 4.3.

Generally, they are viruses. The DNA [9] material is multiplied inside the host cell being its part. The vector strategy is finer as it utilizes a particular gene to derive a particular outcome. It results in ideal features.

4.3.3 The Biolistic Method

Prominently, it is known gene gun mechanism. It is mostly utilized for plants, but now, we are advancing for animals as well. Particles such as gold tungsten or silver are used; they are set in the gun and amidst the object and the gun a halfway vacuum is formed. The particles are fired, and hence, the DNA is successfully acquainted in the cell as shown in Figure 4.4.

Gene therapy or therapeutics is used for effective treatment of recessive gene disorder or acquired hereditary diseases; its target is to modify and comprehend to improve or alter the incorrect genes.

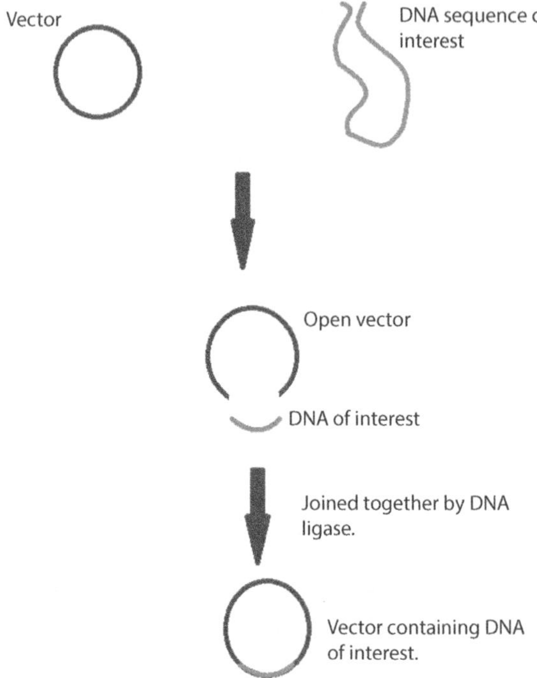

Figure 4.3 Cloning DNA of interest using the vector method.

Viral nanostructured and plasmodial can be the type of vector frequently utilized because of its effectiveness in attacking cells and introducing its hereditary material.

4.4 Food and Agriculture

Human consumption of GM food was primarily agreed in the USA and gradually cotton soybean and corn planted in large % were GM. The development of large number of GM crops was in the US.GM crops enveloped around 1.8 million sq.km of area and extended in more than 24 countries worldwide toward the end of 2014.

A bacterium, Bacillus Thuriengiensis, that itself delivers an inherent insecticide known as Bt toxin is being provided in numerous areas developing crops like corn and potatoes, and it gradually and effectively diminished the use of broad-ranged chemical insecticide. It also enhanced the capacity to overcome bollworm pervasion. Popularly in Bt cotton, as

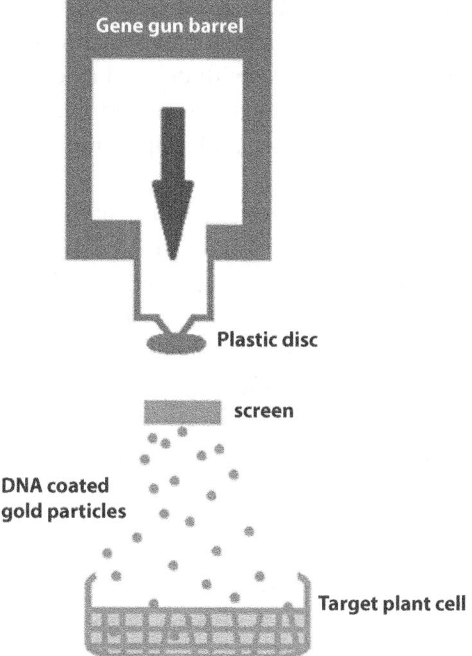

Figure 4.4 Biolistic gene gun.

shown in Figure 4.5 (source: https://www.https://pixabay.com/photos/cotton-bt-cotton-gmo-biotech-cotton-4220654/).

Several different plants are aimed and are target specific shielding from a bug or weed. There are also herbicide-resistant crops aimed for safeguarding from a certain synthetic herbicide.

Figure 4.5 BtCotton.

Calgene in 1994 designed the first genetically engineered food endorsed for carry out release the tomato named Flavr–savr as shown in Figure 4.6 which has a prolonged time for use with delayed ripening.

Others were changed oil arrangement of canola, Bt maize, Bt cotton, soybeans tolerance to glyphosate, and imperviousness of cotton from bromoxynil.

A daffodil's (Narcissus pseudonarcissus) quality gene was incorporated in an altered rice genome which enhanced the amount of beta-carotene convenient to vitamin A as compared to the normal rice thus giving rise to the production of the GOLDEN RICE as shown in Figure 4.7 (source: https://en.wikipedia.org/wiki/Golden_rice).

The gene consisted of the chemical phytoene synthase and also phytoene desaturase out of the bacterium Erwinia uredovora. In 2011, the creation of GM nourishments was carried forward by the US getting 25 GM

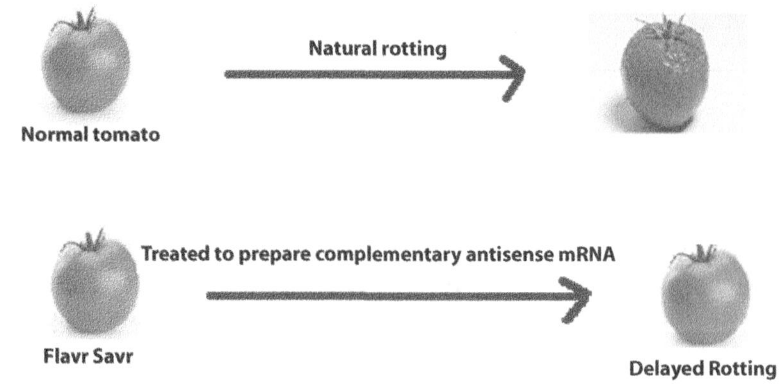

Figure 4.6 Flavr-Savr.

Figure 4.7 Golden rice as compared to normal gene rice.

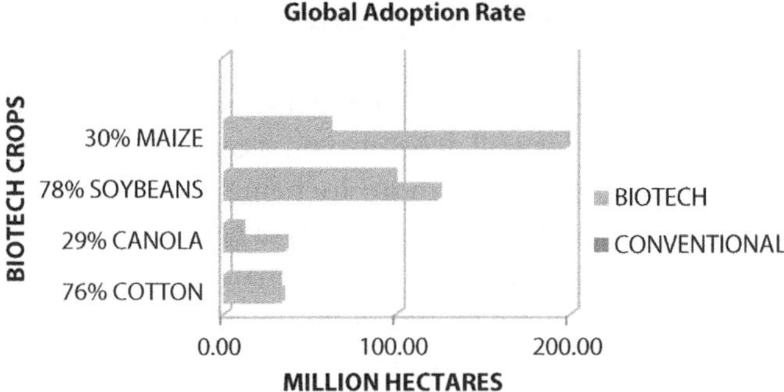

Figure 4.8 Global adoption rates for biotech crops (million hectares).

crops approved administratively. In 2015, US hereditarily altered strains to 92% of corn, 94% of soybeans, and 94% of cotton which was delivered to them. Global adoption rates as far are as shown in Figure 4.8. This graph has been adapted from [10].

AquaAdvantage Salmon is the first-ever genetically altered animal approved for food use in 2015. It was developed from a Pacific Chinook Salmon with hormone managing quality, which was being designed the whole year.

With the help of CRISPR procedure explained further, a white button mushroom was changed in 2016 which got recognized and received *de facto* approval for endorsement in the US. Since the altering procedure did not include incorporation of outside DNA the mushroom was absolved in light which was considered by the office.

4.5 Impact on Farmers

The control of utilization and dissemination of genetically engineered seeds was done by biotechnology organizations which had acquired licenses to do so. Wherever GMOs are developed or grown, it poses a danger to farmer's power as well as to the national food security.

Farmer faces economic loss which is a burden related to money; it usually occurred when GMO sullying was critical. A portion of the expenses to ranchers was used to compensate for the loss of access to the market dangers, and the cost of setting up deterrent measures to keep away from tainting. Buffer areas were made around the region for protection purposes.

Aside from the danger by defilement, already licensed GMO seeds if accidentally grown or gathered crossbred by the ranchers may land them into trouble and confront expensive claims for seed theft.

4.6 Diseases: Gene Editing and Curing

To end the circulation of deadly incurable diseases, human genetic engineering is developed and is well depended on. Issues such as diabetes, dystrophy, fibrosis cancer, and many more are being overcome by employing the use of genetic engineering. Recent trends of gene therapy research and clinical trials are as shown in Figure 4.9. The main focus of the clinical trials was found to be treating cancer, immune, digestive, and genetic diseases (Figure 4.9a) [11]. A relatively large number of clinical trials are recruiting cancer patients for testing different gene therapy–based medicines (Figure 4.9b) [11].

One of the greatest examples that revealed that genetic engineering has the power to improvise the attribute of a living being is now treatable deadly disease the "bubble boy" disease (Severe combined Immunodeficiency) and thus provides a greater life expectancy.

Hence, it's one of the greatest benefits is the idea of curing diseases in unborn children. Hereditary screening with a baby took into account the treatment of the unborn. This can affect in the long run for the developing spread of illnesses later on ages.

The group of DNA arrangements rooted out in prokaryotic life forms genes is CRISPR (Clustered Interspaced Short Palindromic Reshashes).

It was first utilized as a gene-editing tool in 2012. In only a couple of years, the innovation has detonated in prominence because of its making gene editing a lot quicker, less expensive, and simpler than at any other time.

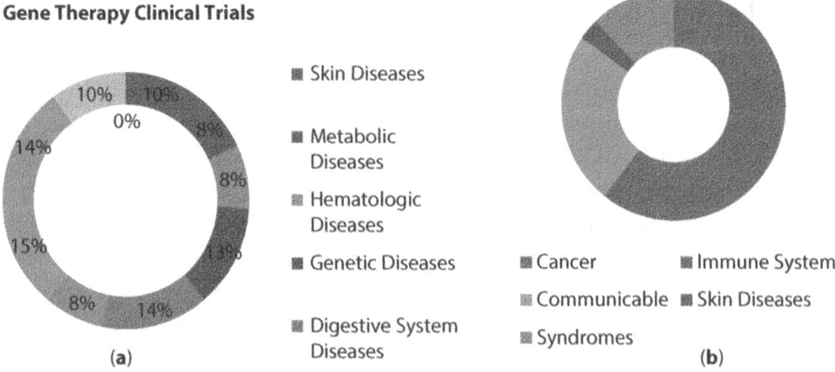

Figure 4.9 Recent trends in gene therapy research and clinical trials. (a) Different diseases being treated by gene therapy in clinical trials. (b) Clinical trials actively recruiting patients for testing gene therapy-mediated medicines in curing diseases.

CRISPR has just changed how researchers do look into it. Theoretically, it could let us modify any hereditary change. Its brief mechanism is as shown in Figure 4.10 (source: https://www.scielo.br/scielo.php?script=sci_arttext&pid=S1679-45082017000300369).

Though essentially, we are exactly toward the start of its turn of events. In food and cultivation, CRISPR would be implemented to inoculate modern societies to contamination. CRISPR-based methodologies using Cas12a have as of late been used in the fruitful alteration in a wide variety of plant species.

A 34-year-old was tentatively cured with hereditary issue earlier having sickle cell sickness last year. Earlier this year to cure Leber innate amaurosis a patient's eye was infused with CRISPR changed infection. Extinct species or newly found species can be designed with the help of CRISPR.

Starting in the resistant versatile arrangement of prokaryotes, this component perceives the attacking hereditary material, divides it into little pieces, and coordinates with its DNA. Secondly, the accompanying arrangement happens: locus translation, managing of RNAm, and making of little pieces of RNA that structure [7] edifices with the Cas proteins, and these perceive the outsider nucleic acids and lastly crush them. Given this regular component, the CRISPR strategy was created empowering altering of the objective explicit DNA succession. The translational testing of human somatic cells has given a quick headway utilizing modification through CRISPR. CRISPR technology can reach around more than 10,000 diseases previously depicted.

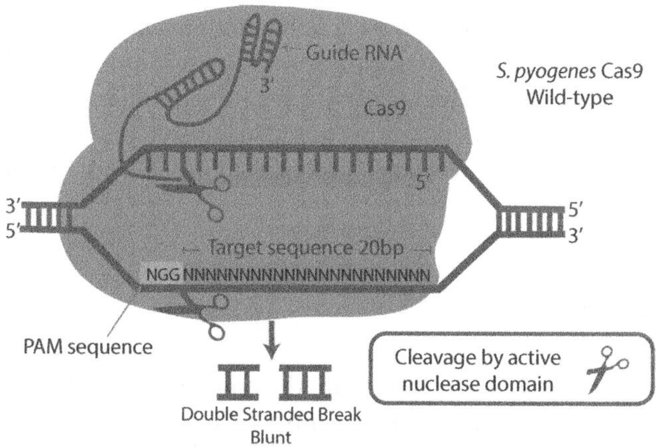

Figure 4.10 CRISPR technology mechanism.

Alessandro Marcello, Group Leader, Molecular Virology lab, arrived at a significant objective in the fight against coronavirus, confining and sequencing the full genome of SARS-Cov-2 on 20 March 2020. The full-genome sequencing of viral detaches is required to comprehend the hereditary development of the infection during the pandemic and to track the inception of the infections that arrived at the region. The accessibility of viral isolates permits research on analytic, antivirals, and immunizations to happen viably. To rapidly make potential antibodies against COVID-19, specialists are utilizing genetic engineering instead of conventional techniques, which can take years. Three different methods dependent on DNA and RNA molecules are speeding to human trials, yet whether they will work, or can be scaled up to a large number of portions, is unclear.

4.7 Conclusion

Genetic engineering has been proven to be a helpful and efficient way to improvise the modernization be it in any field. It is improving certain areas by altering compositions affecting productivity, efficiency, and ability to face various stresses. RNAi, antisense, and various other technologies can overexpress strategies. Knowledge regarding plant and animal biology and the most important technological innovations needs to be enhanced significantly. Bioinformatics is also paving its way used in methods of genetic engineering for more efficient and rapid outcomes.

The function of genetic engineering in the agricultural area for resistance and self-enhancement has been successfully disseminated. Therapeutic cloning and gene editing have concluded and is advancing successfully the promise of incurable disease treatment and a better future to look upon.

What is sure is that individuals will have the option to settle on choices about their lives in manners that were inconceivable previously, when we depended more on arbitrary development than pondering. In other words, we are "Hacking Darwin".

4.8 Future Scope

A GMO keeps on forcing and pushing the constraints of ultimate discoveries and technology and further invents alternatives to enhance the abilities and qualities of the living beings. By controlling genes and the ability to improve it humans can present the blessing of hereditary to the future generations. It assures of better sustainable future keeping in track all the safety and ethical issues and measures. GMOs can be recognized as the explanation of several environmental challenges with the existence of various loopholes also. It can largely change the future because of diverse complexity and precision. Slowly and gradually it is marking an end to conventional strategies and paving way for even faster easier future.

Certain emerging technologies in the future can be [3] TALEN CRISPR-for genome editing, advanced molecular biology, artificial and synthetic chromosomes, gene drive systems, and qualitative as well as quantitative editing traits. Several genetic analysis programs are being initiated in India concerning the Indian population giving rise to various inherent diseases. Also, major steps would be taken for understanding better in terms of new methods of diagnosis. To resist different types of infections and speed up breeding marker resistance selection is introduced. Gene editing policy for medical and agricultural prospects is also under consideration to evaluate. It is focusing on decreasing the allergenic capability and tackling the feasible effect of GM food and medical area carefully following the protocols and labeling.

References

1. Gori, J.L., Hsu, P.D., Maeder, M.L., Shen, S., Welstead, G.G., Bumcrot, D., Delivery and Specificity of CRISPR/Cas9 Genome Editing Technologies for Human Gene Therapy. *Hum. Gene Ther.*, 26, 7, 443–51, 2015.
2. Mukherjee, S., Chap. 34 Genetic therapies: posthuman gene therapy, in: *The gene: an intimate history*, p. 415, Scribner, Nova York, 2016.
3. Sanagalaab, R., Moola, A.K., Diana, R.K.B., A review on advanced methods in plant gene targeting. *J. Genet. Eng. Biotechnol.*, 15, 2, 317–321, 2017.
4. Britannica, T., Editors of Encyclopaedia (2021, July 30). Genetic Engineering. *Encyclopedia Britannica.* https://www.britannica.com/science/genetic-engineering
5. Badal, S. and Delgoda, R., Book *Pharmacognosy*, Science Direct, University of the West Indies, Kingston, Jamaica, 2017, https://doi.org/10.1016/C2014-0-01794-7.
6. Sharma, D., Singh, S., Chand, T., Chapter 42 of Book RNA Interference Therapeutics and Human Diseases, in: Book, "*Encyclopedia of Information Science and Technology*", Fourth Edition, pp. 477–490, PEC University of Technology, India, 2017.
7. Sharma, D., Singh, S., Chand, T., Kumar, P., Chapter RNA Secondary Structure, Prediction and Visualization Tools, in: Book, *Intelligent Communication, Control and Devices*, vol. 624, pp. 335–345, Springer, Singapore, 2018.

8. Giassetti, M., II, Maria, F.S., Assumpção, M.A.O.D., Visintin, J.A., Book Chapter- Genetic Engineering and Cloning: Focus on Animal Biotechnology, in: *Genetic Engineering*, May 22nd 2013, https://www.intechopen.com/books/genetic-engineering/genetic-engineering-and-cloning-focus-on-animal-biotechnology.
9. Kumar, P. and Sharma, D., String Algorithms for Counting DNA Nucleotides, Transcribing DNA to RNA and Complementing a Strand of DNA, in: *International Conference on Data Acquisition Transfer Processing and Management (ICDATPM-2014)*, held at Lingaya's University, Faridabad, pp. 244–247, on 28–29 March, 2014.
10. ISAAA, *Global Status of Commercialized Biotech/GM Crops: 2018*. ISAAA Brief No. 54, ISAAA, Ithaca, NY, 2018, https://www.isaaa.org/resources/publications/pocketk/16/.
11. Goswami, R., Subramanian, G., Silayeva, L. *et al.*, Gene Therapy Leaves a Vicious Cycle. *Front. Oncol.*, 9, 15, 2019.

5

Digital Investigative Model in IoT: Forensic View

Suryapratap Ray and Tejasvi Bhatia*

Department of Forensic Science, Lovely Professional University, Jalandhar, Punjab, India

Abstract

The multidisciplinary branch of science that is forensic science almost implicates all different disciplines of science to deal with various cases scientifically. The approach nowadays is very much efficient than it was used to be. Now, in the digital era where the use of various technologies is getting more popularized, forensic sciences got its own branches such as digital forensics, mobile forensics, and cyber forensics. Now, the application of artificial intelligence, machine learning, etc., is also engaged in this branch. The scope of this article suggests the use of artificial intelligence in forensic science in various cases as of now. This involves the application in blood spatter analysis, crime scene reconstruction, image examination, audio/video analysis, satellite monitoring, etc. We can observe a high potential of precession during the crime scene investigation till the verdict in court of law when implicating artificial intelligence. However, the article also pointed out the challenges and threats to the forensic domain as well as human being.

Keywords: Artificial intelligence, machine learning, forensic science, AI in forensic science, ANN

5.1 Introduction

When it comes to criminal justice delivery, forensic science puts forwarded numerous cases as example of its efficiency and the importance

**Corresponding author*: tejasvi.25999@lpu.co.in

Anita Gehlot, Rajesh Singh, Jaskaran Singh and Neeta Raj Sharma (eds.) Digital Forensics and Internet of Things: Impact and Challenges, (59–72) © 2022 Scrivener Publishing LLC

in a criminal case investigation [1]. To elaborate forensic sciences in simple terms, we can say that it is a multidisciplinary branch of science which efficiently uses various scientific principles to handle criminal cases and help to deliver justice in the court of law. The extensive use of artificial intelligence or AI can be observed nowadays which is efficient enough. Further discussion will illustrate various application of AI in forensic science [2]. AI can be defined as the ability of machines or computer to show case intelligence which can be compared to the intelligence of human or any other animal. Hence, it can be considered as "Machine Intelligence" [3]. The major aim to develop AI is to develop a machine to collect information from the environment as an input and act accordingly to reach the desirable results. This system can be compared to the ability of humans to learn and implementing. As the enhancement of AI is impactfully contributing various sectors, we can encounter various application of AI in crime scene reconstruction, blood spatter analysis, cyber forensics, data management and processing, data acquisition, pattern recognition, puzzle solving, questioned document analysis, ballistics (analysis of various firearms and projectiles), forensic medicine, forensic toxicology, pharmacological analysis, record maintenance, improving contact between individuals during an investigation, etc. [4]. Apart from all this, in forensic medicine, "virtual autopsy" is introduced. Virtual autopsy is the process in which the examination of dead body will be done without performing incision in the body. This is having various advantages over the traditional autopsy. However, this technology still needs special attention for the enhancement. Further discussion figured out the challenges that need to be eliminated for future enhancement of such technology. But sticking to the AI, the virtual autopsy uses AI technology to perform accordingly.

5.1.1 Artificial Neural Network

Artificial Neural Network or ANN is also implicated in the forensic investigations. ANN can be compared to human brain and the nervous system [5]. This technology basically runs independently after certain data are processed in terms of example, such as image recognition or object recognition in an image. To elaborate this, the system is given samples of dog images [6]. The system now will get various features that a dog possesses. Here upon the analysis when even the system will be deployed for any such task where a dog needs to be located, it will give the results from past learnings. Here, one complication can create hindrance that is the similarity of objects. For example, another such image having the similar features of dog is given to be analyzed. The system may give wrong answer or results. But in order to overcome this, the analysis can take place in pixel level [7]. The image that has been shown to the system will be processed initially in the pixel level. Further the results will be given after analyzing pixels of given image [8]. This really makes the error precise in results. The most advantageous thing in such technology is the less coding procedure. Unlike traditional systems which need various coding in order to take input and give output, it works with less coding and programming [9].

Considering forensic sciences, we do have seven laws in this branch. The following are the seven laws:

a) Law of Individuality
b) Locard's principle of Exchange
c) Principle of Comparison
d) Principle of Analysis
e) Principle of Probability
f) Principle of Progressive Change
g) Principle of Circumstantial Facts

Using any technology and following these principles can be helpful in crime scene and in the court of law as well. We can consider the Law of Exchange, which is also known as Locard's principle of exchange that is a very basic principle. AI can analyze a fingerprint or bloody impression to connect with the suspect and to explain scientifically in the court room as well. Using AI and ANN properly can be efficient even more. As of now various applications of AI already have been introduced and are explained as follows.

5.2 Application of AI for Different Purposes in Forensic Science

5.2.1 Artificial Intelligence for Drug Toxicity and Safety

Basile, Yahi, and Tatonetti explained about the preclinical drug safety and post-marketing surveillance of ADRs with an advanced technique that will be focused on machine and Deep Learning. There are two methods to monitor, detect and prevent the future toxicity and drug safety challenges [10]. Those are AI and traditional methods. The main approach of traditional methods has assessing for preclinical safety like "Quantitative Structure

Activity Relationships" (QSAR), which is largely moving toward group of machine learning and deep learning. Post-marketing pharmacovigilance (PV) relies on a variety of data source such as molecular, chemoinformatic, and clinical database as well as social media and biometrics literature [11]. DL-powered natural language processing (NLP) technique was embedding in attention mechanism including word to extract drug's advance effect (AE) relationship in text data [5]. The main approach at predicting ADES has been using annotated datasets that have exclusive use of supervised model limit and predicts novel and unknown drugs effect that cannot rely on labeled data. The down of AI ensemble the numerous questions in supervised modeling task like how incorporate unsupervised approaches in PV studies and how techniques such as GANS will be addressing these concerns. The main motive of this review is to promote the development of safe medical device, using AL algorithm in drug assessment an essential and pressing for development and safety in the future [12]. We need to establish data centres to control the risk of false positive. In the PV, implication of AI is having low risk assessment and also having high beneficial impact on healthcare in various aspects [13].

5.2.2 Crime Scene Reconstruction

In forensic investigation to maintain record, various methods have to be considered which further helps in crime scene reconstruction and to maintain the chain of custody as well. Methods including sketching of crime scene, photography, and other documentation are followed. But AI in the similar situation can help analyzing multiple videos, which must be captured before the collection evidence process. Analyzing multiple videos captured from different angles and giving a result as an animated crime scene video can be helpful in various aspects. Human mind cannot remember all the minute details simultaneously, but computer can do the same. Animated graphics can put forward much more detailed information in a crime scene with a 3-D representation [14].

5.2.3 Sequence or Pattern Recognition

After an initial investigation, the collection of data needs to be analyzed. Analysis can be done for various purposes such as data validation, shortlisting, and, in some case, identifying a desired object from the collection. One common aspect that all the information follows is the sequence or pattern. In some puzzles or riddles, we need to recognize the specific pattern in order to solve that. So, what AI's contribution in such cases is, it can use certain algorithms to solve or just to recognize the pattern followed. It helps in saving time and increases the accuracy as well. So, the basic mechanism that a system can follow is- at the initial stage it provided with various test patterns with given results [15]. AI analyzes the provided information at the initial stages and various test patterns are introduced thereafter. After this, during the training of the system, it is expected to recognize some other related patterns and the performance is examined. This programmed algorithm now can help solving and recognising various patterns in real time.

5.2.4 Repositories Building

The collection of crime records to maintain file and analyze past cases whenever needed is one of the important tasks that forensic experts or forensic scientist do. In such case using a compact disc, memory card, HDD, or any other such storage device can create hindrance. The size as we know cannot be expanded in such devices. But using AI, we can expand the space automatically when the memory needed to be expanded. The data interpretation can also be done simultaneously using such advantageous technology [16].

5.2.5 Establishment of Connection Among the Investigating Team

We can observe multiple involvements of various individuals from different organizations while investigating a crime, such as the investigating officers, medical officers, scientific team, police, and other persons whose involvement is needed. In such cases, the misunderstanding due to lack of communication or incomplete data sharing can easily happen. This situation can be minimized using various application of AI. Using various software that can help assist and build direct connection between all the individuals or responding officers, the direct virtual connection can be established. This will reduce the chances of error and mishandling of cases [17].

5.2.6 Artificial Intelligence and Expert System in Mass Spectrometry

Advance technologies of AI and expert system (ES) are operated by some of the aspects of mass spectrometry as reviewed by Li and Wang (2019).

Nowadays, with an evaluation of hardware competencies and computer software, both of these fields are growing quickly. Modern mass spectrometers have grown into essential parts of life with a particular attention to reward its importance on depending on AI and ESs. This article covers history of computer, data system, factor analysis, principal component analysis (biological applications), and techniques of optimization in MS and ANNs. Basically, AI and ESs are applied in MS techniques. ESs are method or program to fixed data or rule that will be control the method, data analysis and cause a result [18]. AI is connected with advanced scholarly practices like the ability to reason, generalize, discover, and learn are all connected with AI. Now, digital computers have become a crucial component of analytical instruments like MS, and their ability to perform tasks without variation is vital to produce reproducible and defendable in the results of experiments [17]. But they properly maximize instruments and efficiency of laboratory in giving fast end to user results, great sample throughput, and higher profitability. In early work, the data analysis made by conducting simultaneous liner equation results in raw peak conversion into mole fractions of normalized analyte. Seventeen-component sample needed 0.5- to 3-min computer processing time [19]. Today's mixture order of magnitudes more analyte with a reduced amount of time, offering considerably extra information rather than simple quantification of peak. AI to macrospectral interpretation applications worked in DENDRAL that is a list processing language-based code, eight-peak index are most familiar version for Mass Spectrometrists. MS compares or highly analyzes the dimensional multivariate data that have been used for chemometrics and that may give qualitative information from natural system. The application ANNs used in qualitative or quantitative analysis are becoming more acceptable in the MS because neural computational methods have portrayed themselves as an exceedingly effective and valuable tool for the complex data analysis [20]. MALDI/TOF simple calibrations for optimization in mass spectroscopy are easily executable and robust [21]. These results are comparable with polynomial curve fitting for routine applications and the main motive of this article to excel resulting in more hard and tough conditions for instance when sample and calibrants are different fundamentally, when calibrant peaks are correctly assigned or when the range of mass interest is extended past that of the calibration and can be used in a wide variety of application to analyze an accurate result in the complex data [22].

5.2.7 AI in GPS Navigation

In various situations in a forensic investigation and even in other cases, the GPS was found to be an efficient option to carryout various tasks. It helps in shortlisting different routes to a particular location. It also suggests the best route to choose according to the vehicle, weather condition, traffic, and other factors [23]. GPS implicates AI to collect information in real time to provide the best it can (Figure 5.1). The results can vary according to the weather condition, traffics, stop signs, holidays, etc. The given image below (Figure 5.2) is collected from Google Map. Time 5.30 PM IST and the date recorded as 2nd February 2021. It covers

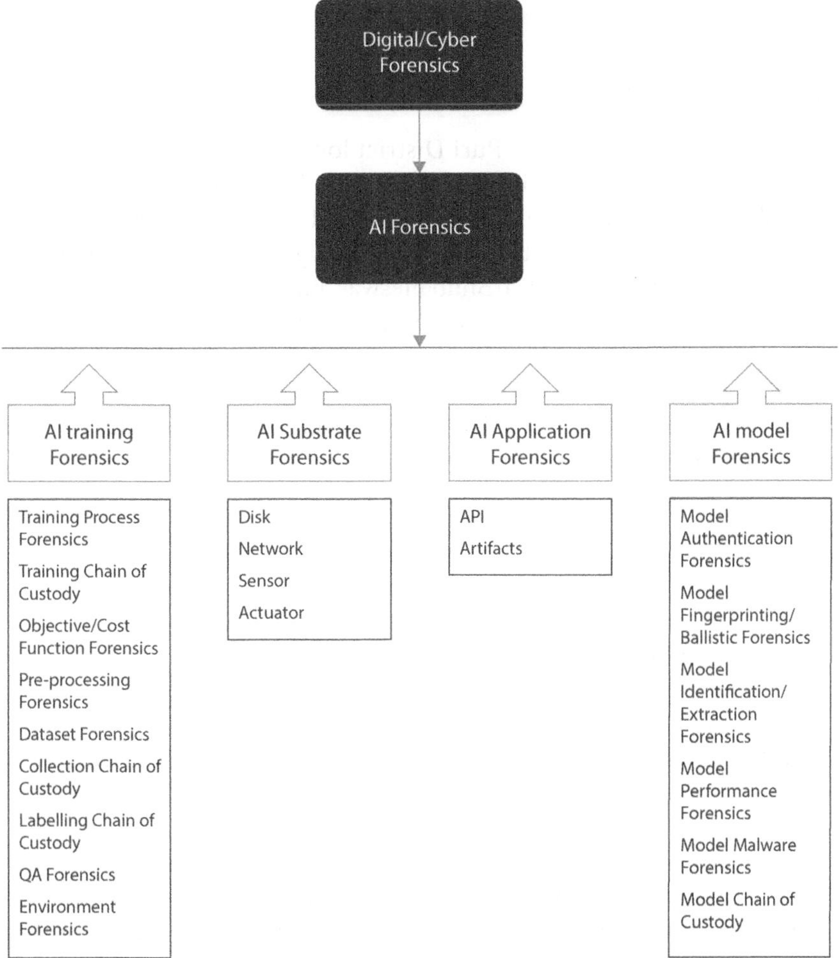

Figure 5.1 Describes the subdomains of AI forensics [3].

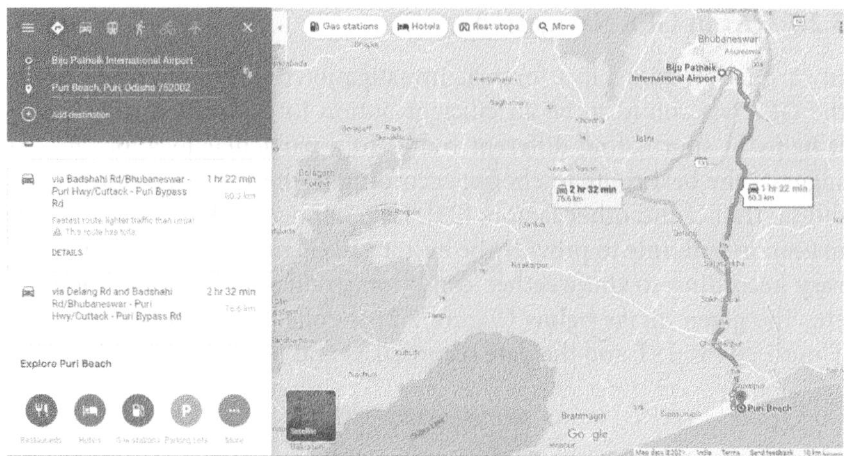

Figure 5.2 AI in GPS navigation.

the Khordha district and the Puri District located in Odisha state, India. The information as per the image is the result derived when the direction was asked from Biju Pattnayak International Airport, Bhubaneswar to Puri Beach. Two routs can be located as highlighted by Google Map. The Blue one (via Badshahi Rd/Bhubaneswar-Puri Highway/cuttack-Puri bypass road) suggests the fastest route which is having toll gates and around 60 km, wherein the other light-colored route (via Delang Rd) is the other possible route which is 76.6 km and no toll gates are there. The map also suggests the time, which can vary accordingly depending on the above mentioned factors [24].

5.3 Future of AI

Although it has various useful features while implicating AI, it also fails in some situations. The GPS in our mobile phones helps Google Map to gather information about the traffic. It can be manipulated intentionally or unintentionally by deploying multiple GPS devices to misguide Google satellites which are collecting information about the traffic. Hackers can also mislead the connection by manipulating the server, etc., with criminal intension.

Numerous applications can be found well evolved and some under developing condition as well. Such as voice analyzing software which uses AI, face recognition feature, and detection of manipulated facial features. Although we consider AI as an advancing and emerging technology, it has lots of aspects to be worked upon for the betterment so as to get flawless results upon demand. The following discussion regarding the challenges can give the idea that we can encounter while using AI in forensics.

5.4 Challenges While Implementing AI

5.4.1 Unexplainability of AI

Sound and evident root origin investigation of failing in AI may desire translucent and definite clarification of the decision-making practice which appears in inadmissible behavior [25]. Though, the study on the explainability of complicated AI systems is still at its initial stages, and it is quite difficult to solving the problem of explainability. Additionally, some recent information disagreed that as the AI technology and proficiency progress over time; it can be tougher or even impossible for AI systems to be understandable [26]. In this condition, simpler abstractions of the decision-making process can intensify the forensic inquiry of such failing. For example, recommend a psychopathological abstraction for complicated AI security problems. Same abstractions can be desired to facilitate scientific forensic investigation of advances AI [27].

5.4.2 AI Anti-Forensics

In the sphere of digital forensics, culprits continually modify to the state of the technology and promote techniques such as decoys, false evidence, or forensic cleaning to retard the forensic analysis [28]. It is feasible that such anti-forensic techniques can be assumed and modified by culprits to employ AI forensic analysis. Proactive description of such techniques and advancement of alleviate solutions will become a progressively necessary area of research in this sphere. A new anti-forensics general taxonomy was formulated by the researchers. So far, anti-forensics was not included in the taxonomy [29].

5.4.3 Connection Interruption Between the Cyber Forensics and AI Communities

One of the tremendous challenges faced is the disconnection between the AI safety and cyber forensics communities (Figure 5.3). Researchers from those spheres are not working together. Though, the sphere of AI forensics has not been accepted and is prepared for future research. This disconnection was supposed in a new survey study, where the maximum number of digital forensic practitioners was agreed or neutral on their proficiency in data science [29, 30].

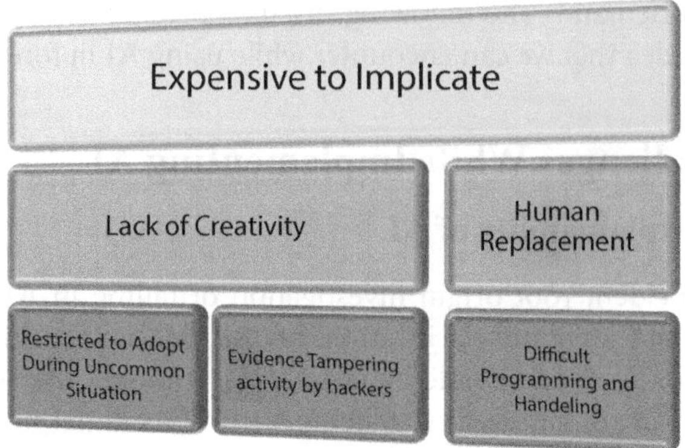

Figure 5.3 Challenges on implication of AI.

5.4.4 Data Analysis and Security

Implementing various technologies, it has been easy to increase storage capacity in various ways upon needed with no time. Storage over cloud and physical devices such as HDD can be easily upgraded. But the main concern is to analyze the huge size of data and to provide security. It is very challenging to analyze this source of data without more manpower and advanced technology. Apart from this, cyber-crimes can be a threat. Keeping the fact in front that the number of cyber hacking activities was found to be increasing at a high rate, hackers can steal data in a single run when we keep our data saved in a single storage space. Also, hackers tend to evolve frequently according to the frequent development and enhancement in the security. The advancement in technology needs further advancement for the safeguarding of information [6].

5.4.5 Creativity

It can be easily noted that the creativity and critical thinking considering the situation to be dealt can create a huge difference when we compare human and the AI technology. Humans can train to be more creative and can adopt to deal with numerous situations [31].

5.5 Conclusion

From the above discussion, it is clear that we are using AI and ANN in different techniques combinedly to get better accuracy and reliability in our results. However, it can also be observed that we have a lot of challenges to face and overcome while using such advanced technology as well. The current studies on the same area are trying to overcome such challenges either by minimizing them or by enhancing the AI technology. Various new technologies based on AI are still under development and in some case under continuous controversy. But it is clear that the future of AI in forensic science is well enlightened with the contribution of various researchers. Already we are able to implicate AI in most of the cases in forensic techniques as mentioned above and many more. The continuous effort will be a grate breakthrough in overcoming and enhancing the technology.

References

1. Bishop, C.M., Neural Networks for Pattern Recognition. Oxford University Press, Inc., USA, 1995.
2. Costantini, S., De Gasperis, G., Olivieri, R., Digital forensics and investigations meet artificial intelligence. *Ann. Math. Artif. Intell.*, 86, 1–3, 193–229, 2019.
3. Duce, D.A., Mitchell, F.R., Turner, P., Haggerty, J., Merabti, M. (Eds.), Digital forensics: Challenges and opportunities. Liverpool John Moores University, UK, 2007.
4. Farquhar, A., Fikes, R., Rice, J., The Ontolingua Server: a tool for collaborative ontology construction. *Int. J. Hum. Comput. Stud.*, 46, 6, 707–27, 1997.
5. Hoelz, B.W.P., Ralha, C.G., Geeverghese, R., Artificial intelligence applied to computer forensics, in: *Proceedings of the 2009 ACM symposium on Applied Computing - SAC '09*, New York, ACM Press, New York, USA, 2009.
6. Kadam, P., Artificial intelligence in digital forensics. *Digit. Forensics (4N6)*, 2020 August.
7. Kamdar, S.R. and Pandey, A., The Scope of Artificial Intelligence in Forensic Science. 58, 3, 48–51.
8. Lipmann, RP., An Introduction to Computing with Neural Nets. *IEEE ASSP Mag.*, 4, 4–22, 1987.
9. Turner, P., Unification of digital evidence from disparate sources (Digital Evidence Bags). *Digit Investig.*, 2, 3, 223–8, 2005.
10. Basile, A.O., Yahi, A., Tatonetti, N.P., Artificial intelligence for drug toxicity and safety. *Trends Pharmacol. Sci.*, 40, 9, 624–35, 2019.
11. Ma, J., Sheridan, R.P., Liaw, A., Dahl, G.E., Svetnik, V., Deep neural nets as a method for quantitative structure-activity relationships. *J. Chem. Inf. Model.*, 55, 2, 263–74, 2015.
12. Willighagen, E.L., The Chemistry Development Kit (CDK) v2. 0: atom typing, depiction, molecular formulas, and substructure searching. *J. Cheminform.*, 9, 33, 2017.

13. Kuhn, M., Campillos, M., Letunic, I., Jensen, L.J., Bork, P., A side effect resource to capture phenotypic effects of drugs. *Mol. Syst. Biol.*, 6, 1, 343, 2010.
14. Amamra, A., Amara, Y., Boumaza, K., Benayad, A., Crime scene reconstruction with RGB-D sensors, in: *Proceedings of the 2019 Federated Conference on Computer Science and Information Systems*, IEEE, 2019.
15. Kim, H., Kim, I., Kim, K., AIBFT: Artificial intelligence browser forensic toolkit. *Forensic Sci. Int.: Digital Invest.*, 36, 301091, 301091, 2021.
16. Venulet, J., Ciucci, A.G., Berneker, G.C., Updating of a method for causality assessment of adverse drug reactions. *Int. J. Clin. Pharmacol. Ther. Toxicol.*, 24, 10, 559–68, 1986.
17. Baggili, I. and Behzadan, V., Founding The Domain of AI Forensics. arXiv [Internet], 2019, Available from: http://arxiv.org/abs/1912.06497.
18. Polyakov, V.V., Bespechniy, O.V., Neymark, M.A., Artificial intelligence as an object of forensic study: perspectives from a border region, in: *Proceedings of the International Conference on Sustainable Development of Cross-Border Regions: Economic, Social and Security Challenges (ICSDCBR 2019)*, Paris, France, Atlantis Press, 2019.
19. Zhang, J., Gu, Z., Jang, J., Wu, H., Stoecklin, M.P., Huang, H. *et al.*, Protecting intellectual property of deep neural networks with watermarking, in: *Proceedings of the 2018 on Asia Conference on Computer and Communications Security - ASIACCS '18*, New York, ACM Press, New York, USA, 2018.
20. Li, J.-H., Cyber security meets artificial intelligence: a survey. *Front. Inf. Technol. Electron. Eng.*, 19, 12, 1462–74, 2018.
21. Behzadan, V., Yampolskiy, R.V., Munir, A., *Emergence of addictive behaviors in Reinforcement Learning agents*. 2018, Available from: http://arxiv.org/abs/1811.05590.
22. Santoso, D. and Jeon, H., Understanding of GPU architectural vulnerability for deep learning workloads, in: *2019 IEEE International Symposium on Defect and Fault Tolerance in VLSI and Nanotechnology Systems (DFT)*, IEEE, 2019.
23. Ramakrishnan, P.N., Forensic analysis of navigation system (GPS) – A case study. *Forensic Sci. Criminol.*, 3, 1, 1–6, 2018.
24. Yampolskiy, R.V., Artificial intelligence safety and security. Chapman and Hall/CRC, USA, 2018.
25. Yampolskiy, R.V. and Spellchecker, M.S., Artificial intelligence safety and cybersecurity: A timeline of AI failures. 2016,
26. Farrell, M.G., Merrell Dow Pharmaceuticals D, Inc.: Epistemilogy and Legal Process. *Cardozo L Rev.*, 15, 2195–2196, 1993.
27. Chen, X., Liu, C., Li, B., Lu, K., Song, D., Targeted backdoor attacks on deep learning systems using data poisoning. 2017, Available from: http://arxiv.org/abs/1712.05526.

28. Grajeda, C., Sanchez, L., Baggili, I., Clark, D., Breitinger, F., Experience constructing the Artifact Genome Project (AGP): Managing the domain's knowledge one artifact at a time. *Digit. Investig.*, 26, S47–58, 2018.
29. Sanchez, L., Grajeda, C., Baggili, I., Hall, C., A practitioner survey exploring the value of forensic tools, AI, filtering, & safer presentation for investigating child sexual abuse material (CSAM). *Digit. Investig.*, 29, S124–42, 2019.
30. Gogolin, G., The digital crime tsunami. *Digit. Investig.*, 7, 1–2, 3–8, 2010.
31. Patlewicz, G. and Fitzpatrick, J.M., Current and future perspectives on the development, evaluation, and application of in silico approaches for predicting toxicity. *Chem. Res. Toxicol.*, 29, 4, 438–51, 2016.

6

Internet of Things Mobility Forensics

Shipra Rohatgi[1]*, Aman Sharma[2] and Bhavya Sharma[3]

[1]Amity Institute of Forensic Sciences, Amity University, Noida, India
[2]Digital Forensic Division, Directorate of Forensic Science, Junga, Shimla Hills, India
[3]M.Sc. Forensic Science, Punjabi University, Patiala, India

Abstract

The Internet of Things has made it all possible to connect appliances with the internet. The built-in sensors get connected to the internet and transfer all the integrated data to the application. This transferred data helps in the management of the smart devices and controls the particular functions that need to be performed. Forensic science deals with the applications and techniques for the analysis of evidence obtained from the scene of crime, for the purpose of law. Whereas, mobility forensics deals with the software, tools, and techniques for the analysis of mobile phones and smart devices for the purpose of law. In the last few years, the easy approach to smart devices has resulted in the exponential growth of cybercrime. Here, it becomes important for the forensic examiner to perform analysis by maintaining the protocol. Forensic analysis requires highly sensitive and rational techniques so that the data is not at all manipulated due to any error. The IoT devices have the most special feature of transferring all their data to one source. This could help the forensic examiner to extract the data from a single source that will result in rapid examination. The usage of IoT-based data would help the investigation team in most ways. As the amount, nature, and sensitivity of data are large, it provides a wide range of possibilities in the investigation. It requires focusing on the techniques used for the analysis of IoT data.

Keywords: Internet of Things, mobility, forensics, cybercrime, analysis

**Corresponding author*: shiprarohatgi8@gmail.com

Anita Gehlot, Rajesh Singh, Jaskaran Singh and Neeta Raj Sharma (eds.) Digital Forensics and Internet of Things: Impact and Challenges, (73–86) © 2022 Scrivener Publishing LLC

6.1 Introduction

"Hello, Google" or asking Alexa to operate has made it easy for us. A man jogging, walking, running, or doing a day-to-day activity is capable of tracking the health parameters [5]. A person sitting in a car can turn on/off home appliances by using a smartphone. A car can be controlled by the operator sitting in a room kilometer apart. Whether it is about monitoring a human, appliances, or a machine, the Internet of Things (IoT) is the key for all.

The word internet means "a network that connects devices" and things mean "different appliances". Thereby, the IoT could be understood as a network that connects the different appliances [4]. To understand the meaning of the IoT, we need to focus on the origin and the ultimate source. In the last two decades, a sudden rise in technology was observed. With the invention of computers to laptops, button mobile phone to a fully smartphone, and the journey of the internet from 1G to 5G the world has witnessed the growth of technology. The end-to-end traditional methods of connecting devices have been overcome by the invention of the IoT [12].

IoT can connect the devices at a much broader range. The connectivity is no more restricted within an area of cables. It is essential to understand that invention of the IoT has made lives trouble-free. The traffic signal, street lights, and home appliances such as air conditioners, televisions, car locks, car mobility, Goggle Homes, and Amazon Alexa, all are based on the principle of the IoT [14]. It consists of specialized micro sensors that work on a specific idea. Also, it provides a user-friendly approach, and numerous features in a device help in the customization accordingly.

With the rise in technology, crime related to technology also increases rapidly. Every day, the rate and nature of cybercrime expand that consequently generates the requirement of up-gradation in forensic technologies. Presently, data extraction in logical and physical guise from mobile phones is a vital task for forensic analysts. There is few internationally manufactured software specifically for forensic data extraction from internal and external storage devices and mobile phones.

Mobility forensics is an expression used to describe the need for forensic science that focuses on the data recovery from mobile phones, smartphones, and internal and external storage devices. It also focuses on the necessity to have different software, tools, and techniques according to the nature of the device that can help in data extraction and analysis as mentioned in Figure 6.1 [3].

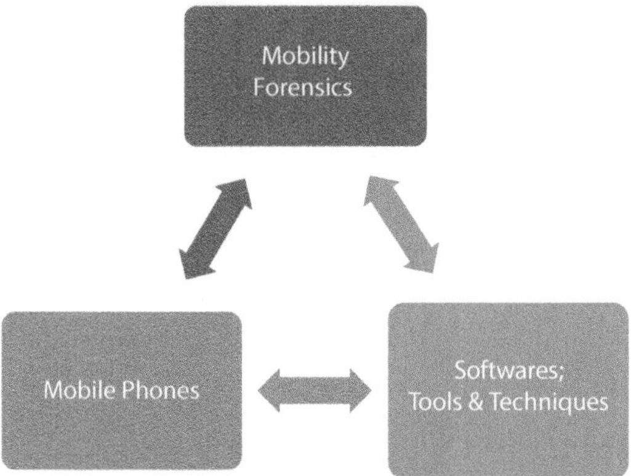

Figure 6.1 Model explaining the interrelation of mobility forensics with mobile phones and software's, tools and techniques.

IoT uses sensors that connect with the devices even from a distance. The sensors help in the localization, tracking, data storage, and identification of required factors [9]. Let us understand this by an example of "Apple Home Kit". It allows the management of all the smart devices such as lights, air conditioners, thermostats, home locks, and CCTV cameras. Apple Home Kit is the central platform for managing all the movements of sensors. The sensor is the primary part that senses, tracks, and transfers data to the central platform. Whenever a crime is committed in a house or with a person using the framework Apple Home Kit, a lot of data can be removed and that data can help in the investigation procedures on great terms.

Likewise, there are numbers of IoT that help the forensic investigation. The IoT are generally connected and worked using a smart device that could be a smart mobile, tablet, or any other mobile device.

6.2 Smart Device and IoT

A smart device is a machine that works smartly. Whether it is a smartphone, tablet, or even a smartwatch, they all consist of sensors. Sensors in smart devices are specialized microchips that detect the changes happening and respond accordingly to the other system. The changes sensed by the sensors are transferred in the form of digital signals that further transfers them into human-readable form. If seen as architectural, then they all have a similar internal architect though the difference occurs in the functions they are required to perform. The structure of smart devices

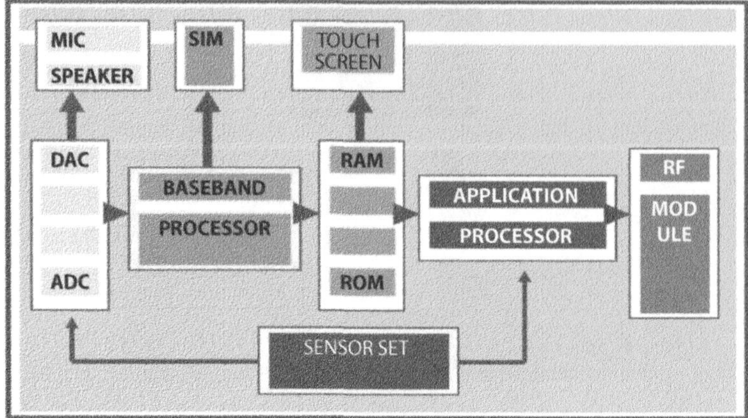

Figure 6.2 Diagrammatic representation of internal structure of smart devices.

is largely classified into two parts the application processor and the sensor set. The interfacing parts such as analog-to-digital converters (ADCs) and digital-to-analog converters (DACs) connect the application processor to the sensor [8]. The nature of functioning, speed, and all other features depends upon the total number of processing units present in the smart devices. Whereas, the sensors enhance the usability, controllability, and management of the device. The basic structures of smart devices are diagrammatically explained in Figure 6.2.

6.3 Relation of Internet of Things with Mobility Forensics

In the modern world of technology, we all are surrounded and dependent on gadgets, appliances, and smart devices. Having a mobile phone, using the internet for different purposes is such a common phenomenon in the 21st century. It would not be incorrect to say that we do not use machines anymore; instead, slowly machines have started using us.

Using a smart device and application is itself permission for the sources to capture all essential information and data that we store in the device to be transferred unethically. It does not matter that how much security a source assures you to protect your data, the unethical hacking and sources are enough capable of recovering it. Adding to this when the IoT-based smart devices are used and linked to the prime source smartphone, the sensors of smart devices transfer all the data to smartphone.

Now, here, smartphone is the center to collect and combine all the data. In general, smart devices are used to make lives easier and more functional. But, at the same time, the security and privacy of data linked with the IoT devices is a huge issue that needs to be protected.

6.3.1 Cyber Attack on IoT Data

Traditionally, the cyberattacks were restricted to certain data or information. The technology working with advancement is also looking upon to strengthen the security and privacy of the device and data. But as the security increases, the techniques to hack the device also update. If we are updating the techniques to tackle cybercrime, then the criminal is also updating its techniques and vice versa. And now, not just to be restricted with traditional devices, the crime against the IoT has been increased. The traditional method of protecting the device from ransomware attacks is no more suitable for IoT devices because it requires more computing and resources for protection [5].

The cyber attackers look toward the IoT devices as a gold mine. When we compare the traditional cyber systems with IoT cyber systems often called cyber-physical systems, there is a major difference in the manner of data storage. In the traditional method, all the data gets stored within the system [13. But in IoT devices, the data from the sensor is transferred to the connected center source. The sensors transfer all the data to a center called decentralization that comes with numerous benefits and disadvantages. All the data can be collected from a single source that is why it is an attractive field for cyber attackers. The nature of the physical sensors provides a highly vulnerable opportunity for the security and privacy of the data.

Let us understand the whole concept using a real-life situation. When we install an application on smartphones before starting, we have to provide them access by sharing location, photos, and other information. Whenever we book a cab the location is to be shared in the application. By attaching the physical sensors in the smart devices connected to the smartphones also ask for access to data. We often share collaborated mails, data, documents, information with friends and family, that we are providing full access to the shared data. Under such circumstances, it is such an easy process for the hacker to hack and extract all the data.

The data can be therefore utilized for any erroneous act. Suppose the car sensors are attached to the source of the hacker and now he can control all the possible functioning of the car. It thereby can lead to a catastrophe.

You might have observed certain mails on your email id that goes directly to the spam folder or certain emails assuring that they are providing you

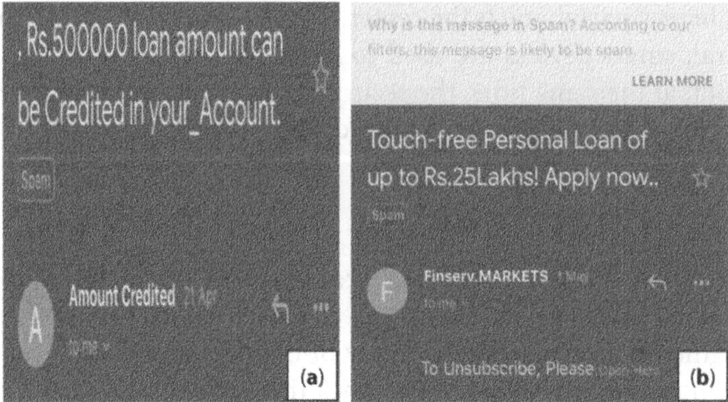

Figure 6.3 (a) The email says "referring email id that Rs. 5,000,000 loan amount can be credited in your account". It provides with a tempting offer and a link below to click on. (b) In the second email, it provides you with an option to "unsubscribe" and click on the "Open here" option.

money as you have won a lottery. Also, it can be someone calling you referring that they are from your concerned bank and asking for an OTP to reactivate your ATM card. All of these aspects are general tricks to get access to your device and hack all the information from your devices. Your smartphone is the center for all the data and information for IoT devices, and by getting trapped in such a situation, you provide full access to the data as shown in Figure 6.3.

All these are the basic methods by which the attackers can get access to the data.

6.3.2 Data Recovery from IoT Devices

Whenever a crime is committed, the investigator preserves the scene of crime and starts searching for the evidence. The evidence will be the basis for the victim to get justice and the criminal to get punishment; it becomes important to search for them correctly. Cybercrimes are new to the world and are still evolving. The cases in which evidence related to mobile phones, storage devices, or any other smart device is found is directed to the forensics for the analysis [8]. There are sufficient digital forensic laboratories that help in the extraction of data from the recovered mobile phones.

An investigator indeed relies on digital evidence more than any other evidence. The reason behind this is the amount of data and information digital evidence can give which is non-comparable to others [9]. Smartphones linked with IoT devices are themselves a huge data source.

For example, suppose a crime is committed inside a house which is having security sensors at the gate and the criminal was unaware of that. The sensors were capable of recording the picture, video, timing, and all other movements around the gate. The security sensors were linked with the mobile phone of the owner. The forensic team here can extract the data of the security sensor from the Smartphone using forensic tools and techniques. That would help the investigation team to encounter the criminal. But is it so easy to extract data from IoT devices? The answer is no. There is still a long way for forensics to generate all the data from the IoT devices. The volatile nature and the attacks over the data make the whole process a bit complicated.

Software such as Cellebrite UFED, Access Data FTK, XRY, and Oxygen are generally used for data extraction from mobile and smart devices. This mentioned software's help in the extraction of all the logical and physical data from mobile phones. But this software is not fully designed to extract all the data and information from the application or framework controlling the smart IoT devices.

The IoT devices are managed by the applications or a framework installed and linked with the sensor on the smartphone. The nature of data extraction completely depends upon the strength of security and privacy the application or framework provides. The sensitivity of the center to store all the data and the manner of storage of data will decide that how the data will be extracted, how much data will be extracted and the nature of data that needs to be extracted. The "Goggle Cloud IoT Core" is software that helps one to manage all the IoT data, device tracking status, locations, and all other important information. It provides and promises complete security and privacy to the data.

6.3.3 Scenario-Based Analysis of IoT Data as Evidence

With the introduction of the IoT, lives have for sure become easier. The data transferred from the IoT sensors to the applications controlled by smartphones or to the cloud can be recovered directly from the device using logical methods. There are certain cases where the investigation team could only solve the case by using the information stored by the sensors.

Case Study 1: A group of tourists was traveling from one region in India to another by using a rented car. The company that owns the rented car has used a sensor that can control and monitor the car. The tourists were traveling to the mountains and the car went missing. Then, the police contacted the rented car company and got all the location and information regarding the travel of the car. The car was found in one of the ditches of the mountains. All the dead bodies were recovered. Also, it was found that when the accident happened the speed was more than 60 Km/h that was sensed by the sensor and transferred to the source.

Case Study 2: A 60-year-old man was found dead in his house. He used to live with a servant. The family was accusing the servant of the death. When the investigating team reached the scene of a crime, the body was lying on the bed in the same condition in which death occurred. They observed a watch on his hand. He was wearing a smartwatch that can track his health parameters and whenever any misconduct will be sensed it will transfer the information to linked contacts asking for urgent help. The investigator searched the watch followed by the Smartphone. It was found that the pulse rate was abrupt from 10:37 PM to 11:04 PM before the death, and around 11:04 PM, the pulse stopped. It was clear that it was not a murder. Further on postmortem, it was found that the death occurred due to cardiac arrest and not murder.

Case Study 3: A burglary case was registered in 2021. When the investigation team reached the scene of the crime, it was found that the house was equipped with several security sensors and hidden cameras. All the sensors were connected to the cloud storage in the owner's house. The data was not stored in the mobile but was directed to the cloud directly. The limit of the cloud to store data was only 5 GB, and after getting new files, it directly deletes the older ones. The data was recovered and it was found that the security guard tried to control the sensors and introduced a thief inside the house when no one was present there. The door sensors recorded even the minor moments and the graphs of the moments were collected from the cloud storage. The pictures and video were also collected. The case was directly solved using this evidence, and further, the criminals were found and subjected to punishment by a court of law.

6.4 Mobility Forensics IoT Investigation Model

The investigation of mobility forensics works as same as any other evidence. But the method used for the analysis differs [1, 10]. The common model for the forensic investigation of IOT-based devices diagrammatically explained in Figure 6.4 and is explained as follows:

a) Pre-Investigation: Whenever the crime is committed till the investigation team reached the crime scene, it all comes

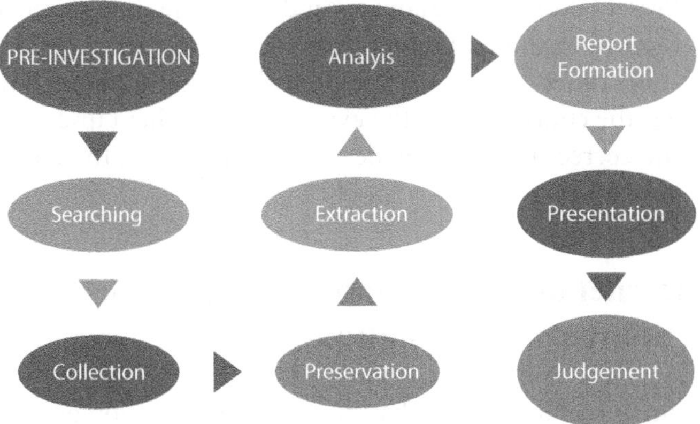

Figure 6.4 Common model explaining the process of forensic investigation for IoT-based devices.

under pre-investigation. The sealing of crime scene, photography, videography, and note-making is the essential part of pre-investigation.

b) Searching: Completing the pre-investigation, the investigation team goes for the searching of evidence. In the IoT-based crime cases smart devices, their central sources are the main evidence.
c) Collection and Preservation: After recovering evidence, the most essential step is to collect the evidence in the most suitable manner. A wrong collection method can, however, manipulate the evidence and that is unlawful for forensic examination. The prime collection should focus on the central source of sensors transferring data. The collected devices should be carefully preserved in a faraday bag, to avoid the interaction of the device with networks.
d) Extraction and Analysis: By following the methods and true ethical softwares, the data of IoT devices can be extracted. It is the main step of the investigation that will decide the further accomplishments in the investigation. The data extracted should be carefully analyzed by the forensic examiner.
e) Report Formation: Using the software itself, the report should be generated attaching the meaningful data found during analysis. That will help the investigation team to explain the details easily in the court of law.

f) Presentation in Court of Law and Judgment: If required, the forensic examiner presents his report in the court of law. At some times, due to a lack of knowledge on concerned topics, the court requires the expert to make them understand the correct nature of evidence. Based on that, the court of law makes its final verdict.

6.5 Internet of Things Mobility Forensics: A Source of Information

The introduction of IoT devices has made the investigation procedure a bit uncomplicated. It cannot be seemed as unique or idiosyncratic but is possibly called contemporary related to forensic analysis. For sure, its nature of providing a large amount of data and information is a treasure. The reason for the analysis of IoT devices is no different than other evidence, but a difference occurs in the method of analysis. The template for the information to be collected from forensic analysis of IoT device data is as shown in Figure 6.5.

6.6 Drawbacks in IoT Devices Data Extraction

The tools, techniques, and software are used to extract data from smartphones. The ongoing upgrading of chipsets in smartphones on regular

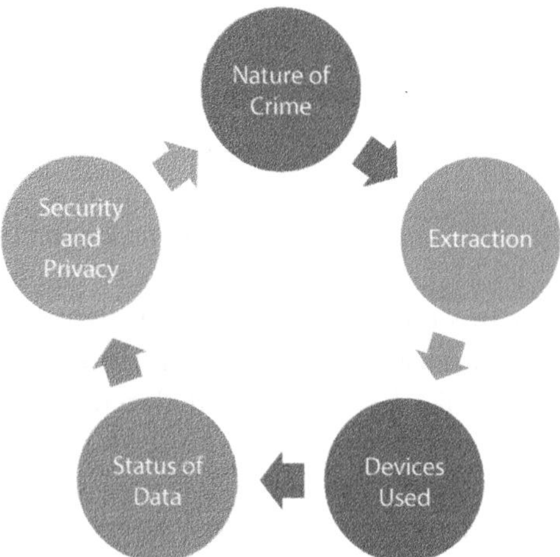

Figure 6.5 Factors related to the IoT mobility forensics.

basics is becoming a problem for the extraction of data. The companies of smartphones are coming with new models of Android and IOS devices try to help the customers with a high-security barrier [2]. Forensic scientists are still struggling to extract physical data from Smartphones. In all of this, now, there is one more struggle of extracting data of IoT devices from smartphones. The drawback of IoT in forensics is explained using Figure 6.6.

1. Manipulation of Data: The lack of security and privacy makes the data vulnerable to the attacking sources. Whether the data gets attacked by malware, spyware, and any other such source or the attacker gets access to it, it completely changes the nature of data. This change in nature, therefore, alters the data and hence can hinder the investigation policies. Though this data manipulation can be preserved by the forensic analyst by using the methods to lower IoT platforms power.
2. False Negative and False Positive: The high sensitive nature and human involvement often result in several false negative and positive results. There is no defined reason or solution for the problem. Human error is though considered as one of the reasons for its occurrence. So, why analyzing data

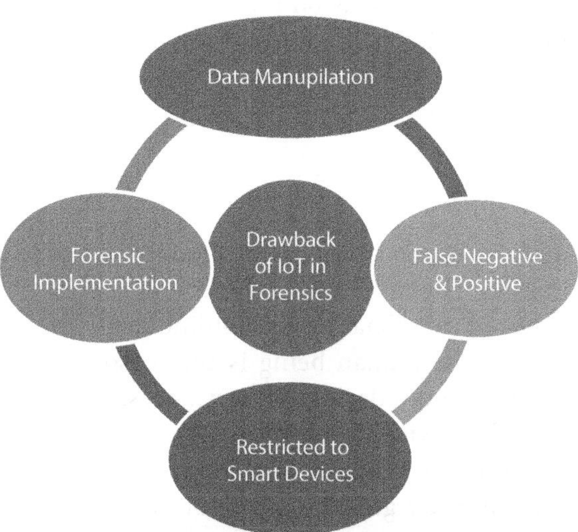

Figure 6.6 Model explaining drawback of internet of things in forensics.

become important and difficult for the forensic analyst to differentiate between the false and genuine data entries [3].

3. Restricted to Smart Devices: IoT devices provide a lot of information but only in the scenarios where smart devices are being used. In all other conditions where the IoT devices are not present, this phenomenon will not help the forensic investigation [6].
4. Forensic Implemented: Till now, the analysis of IoT-based data is not used on a large scale in forensic investigation. Still, it requires expanded research to implement it completely scientifically [11]. That can only be done, by studying all the advantages and disadvantages in detail. Also, no particular software's are available for forensic extraction and analysis of data based on IoT device.

6.7 Future Perspective of Internet of Things Mobility Forensics

IoT-based devices are constantly emerging with new techniques. Mobility forensics requires to have more forensic software that promises to extract the data easily without manipulating it. The currently used software such as general software such as Cellebrite UFED, Access Data FTK, XRY, and Oxygen are not capable of extracting all the IoT data. Also, a strong system to fight against cyberattacks on the data of IoT devices is required. A verified protocol should be followed for solving IoT-based cybercrime cases.

6.8 Conclusion

The objective of this chapter is to provide an overview of IoT and its role in mobility forensics. Digital forensics deals with several types of crimes that might be related to official data or online data. The easy approach of digital devices to the human being is the reason for accomplishing the crime without any boundaries and territories. The security and privacy provided by the device decides the difficulty level for the attacker to attack on it. Gaining the access of our devices is the major role that it plays. Once the attacker gets the access of device, all our data comes under danger. So, it becomes important for the forensic examiner to deal with such nature of crime. The data of IoT devices is the major advantage and disadvantage of the technique. It requires high security to be protected and, if attacked on, it provides all the essential personal as well as professional details. Mobility forensic here requires new technologies to fight against such crimes in most positive manner.

References

1. Agarwal, A., Gupta, M., Gupta, S. *et al.*, Systematic digital forensic investigation model. *Int. J. Comput. Sci. Secur.*, 5, 1, 118–131, 2011.
2. Hossain, M.M., Fotouhi, M., Hasan, R., Towards an Analysis of Security Issues, Challenges, and Open Problems in the Internet of Things. *IEEE World Congress on Services*, pp. 21–28, 2015.
3. Rahman, K.M.S. and Bishop, M., Internet of Things Mobility Forensics. *Information Security Research and Education (INSuRE) Conference*, 2016.
4. Clark, J., *What is Internet of Things (IoT)?*, IBM, United States, 2016, Available via Dialog box https://www.ibm.com/blogs/internet-of-things/what-is-the-iot/ Accessed 17 November 2016.
5. Eskofier, B.M., Lee, S.I., Baron, M. *et al.*, An Overview of Smart Shoes in the Internet of Health Things: Gait and Mobility Assessment in Health Promotion and Disease Monitoring. *Appl. Sci.*, 7, 10, 986, 2017. https://doi.org/10.3390/app7100986.
6. Yaqoob, I., Ahmed, E., Muhammad, H.R., Abdelmuttlib, I.A.A. *et al.*, The rise of ransomware and emerging security challenges in the Internet of Things. *Comput. Netw.*, 1389-1286, 444–458, 2017.
7. Conti, M., Ali, D., Katrin, F. *et al.*, Internet of Things security and forensics: Challenges and opportunities. *Future Gener. Comp. Sy.*, 0167-739X, 544–546, 2018.
8. Hou, J., Qu, L., Shi, W., A survey on internet of things security from data perspectives. *Comput. Netw.*, 1389-1286, 295–306, 2019.
9. Masoud, M., Jaradat, Y., Manasrah, A. *et al.*, Sensors of smart devices in the internet of everything (IOE) era: big opportunities and massive doubts. *J. Sens.*, Volume I, 6514520, 2019. https://doi.org/10.1155/2019/6514520.
10. Servida, F. and Casey, E., IoT forensic challenges and opportunities for digital traces. *Digit. Investig.*, S22-S29, 1742–2876, 2019.
11. Qatawneh, M., Mohammad, A., Wesam, A. *et al.*, DFIM: A New Digital Forensics investigation Model for Internet of Things. *J. Theor. Appl. Inf. Technol.*, 24, 1992–8645, 2019.
12. Yaqoob, I., Abaker, I.T.H., Ahmed, A. *et al.*, Internet of things forensics: Recent advances, taxonomy, requirements, and open challenges. *Future Gener. Comp. Sy.*, 0167-739X, 265–275, 2019.

13. Yoo, S.C., The emerging Internet of Things. *Oppurtunity Challenges Privacy Secur.*, 2020. Center for International Governance Innovation. Available via Dialog box https://www.cigionline.org/articles/emerging-internet-things.
14. Hossain, M.M., Fotouhi, M., Hasan, R., "Towards an Analysis of Security Issues, Challenges, and Open Problems in the Internet of Things". *IEEE World Congress on Services*, 2015, pp. 21–28, 2015.

7

A Generic Digital Scientific Examination System for Internet of Things

Shipra Rohatgi[1*] **and Sakshi Shrivastava**[2]

[1]*Amity Institute of Forensic Sciences, Amity University, Noida, India*
[2]*NSHM College of Management and Technology, Kolkata, India*

Abstract
In the age of the Internet of Things (IoT) today, almost every machine, including cars, keys, watches, glasses, and webcams, is connected to the Internet. All machines capable of capturing screens and collecting individual information are continually expanding. These improvements, on the one hand, make human life more comfortable and convenient, but on the other hand, there are numerous legal centralities, the suitability of distinctly collected devices, and the boundaries and boundaries of indistinguishable organizations. As crime and crime rates increase, there are situations where it is not necessary to change the system to deal with violations every time. It is possible for such development and improvements that raise advanced agent issues when IoT devices are properly included in the scene. The drawbacks of security measures depend on the IoT system, where the potential impact of the information being processed is included until cybercriminals and cybercriminals create an irresistible environment in which they carry out attacks and illegal activities. The purpose of this work is to illuminate simple issues and encourage advanced criminal activity checks for IoT-based success.

Keywords: IoT, cybercrime, forensic, real-time scanning

**Corresponding author*: shiprarohatgi8@gmail.com

Anita Gehlot, Rajesh Singh, Jaskaran Singh and Neeta Raj Sharma (eds.) Digital Forensics and Internet of Things: Impact and Challenges, (87–110) © 2022 Scrivener Publishing LLC

7.1 Introduction

This chapter allows a brief understanding of this area of the Internet, computerized quantification, IoT logic, and real-time scanning, which provides a truly stable understanding of crime scenes. Computerized quantification plays a very important role in making a distinction within a true system. The net itself can be part of the web of things (IoT). Despite the fact that the Internet of Things (IoT) did not exist for a particularly long time, in the early 1800s, there was a debate about how machines could communicate, essentially made in the 1830s. Wired phones were an overview of how machines arrange communications. One of Net of Things' most important punctuality occurred when the Coca Cola machine was installed on the Carnegie Mellon College campus. A sub-research (software engineer) organizes the net in a machine by interfering with the machine's refrigerating equipment. Since then, in some respects recently, we have taken steps to ensure that we have cold drinks. Sometime later, in 1999, the term Things Internet was officially named by Kevin Ashton, the US development ace of the IoT field [1–25].

Advanced forensic medicine suggests science and handles obvious crimes that occur at the computer device level. The main reason for advanced forensics is to recognize examples of advanced media, analyze them as evacuation, and prepare for prosecution so that the case appears in court. Other study plans are highly dependent on the type of equipment and environment in which they are used and computerized equipment can have customary computer, mobile phone, switch, and other equipment configurations, so under advanced forensic medicine. We recommend that you have multiple offices. It faces many challenges that prevent it from uncovering pieces of proof in progress by computerized forensics. In recent years, the use of the IoT is rapidly progressing. In any case, there are many weaknesses in the development of IoT, and it is likely that it will lead to cybercrime by contradiction, and it is easy to have little effect on the client. Since many IoT contradiction-related events are expanding, high-level investigations are required to deal with IoT contradiction-related misconduct. Of course, the biggest concern when coordinating the progress of the IoT is not security, but downplaying the evaluation obtained. After that, this gadget will lose a lot of equipment assets. Due to this lack [1–25], most trusted gadgets cannot be displayed on IoT devices. It takes up space and needs to handle tasks, so it is a direct target for cyberattacks. They use these devices as weapons to find ways to attack known or unknown websites.

Cyber offense with the control of IoT development can cross the virtual space to disturb the lifestyle of people, and this leads to the critical increase in the amount of illegal activity, requiring the opening of progressed examinations to shed light on what has happened [1–25].

7.2 Internet of Things

The IoT brings control in internet, data dealing with, and analytics to the veritable world of physical objects. For customers, this suggests affiliation with the around the world information organized without the go-between of comfort and screen; various normal objects and devices can take enlightening from that organize with unimportant human mediations. The term "Internet of Things" are comprised of two words which incorporate "Internet" and "Things". The internet can be around the world computer course of action that gives particular sorts of information, and it comprises interconnected systems that utilize the standard Web tradition (TCP/IP) to supply organizations for billions of individuals inside the world. The "Things", on the other hand, may well be one of a kind inside the honest-to-goodness world. These objects join electronic contraptions and specialized equipment that we utilize day by day, as well as things that we do not commonly think of as computerized at all, such as furniture, clothing, food, and unprecedented things [19].

Agreeing to the IoT building square comprises of five primary sections as the taking after:

1) Sensor and detector section
2) Processing section
3) Communication section
4) Actuation section
5) Communication section
6) Energy section

These modules are supported by the list operations, timer, and storage.

1. **Sensor and detector section:** IoT substances have the function of detecting and responding to the surrounding conditions of the surrounding environment. The detection section can be divided into two parts: control detection and event-driven detection. The previous type is an execution point specified on the client or server side and has the ability to

detect only when there is a request to evaluate the sensor. The last type mentioned is event-driven detection, which is detected by sensors and detectors when there is a change in the surroundings. The role of the sensor is to collect and/or erase information. Information at any given time is written to the Ready/Processing section to perform the task of preparing for the next activity. Each sensor or sensor has a unique identifier and physical address to communicate separately within the IoT framework [19].

2. **Processing section:** This section is central to the IoT system, providing an adjacent brain throughout the sensor and application framework. The most important task is to prepare the data and information that the sensor collects and transmits. When expanded, this area can be controlled and inspected at a very basic level, using command-controlled instruments through this program. To save communication, the preparation applies encryption and descrambling of information. As it may be, it is not a ready-made contradiction, but this module should be placed in agreement with the application [19].
3. **Actuation section:** This segment will trigger devices to leverage the conditions of IoT materials over a wide area. When the planning module prepares the approximate data, the processed data (also known as the result) triggers the actuator to execute the result. There is no data in this segment or no calculation moves occur [19].
4. **Communication section:** The IoT device has an IP address and space as well as the required communication. There is a basic section. Thus, the information and these results can be previously in the sorting section, in an organized environment such as adjacent execution coordinates and wide area orchestration. Organizations are continually doubly shaped because they interact with communication channels between computer programs and adjacent devices [19].
5. **Energy section:** IoT gadgets have limited essential use. In this case, the whole of essentiality opens to each IoT element. Each task recommends certain necessities, such as the identification, derivation of modules, and the consent of each, from processing of communication modules to exhaustion of space [19].

7.3 IoT Architecture

IoT advancement includes a wide combination of program and the utilize of the IoT is creating so rapidly. Depending upon assorted application zones of the IoT, it works in like way since it has been designed/developed. But it has not standard characterized arrange of working which is totally taken after all around.

The building of IoT depends upon its value and execution in a number of divisions. Still, there is an essential arrange stream based on which IoT is built. So, here we will examine the fundamental crucial design of IoT, i.e., four-stage IoT design [14].

The IoT architecture as mentioned in Figure 7.1 is explained as follows:

I. **Sensing Layer:** Sensors, actuators, and gadgets are shown in this Detecting layer. These Sensors or Actuators acknowledge information (physical/environmental parameters), forms information, and transmits information over the arrange [14].

II. **Web Layer:** Internet/Network doors and Information Procurement Frameworks (DAS) are displayed in this layer. DAS performs information conglomeration and transformation capacities (collecting information and accumulating information at that point changing over

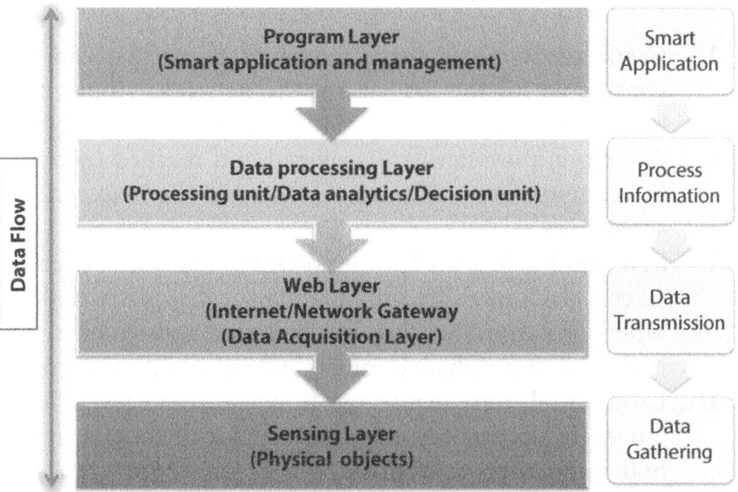

Figure 7.1 IoT architecture to understand data flow.

analog information of sensors to advanced information, etc.). Progressed doors primarily open up an association between Sensor systems and Web and moreover perform numerous essential portal functionalities like malware security, and sifting, moreover, in some cases, choice making based on inputted information and information administration administrations, etc. [14].

III. **Data Processing Layer:** This will be the taking care of unit of the IoT environment. Here, data is analyzed and pre-processed now and then as of late sending it to the data center from where data is gotten to by computer program applications regularly named as exchange applications where data is checked and supervised and help exercises are as well organized. So here, Edge IT or edge analytics comes into the picture [14].

IV. **Program Layer:** Usually, the ultimate layer of the four stages of the IoT plan. Data centers or cloud is the organization organizer of data where data is directed and is utilized by end-user applications like cultivation, prosperity care, flying, developing, and defense [14].

7.4 Characteristics of IoT

IoT comes up with following characteristics which has been summarized:

I. **Connectivity:** The most important thing that can be considered for the IoT case is the network. Things can be transparently associated with other substances. Therefore, they can be discovered and reached by both the components of the atmosphere and the inaccessible substances.

II. **Sensing:** For IoT, the first important fundamental to consider is readiness. The situation may be directly related to other substances. So, they can be found and obtained by both their atmosphere elements and advanced materials.

III. **Communal:** You can integrate things with a variety of heterogeneous components in a wide range of control areas, both human and mechanical.

IV. **Expandability:** The IoT gadget gun is gradually expanding and is destined to relate to information organizations around the world. IoT gadgets need to be planned so that they can effectively scale up or down based on demand. In general, IoT has a changing case of scale as it can be used from successful domestic machines to the mechanization of vast industrial facilities and workstations. Career should plan IoT frameworks based on current and future scale of engagement.

V. **Dynamicity:** Everything can communicate with a variety of things at any time, with any input, with some capacity. They can deliberately enter and exit the orchestration, demanding that they not be confined to a particular physical area, and take advantage of a combination of interference.

VI. **Intelligence:** In about each IoT utilizes case in today's world, the data is utilized to create basic exchange encounters and drive imperative commerce choices. We make machine learning/significant learning models on the beat of this colossal data to urge critical encounters. The analog signals are preprocessed and changed over to an organized on which machine learning models are prepared. We need to be past any question the proper data establishment based on commerce needs.

VII. **Energy:** From conclusion components to network and analytics layers, the total biological systems request a part of energy. While designing an IoT environment, we have to consider plan techniques such that vitality utilization is negligible.

VIII. **Safety:** One of the most highlights of the IoT ecosystem is security. Within the entire stream of an IoT environment, touchy data is passed from endpoints to the analytics layer through connectivity components. Whereas planning an IoT framework we ought to follow legitimate security, security measures, and firewalls to keep the information absent from misuse and controls. Compromising any component of an IoT biological system can in the long run lead to the disappointment of the full pipeline [19].

IX. **Integration:** IoT coordinating different cross-domain models to enhance client involvement. It too guarantees a legitimate trade-off between framework and operational costs [19].

7.5 IoT Security Challenges and Factors of Threat

With the headways of advances, nearly boundless transfer speed, and cheap information rates, the IoT utilize cases are developing quickly over spaces. Besides the expanding utilize cases the carriers moreover need to associate IoT suits with quick ready-to-market capabilities. These things inside and out take off the major security escape clauses behind. In this article, we will go through the major security challenges for IoT utilize cases [19]. Separated from that, IoT has been uncovered to cyber dangers and assaults. Three primary resources of threat in IoT have been distinguished as follows:

I. **Malicious User:** The client of the IoT, gadgets gets attacked just to require within the unmentioned of the producer and get to restricted convenience [19].
II. **Immoral Manufacturer:** The maker of the gadget abuses and employments the innovation to urge the information around the clients and uncovering it to the untouchable [19].
III. **Adversary:** Known as an outsider substance, ordinarily not a parcel of any IoT system and has no authorization to it. He or she, at that point, tries to initiate the sensitive information for harmful purposes. It may cause the breakdown by controlling the IoT substances [19].
IV. **Faulty Programming:** The software design for the IoT apps or IoT contraptions may utilize the prolog codes to do reconnaissance on the user's data. The foremost discernibly horrendous thing is these codes can be remaining unexposed for a long period of time. Separated from that, many creators utilized to ignore to apply the safe programming codes inside the system. It makes it fewer complexes for them mishandle the data [19].
V. **Sensitive Data Violation:** We may collect personal information from unique sources for adversarial event meta-information behavioral research.
VI. **SQL Injection:** Malware injection strategies used to attack information-based applications control the security flaws in the application computer program and adjust the information to give the adversary a parody personality and cause problems of abandonment.

7.5.1 Effects of IoT Security Breach

I. **Losing Sensitive Information:** IoT gadgets are joined in divisions like restorative, protections, and managing an account. Compromising with these frameworks may spill the client's therapeutic data, managing an account, or monetary subtle elements to the dark cap programmers [15].

II. **Business Disruption:** Due to the vulnerability of any hub of the IoT environment, programmers may get a backdoor to get to the total trade server. Due to the speck net transformation, each trade is presently nearly digitized. Mostly compromised nodes can moreover lead to disturbance of the complete trade handle [15].

III. **Manipulating Information:** As we talked about touchy client data stream over the IoT hubs and associated center points. Programmers can control the data on the go which may lead to long-term impacts. Assume in a restorative utilize case in the event that the back entryway gotten to application changes the well-being data, the activities too changed. Without appropriate supervision, this may lead to life-threatening challenges. Nearly each IoT utilize case these days is coordinates with machine learning compute motors. Nourishing or controlling off-base information to these frameworks changes the noteworthy bits of knowledge, which eventually leads to the misfortune of trade [15].

IV. **Untrustworthy Connections:** A few IoT gadgets send messages to gadgets or systems without encoding. To overcome these, engineers have to utilize standard TLS or transport encryption. It is additionally successful to utilize a person

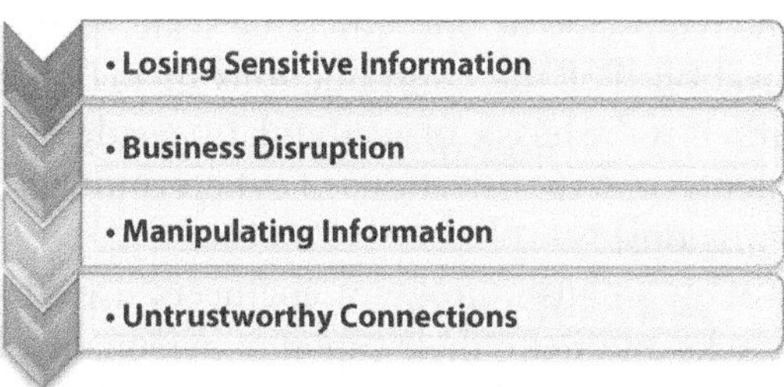

Figure 7.2 The loopholes of the IoT ecosystem.

separation framework for personal associations. It ought to be double-checked that information ought to be transmitted in a secret way [15] as depicted in Figure 7.2.

7.6 Role of Digital Forensics in Cybercrime Investigation for IoT

The IoT innovation is integrating various applications and the IoT is developing very rapidly. Designed/developed for various applications of the Web of Things, it works well. However, it does not have a design that has the standard features of working that is universally fully followed. The behavior of the IoT depends on the value and execution of the IoT in various sections. IoT development can be a mixture of various progress areas such as IoT area, organizer area, and cloud area. These areas can be sources of pieces of IoT progressed evidence. This means that attestations can be collected from smart device competition, internal orchestrations such as firewalls, switches, or external frameworks such as the cloud and software. It is one of the most important targets for recent perpetrators. Therefore, IoT forensics is characterized as the field of computerized science where the handle of most investigations or investigations needs to be IoT-based. This is usually the primary way to start an investigation of IoT-related events that urge system-wide. If so, logically, the review method is fundamental as it runs in the worldview of IoT [14].

7.6.1 IoT in Digital Forensic

Investigation and seizure are likely essential steps in forensic examination. The first challenging step is to identify an IoT or recognize the radical contradiction in an organization or IoT environment. These are physically on the nanoscale or unpredictable scale, as they are computerized in inactivation. For the contradictions of IoT that are part of a better framework, it is the hassle of accumulating gadgets and competent fitness requirements or demonstrations of cybercriminals for typographical errors or omissions.

In the event of an ambush, program engineers use all their aptitudes to cover their tracks and deny their captain's personality. It organizes to encourage some evidence of crime which improve in IoT coherent natural systems. Real investigators should make an effort to analyze the logs that are delaying the main parcels from the handle. In addition to a global view of the target framework perpetrator components, the attacker's possible inspiration is required.

The most important issue of forensics in internet-connected devices is delivered by storing fully computerized scenes of cheating. Gathering information in an entirely exciting environment focused on heterogeneous equipment and program structures, variable assets (compute controlled memory capacity space) is no fewer errands. Many inconsistencies are that when a contradiction occurs, all stored logs are deleted. It refueled and quantified the quantifiable analytical work. The requirements of a real device can be set from start to finish, and protecting certain information collected from sensors is another very difficult task. As everything works some base as in a Framework as depicted in Figure 7.3 which would help in understanding steps to proceed for IoT forensics and a multi- faceted approach as depicted in Figure 7.4 to understand from which sources evidence could be collected [15, 17, 20].

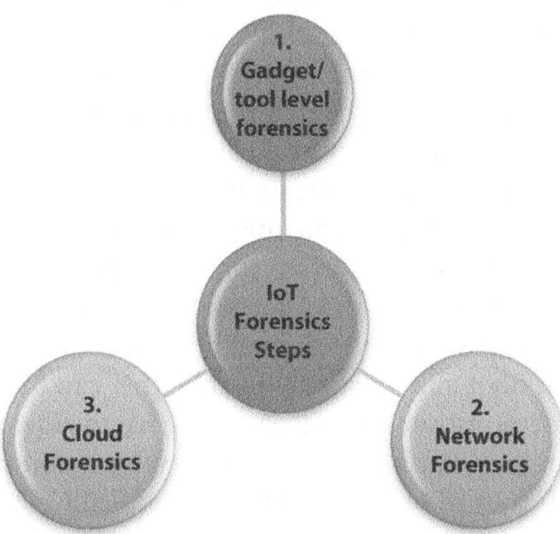

Figure 7.3 Mixture of three digital scientific schemes which helps in understanding steps involved in IoT forensics.

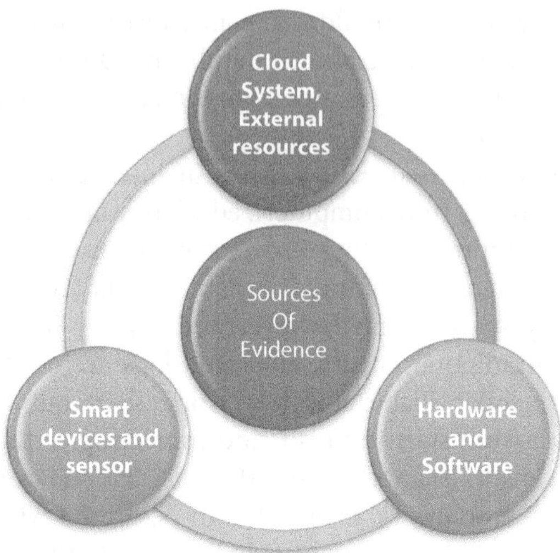

Figure 7.4 IoT Forensics requires a multi-faceted approach where demonstration can be collected from differing sources.

7.6.2 Digital Forensics Investigation Framework for IoT Devices

After so numerous inquires about inside the IoT advertise, brand unused IoT gadgets are as of now being spearheaded and created to form our lives in vogue and simpler. Now, reality suggests that planning have to be continuously attentive against security breaches—and having a strong occurrence reaction arranges input is crucial. A proactive approach that strategizes some time recently, during, and after a potential breach empowers your organization to create the foremost educated choices to protect it. To play down the income misfortune of a security occurrence, you would like a comprehensive see that coordinating security danger insights, occurrence reaction, and remediation. The framework is competent of giving namelessness mystery, and no disavowal of the freely available proves. It to boot able to supply meddle that can be utilized for the obtainment of demonstrate, as well as a contrive to affirm the judgment of the demonstrate utilized all through the examination of wrongdoing. Besides the IoT framework, the computerized legitimate examination framework makes a contrast work together to open critical and critical data, it as well collects and supervise data and makes a distinction you characterize rules, the framework engages analytics and visualization toward the working strategy for computerized forensics [20].

Examination of IoT gadgets employments, the Coordinated and Computerized Forensic Examination System strategy with the takings that come after, has been depicted in Table 7.1.

7.6.3 Road Map for Issues in IoT Forensics

IoT automation has introduced a specific shift of inspection field, specifically, how to get interconnected with the data record. Somehow, there are so many difficulties in context with IoT forensic investigation.

1. Data Location: A lot of information about the IoT extends to many areas that are out of the reach of users. Certain information can be stored inside the cloud on third-party networks, mobile phones, and other gadgets. In addition, IoT forensics, identifying areas of proof, is considered one of the most difficult challenges investigators face to collect evidence. In this way, IoT information can be found entirely in other countries, mixed with data from other users, and represents a change in national acquisitions [17].

Table 7.1 Strategy for investigating for IoT devices which help in proper chain of custody of devices.

1. Pre-Investigative Readiness	• Administration readiness • Technical readiness
2. Preparation	• Notification • Authorization • Preparation
3. Proactive Process	• Securing the scene • Documentation of the scene • Incident triggering • Foresighted preservation, analysis, prior report
4. Reactive Process	• Recognition/identification • Collection and acquisition • Preservation • Examination • Analysis • Documentation
5.Preparation of Report	• Conclusion • Reconstruction • Dissemination

2. Limited Lifespan in Digital Media: Due to the capacity limitation of the IoT gadget, the expected life of the internal information of the IoT gadget is short and the information is overwritten very effectively. Occurred in the possibility of being able to prove that it is in the wrong place [16]. Exchanging information to the nearest center or cloud can be a simple array to explain the problem. It shows another challenge related to securing a storage chain and how to prove evidence that has not been modified or adjusted [17].

3. Lack in Security Service: Proving IoT gadgets can change or eliminate a sense of security need and, accordingly, is likely to prove not strong enough to be accepted by this court. For example, some companies do not often or never upgrade their gadgets in advertising, while others drop their supported device systems around newer items with deprecated frameworks. As a result, these devices can be taken off defenseless because the programmers have discovered a sense of helplessness that is not being used [17].

4. Device Type: Forensic recognizable information procedures allow advanced agents to recognize and obtain evidence at the scene of a prior crime. In general, the proof source is a kind of computer framework, such as a computer or a general-purpose telephone. Sources of proof in the IoT can be objects such as sharp refrigerators and sharp coffee growers. As such, test tubes face several problems. One of these challenges is to distinguish and find IoT devices at crime scenes. The name of the gadget seems to be unspecified because the battery is dead. Searching can be very tedious, especially if the IoT gadget is exceptionally small, hidden, or like an existing gadget. Taking the gadget to the laboratory and finding space can be another challenge that inspectors can face in terms of gadget classification. Extracting the proof frame portion of these gadgets is considered another IoT challenge, as most producers receive their own stages, frameworks, and equipment of work in the extension [17].

5. Data Format: The deployment of data generated by the contradictions of IoT does not place what is stored in the cloud. In development, clients do not have easy access to their data, and the data has emerged in the course of an action that is more certain than it can clean up. In addition, data can be processed to exploit interpretive powers in multiple places. Therefore, in order to be recognized in court, the outline of the data needs to be returned several times in an interesting orchestration if the conduct of the exam is delayed [17].

6. Improper Evidence Handling: Digital certificates are particularly sensitive, basic, and modified/modified or destroyed. You may shut down the device or overwrite/demo it in advance. Most IoT devices store data in the cloud in a selective way to solve limitation issues. The weakness issues demonstrated in the IoT environment are much more complex than existing computing. When the IoT overwrites or compresses recent data to predict its lifespan, the data may not exist locally. To face this challenge, we need methods not used by computerized inspection to track and channel the movement of data in IoT environments [19].

Officers at the scene of a breach must follow rules established by the ACPO to ensure that an information investigation occurs, and that all critical information is gathered in an authoritative and resourceful manner. ACPO (Association of Police Chiefs) directs registration standards for computerized electronic evidence and is registered under the following:

I. **Principal 1:** "Civil servants are required by law not to exercise any activity or by their moderators to modify information stored on computers or media which may thus be subject to the control of the courts."
II. **Principal 2:** "When an individual deems it necessary to obtain unique information stored on a computer or on a competent medium, that individual should be competent to do so and be able to provide evidence to clarify its suitability and operational recommendations."
III. **Principle 3:** It is necessary to establish and protect a review link or other record of all forms related to electronic evidence. A free third party should be able to view these forms and get the same results.
IV. **Principle 4:** The evaluator (record manager) is generally obligated to ensure that these laws and standards are followed [11].

7. Securing the Chain of Custody: Chain of custody is fundamental to assure legitimacy of verification in law. It has a strategy to maintain the chronology of the particular show throughout the main course of the exam. Acceptance of computerized evidence as it can be recognized in good faith in court if the chain of custody can lead to the evidence, how to consider the strategies implemented for the evidence to verify the view review and prepare for the review and appearance of review disclosures [19].

In addition, the management chain absolutely provides consistent observation points to verify and consider all existing computer demonstrations with people where, when, and when they came into contact with the electronic demonstration from each piece of evidence of the test method. You need to prove it. Part of the general area is as mentioned in Table 7.2.

Table 7.2 IoT's chain of custody and challenges faced by investigators.

Chain of custody frame	Challenges faced
Case number	Size of the object matters in forensic terms
Offense, victim, and suspect names	Location that affects easy access, connection possibility with other devices, etc.
Date, time seized and Location when it is seized	Relevancy of identified devices.
• Item number • Description of item • Signatures and IDs of individuals releasing and receiving the items	Legal or judiciary issues
Authorization for disposal	Network traffic boundaries or edgeless network, i.e., no perimeter, or less clearly defined perimeters.
• Witness to destruction of evidence • Release to lawful owner	Availability of tools—is it sufficient for examination and investigation or not? Is every data encrypted? Does the device still consists of data or is it simply middleware?

7.7 IoT Security Steps

In a very large sense, the contradictions in IoT are rarely specific to each other, and what protects them also depends on the type and manifestation of the contradiction. The interior of the office building has a sharp light bulb that belongs to a specific vendor rather than a smart printer. And in most cases the control system that performs the entire office has a special working system. A comprehensive multi-layered security set of measures and a firm back are essential to successfully safeguard all of these various IoT contradictions [12].

Security organizations should essentially ensure more endpoints through their efforts; IoT security breaches can cause rapid damage to IT and physical systems. The IoT emphasizes the need for today's efforts to focus on cyber adaptability. It is the ability to successfully sustain change and effectively sustain it against a wide range of threats from insiders from the nation's guilty party competitors [12].

There are five important security steps for organizations to follow while setting up an IoT devices:

a. Change the default password to change the security settings to suit your specific requirements.
b. Unnecessary features should be turned off or disabled.
c. For devices that have the ability to use third-party applications, we have used true blue applications from real vendors.
d. Update your gadget firmware and applications to protect your gadget from known security vulnerabilities.
e. Investigate the consent required from the perspective of setting up applications on gadgets and limit acquisitions to these applications [12].

7.7.1 How to Access IoT Security

In order to realize IoT cyber flexibility, all existing IoT-related assets are recognized as existing internal operations, and organizational units, Sharp, and IoT devices are instructed throughout the life cycle, focusing on their personality, in advance. It must be launched with careful consideration to provide the event for response and progress confirmation [13].

1. Risk assessment: As part of the hazard inspection, the organization considers how IoT security events will affect the exchange. At that point, you can take reasonable action, considering the approach and form needed to recognize the scene and modify it accordingly. Overview whether your ability to respond to IoT events meets that reason-search for ace accessories if they do not, or quickly improve your aptitude. Crisis response recreation will be conducted to guide the ability to respond to IoT attacks.

The reality that IoT's contradictory disillusionment can inadvertently bring happiness and security must be considered when choosing to track response times. You need to ensure that your orchestrations are characterized and filled with the movement of commerce and large disaster recovery goals to provide the required level of cyber flexibility. In the midst of the IoT compromise, hurtful, working on disaster recovery plans [13].

2. Asset identification and management: Asset composition begins with an understanding of the system that directs it. Thus, the basic procedure for IoT security is to discover and deploy IoT devices in your organization. Given the universality of IoT devices, have the ability to judge that such stocks can certainly be on a larger scale than what is currently being implemented [13].

You can search in several ways.

- Using forensic accounting: Capital and operating cost analysis.
- Technically active or passive network analysis.

1. **Active analysis** relies on software to detect various network subnets and issues related to networks. However, these checks are not generally recommended as they may cause unexpected malfunctions in the device and may not respond as expected.
2. **Passive analysis** relies on placing network probes at well-designed choke network points. It provides all the information about device identification and network usage patterns.

As assessments are added, they are organized and backed by the appropriate approaches and phrase to overcome and low down the risk in response to the organization's risk demands [13].

3. Incident response: In IoT systems, internal agitation, security, and openness are top priorities. Event responders should examine whether an attacker can cause complaints that pose little risk to life, or whether it has an intrinsic advantage, such as an essential age, with little to no anxiety impact on the client. The destabilizing impacts of IoT and the quality of responses to ambush are particularly relevant for inclusiveness as businesses prepare to respond. The IoT security plan required that exchanges be treated the same as the fire security plan. Documentation, training, and recovery from failures should be reviewed within the scope of any event improvement.

Incident response has three key priorities:

- Stop spreading: Anticipate an attack or unstable effect that jeopardizes the help system. Take proactive steps to predict the progression of an ambush and turn off systems or systems as needed.
- Please prevent damage: Security must remain the most important requirement, as well as stop an attacker from communicating with the infected system and executing dangerous commands.
- Remove the danger: Take defensive measures that can anticipate aggressive compromises, freeing from the causes of attacks and the effects of anxiety [13].

The IoT framework offers legal examiners a number of exciting challenges. These are as follows:

- **Legacy systems:** It is brutal that the amplified resurrection cycle gear is decades old and may not be suitable for measurable investigation.
- **Custom-built architectures:** A number of IoT frameworks are customized for each user. Given its ambiguous nature, it is often held captive, as were the chosen few in the engineering business. Due to high employee turnover, information is often misleading—there are inspection and recovery challenges.
- **Physical access:** IoT frameworks vary in size from small to very widespread and large, and some may actually be portable. Therefore, choosing a physical get-to can be difficult.
- **Absent or unhelpful logging:** If you are not a security expert and the IoT logging that engineers regularly describe is completely inaccessible, then your security experts will be limited to regular use.
- **Proprietary protocols:** Standardization of conventions is progressing in the world of IoT, but there is no absolute one. Often, sorting communication surveys is complicated by the fact that few people can handle transactions that occur between machines.
- **Inability to rebuild:** Re-imaging of IoT elements such as programmable rationale controllers is often incomprehensible. After that assault recovery is time consuming and can be a very special treatment if it is unlikely to be achievable [13].

4. Security monitoring: Security is an energy-filled situation. Apart from checking the framework when vulnerability is discovered, it is essential to screen the framework, identify the problem, respond to it, solve the problem, and thwart the enemy. The checks and responses that can be performed in an IoT environment are not fully constructed teachings and can be decisive. You need to consider the placement and shipping of unused IoT systems. Fortunately, various IoT devices are located in a single purpose system that basically has well-defined behavior. This suggests that once observations are built, there is far less demanding to recognize strange behavior than the contradictions of common computing.

What steps should the CISO take? Here are the most important actions that a chief information security officer (CISO) can take to mitigate risk to IoT systems:

- **a.** Undoubtedly, the Board recognizes the security risks associated with the IoT framework and, in particular, to mitigate and supervise them by ensuring that security is summarized in all modern frameworks. Ready to raise money.
- **b.** Established universal measures and sectoral rules (such as those issued by the Nutrition and Comfort Organization of the United States) are being applied to monitor obsolete enactment and management in the region.
- **c.** Identify your IoT frameworks and resources and stock them.
- **d.** Assess the risks of an inventory of IoT frameworks and build appropriate perspective and strategies to mitigate them.
- **e.** Make sure that the IoT gadget is recognized in an array, which means it is an input to monitor and control access to permissions.
- **f.** Use IoT gadgets that are known to be secure as-is and inspect them frequently to meet changing risk profiles.
- **g.** Use it because it is a trusted provider that powers your entire lifecycle IoT framework.
- **h.** Ensure that you simply have an IoT occurrence reaction arrange input—which is looked into and tested regularly.
- **i.** Make sure you can see the IoT gadget in the observation framework that strange behavior is detected.
- **j.** When responding to the IoT outbreak, take a "safety first" stance and make sure that you may demand quick and actionable activities when needed [13].

5. Steps for Securing Networks and Routers: In an IoT responsive environment, it is also a cause for concern, which may constitute inconsistencies and switches. It is thought that exploiting one of the inconsistencies of the compromised IoT will spread malicious code to other contradictions related to the same course of action. For example, a sharp printer can be used to contaminate office computers and other sharp devices in the process of doing the same. Also, if the switch is at risk, then any contradiction associated with it can be propagated with malware. Later, measures can protect your system and router:

a. **Map and monitor all connected devices:** Settings, entitlements, firmware forms, and patches after that are famous. This step can provide assistance for the client to evaluate the security measures to be taken and to determine which appliances need to be replaced or serviced.
b. **Apply network segmentation:** Use organizational segmentation to prevent escalation of assault and isolate high-risk devices that cannot be taken offline immediately.
c. **Make sure network architecture is secure:** Clients need to install the switch using VLAN or DMZ. This is a segmentation and separation mechanism that includes an additional layer of security in the system.
d. **Follow router-specific best practices:** Strengthening switches, firewalls, weakening WPS, strengthening WPA2 security rules, and using the sure secrets of Wi-Fi get are some of these practices.
e. **Disable unneeded services like Universal Plug and Play (UPnP):** UPnP used and not effectively deployed switches is a recent assault, highlighting the need to compromise or disable unnecessary features or management to prevent security incidents. They ensure that the critical procedures required for secure IoT devices are fair [12, 26].

7.8 Conclusion

To properly handle the contradictions of IoT from a legitimate point of view, it can be changed by experts and legal advisors with specialized computerized legal capabilities. The abundance of quantifiable advisors is being opened to fields beyond computerized forensics, providing courses and expertise throughout investigation planning, in which sources of proof and logical shapes are probably most important to their case, and the ace inside. Calculate what questions to ask legitimate science asks about the office.

In a perfect world, digital/multimedia logic advisors are not limited to advanced disciplines and need to demonstrate a wide range of capabilities within a particular area of forensic medicine. Cross-cutting instructions allow them to support the exam and know when they need to be encouraged with a professional star for a detailed exam. Will this procedure open up advanced forensic capabilities that can truly evaluate the demonstration of large IoT device sets, requesting almost any other major device?

Potential criminal misuse of IoT devices should also be considered. Criminals can use data generated from IoT devices to stalk victims, arrange for theft (determined when the owner is not in place) and abuse it, or monitor cameras where they abuse it. You can prepare for the same assaults that access and other IoT frameworks. IoT devices to anticipate records related to torts or illegal activities are involved [14, 26].

References

1. Castelo Gómez, J.M., Carrillo Mondéjar, J., Roldán Gómez, J. *et al.*, A context-centered methodology for IoT forensic investigations. *Int. J. Inf. Secur.*, 20, 647–673, 2020, Spinger Publication. https://doi.org/10.1007/s10207-020-00523-6.
2. Montasari, R., Jahankhani, H., Hill, R., Parkinson. S., *Digital Forensic Investigation of Internet of Things (IoT) Devices. Advanced Sciences and Technologies for Security Applications*, 2021, from https://pure.hud.ac.uk/en/publications/digital-forensic-investigation-of-internet-of-things-iot-devices.
3. Servida, F., Casey, E., IoT Forensic challenges and opportunities for digital traces, *Digital Investigation*, Volume 28, Supplement, 2019, Pages S22-S29, ISSN 1742-2876, from https://doi.org/10.1016/j.diin.2019.01.012.
4. Hou, J., Li, Y., Yu, J., Shi, W., "A Survey on Digital Forensics in Internet of Things". *IEEE Internet Things J.*, 7, 1, 1–15, Jan. 2020. Retrieved 5 May 2021, from https://ieeexplore.ieee.org/document/8831387.
5. Abomhara, M., and Køien, G.M., "Cyber Security and the Internet of Things: Vulnerabilities, Threats, Intruders and Attacks", *Journal of Cyber Security and Mobility*, 4, 65–88, doi: https://doi.org/10.13052/jcsm2245-1439.414
6. Kumar, G., Saha, R., Lal, C., Conti, M., Internet-of-Forensic (IoF): A blockchain based digital forensics framework for IoT applications. *Future Gener. Comp. Sy.*, 120, 13–25, 2021. from https://www.sciencedirect.com/science/article/abs/pii/S0167739X21000686.
7. Agarwal, R. and Kothari, S., Review of Digital Forensic Investigation Framew orks, in: *Information Science and Applications. Lecture Notes in Electrical Engi neering*, vol. 339, K. Kim, (Ed.), Springer, Berlin, Heidelberg, 2015, https://link.springer.com/chapter/10.1007%2F978-3-662-46578-3_66#citeas.
8. Wikipedia, *Internet of things*, 2018, Retrieved 5 May 2021, from https://en.wikipedia.org/wiki/Internet_of_things.
9. *What is an IoT Platform & What Role Does it Play In Your Business?*, 2021, (online article). accessed on 5 May 2021, from https://www.business.att.com/learn/research-reports/whats-an-iot-platform-and-what-role-does-it-play.html

10. Boricha, V., Packt Hub (online), *IoT Forensics: Security in connected world*, 2018, accessed on 5 May 2021, from https://hub.packtpub.com/iot-forensics-security-connected-world/.
11. MacDermott, Á., Baker, T., Shi, Q., *IoT Forensics: Challenges For The IoA Era*, 2018 9th IFIP International Conference on New Technologies, Mobility and Security (NTMS), 1–5, 2018, doi: 10.1109/NTMS.2018.8328748 from https://core.ac.uk/download/pdf/146487345.pdf.
12. Security news in IoT section, *The first steps in effective IoT device security*, October 31st, 2019, (online) at https://www.trendmicro.com/vinfo/us/security/news/internet-of-things/the-first-steps-in-effective-iot-device-security.
13. Manfredi, L., Davies, R., Hatala, L., Ward, J., *10 steps to securing the internet of things*, (online) (2021) accessed on 5 May 2021, from https://www.dxc.technology/security/insights/144647-10_steps_to_securing_the_internet_of_things.
14. Rani, S., Kataria, A., Sharma, V., Ghosh, S., Karar, V., Lee, K., Choi, C., Threats and Corrective Measures for IoT Security with Observance of Cybercrime: A Survey. *Wirel. Commun. Mob. Com.*, 2021, 5579148, 30, 2021. https://www.hindawi.com/journals/wcmc/2021/5579148/.
15. Sathwara, S., Dutta, N., Pricop, E., "IoT Forensic A digital investigation framework for IoT systems". *ECAI 2018. International Conference – 10th Edition*, 2021, Retrieved 5 May 2021, from https://arxiv.org/ftp/arxiv/papers/1909/1909.02815.pdf.
16. S. Sathwara, N. Dutta and E. Pricop, "IoT Forensic A digital investigation framework for IoT systems", *2018 10th International Conference on Electronics, Computers and Artificial Intelligence (ECAI)*, pp. 1–4, 2018.
17. Alabdulsalam, S., Schaefer, K., Kechadi, T., LeKhac, N.A., *Chapter 1 Internet of Things Forensic: Challenges and Case Study*, 2021, Retrieved 5 May 2021, from https://arxiv.org/ftp/arxiv/papers/1801/1801.10391.pdf.
18. Khanafseh, M., Qatawneh M., and Almobaideen, W., "A survey of various frameworks and solutions in all branches of digital forensics with a focus on cloud forensics", *International Journal of Advanced Computer Science and Applications (IJACSA)*, 10(8), 2019. http://dx.doi.org/10.14569/IJACSA.2019.0100880
19. Zulkipli, N.H., Alenezi, A., Wills, G.B., *IoT Forensic: Bridging the Challenges in Digital Forensic and the Internet of Things*, Published in IoTBDS 2017, accessed on 5 May 2021, from https://www.scitepress.org/Papers/2017/63087/63087.pdf.
20. Rizal, R. and Hikmatyar, M., Investigation Internet of Things (IoT) Device using Integrated Digital Forensics Investigation Framework (IDFIF). *J. Phys. Conf.*, 1179, 012140, 2019, https://iopscience.iop.org/article/10.1088/1742-6596/1179/1/012140/pdf.
21. Kebande, V.R. and Ray, I., A Generic Digital Forensic Investigation Framework for Internet of Things (IoT). *2016 IEEE 4th International Conference on Future Internet of Things and Cloud (FiCloud)*,

pp. 356–362, 2016, from https://www.semanticscholar.org/paper/A-Generic-Digital-Forensic-Investigation-Framework-Kebande-Ray/e65638c441a46b889547428cfbd65fb03ca9a3b2.

22. *Incident Response Services and Threat Intelligence*, (Online). Retrieved 5 May 2021, from https://www.ibm.com/security/services/ibm-x-force-incident-response-and-intelligence.
23. Shmulik Regev, co-authored by Assaf Regev, Innovative New Solutions for Securing the Internet of Things (Online article), February 22, 2016, from https://securityintelligence.com/innovative-new-solutions-for-securing-the-internet-of-things/%20,https://securityintelligence.com/innovative-new-solutions-for-securing-the-internet-of-things/.
24. *Smart Forensics for the Internet of Things (IoT)*, 2017, (online) Retrieved 5 May 2021, from https://securityintelligence.com/smart-forensics-for-the-internet-of-things-iot/.
25. Alharbi, R., *Collection and Analysis of Digital Forensic Data from Devices in the Internet of Things*, 2015, accessed on 5 May 2021, thesis from https://repository.lib.fit.edu/bitstream/handle/11141/2657/ALHARBI-THESIS-2018.pdf?sequence=1&isAllowed=y.
26. V, N. P. S., Samm, A., and Joseph, D., *Digital Forensics with Kali Linux: Perform data acquisition, digital investigation, and threat analysis using Kali Linux tools*, 2017.

8

IoT Sensors: Security in Network Forensics

D. Karthika

Department of Computer Science, SDNB Vaishnav College for Women, Chennai, Tamil Nadu, India

Abstract
IoT forensics is a branch of digital forensics which deals with IoT-related cybercrimes. It includes investigation of connected devices, sensors, and the data stored on all possible platforms. The motive is to identify, collect, analyze, and present digital evidence collected from various mediums in a cybercrime incident. There is no specific method of IoT forensics that can be broadly used so identifying valuable sources is a major challenge. IoT forensics requires a multi-faceted approach where evidence can be collected from various sources. These include variance of the IoT devices, data present across multiple devices and platforms, and data that can be updated, modified, or lost. Data is stored on cloud or a different geography for data to be retrieved. This chapter focuses on with ever evolving IoT devices that there will always be a need for unique, intelligent, and adaptable techniques to investigate IoT-related crimes. Forensics experts will have to develop skill sets to deal with the variety and complexity of IoT devices to keep up with this evolution. There are high possibilities the data on cloud can be altered which would result to an investigation failure. Cybercrime keeps evolving and getting bolder by the day. No matter the challenges one faces, there is always a unique solution to complex problems.

Keywords: Cloud computing, Internet of Things (IoT), networks, sensors, forensics

8.1 Introduction

The Internet of Things (IoT) is having a significant impact on organizations, customers, business innovation device owners, and foundation administrators. The push to make all electronics "smart" is fueling a frenzy

Email: Karthika.d@sdnbvc.edu.in

Anita Gehlot, Rajesh Singh, Jaskaran Singh and Neeta Raj Sharma (eds.) Digital Forensics and Internet of Things: Impact and Challenges, (111–130) © 2022 Scrivener Publishing LLC

of opportunity for digital hoodlums, country state on-screen actors, and security scientists. According to a security expert, the track record in cybersecurity is terrible. The IoT is a quickly expanding field of technology and gadgets that might endanger the economy, partnerships, commercial exchanges, individual security, and wellness.

While the development is mechanical, distinct people have ever-present human inspirations and inclinations to try, intentionally or inadvertently, to misuse those advancements. They confirmed that they are on the approach of experiencing a security nightmare. What does this mean exactly? For one reason, IoT innovation is outpacing IoT security knowledge and awareness. New physical and digital frameworks, gadgets, and connections that were unimaginable 5 years ago are rapidly straining human morality to its limit. Consider a comparable topic that allows us to draw parallels: bioethics and the new, uncommon hereditary building talents that people now possess [1]. They may now be able to produce novel traits in animals and humans by spontaneously mixing DNA from carefully sequenced nucleotide sequences. Just because they can do something does not imply that they should do it all the time. The fact that they can connect to another device does not indicate that they should. That is exactly what the IoT is doing. The necessity to reconcile all the fantastic, confident forecasts about humanity's future with the truth that human intellect and conduct have consistently and will continue to miss the mark when it comes to idealistic aims. There will always be blatant and hidden criminals; regular individuals who become embroiled in conspiracies, financial disasters, and extortion; tragedies; and profiteers and con artists ready to damage and profit from others' pessimism. To put it another way, a few people will always be driven to break in and take gadgets and frameworks for the same reason that a burglar would always be motivated to break into a house and grab the most expensive belongings.

8.2 Cybersecurity Versus IoT Security and Cyber-Physical Systems

It is not common to associate IoT security with cybersecurity, yet it is a combination of both. Small data, servers, organizational structures, and record security are only a few of the components of IT. Internet-linked key frameworks may also be monitored and overseen by the government in an instant or suitable manner. Also known as digital important structures, this item has become a crucial distinction between IoT and cybersecurity.

Unless otherwise specified, cybersecurity typically ignores the physical and security components of the equipment device, as well as any essential international communications it may have. Unlike most other technologies, the IoT has a unique security need that extends to actual devices and equipment that begin and receive data in the real world. Physical and basic components make up the IoT. In addition to being physical objects, a substantial percentage of IoT devices may represent security risks [2]. Such contraptions can, therefore, cause bodily harm, property destruction, and death.

There was no one, static set of meta-safety rules that applied to all devices and hosts at the time. Every IoT device must have a completely engaging application, and there must be a set of frameworks in which IoT devices may be used. Even though IoT devices come in a variety of shapes and sizes, they all have the following characteristics: Possibility of directly or indirectly transmitting data through the internet in the device's medium or state, manipulates or displays anything tangible, such as the segment itself, or a rapid association with a factor. A physical device might be an IoT device if it has sophisticated interfaces to connect to the Internet as shown in Figure 8.1. So, the health of an IoT device depends on its use, the physical strategy it employs, and the conditions it is subjected, and the affectability of the frameworks with which the device interacts.

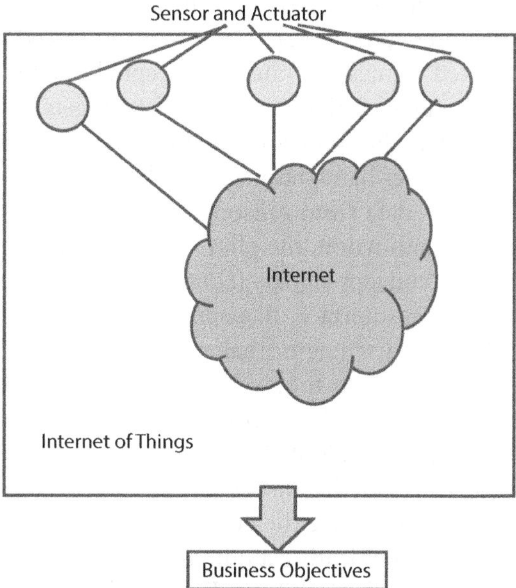

Figure 8.1 IoT sensors over business objectives.

Consider the IoT to be a superset of the cycle, as the cycle will be incorporated into the IoT merely by its web connectedness. A cycle is first and foremost a well-designed system that promotes safety, security, and usability. Developing business IoT deployments should learn from the cycle's rigorous rigor.

8.3 The IoT of the Future and the Need to Secure

We are always inventing new techniques for dealing with large-scale challenges, even as today's IoT technologies continue to push the boundaries by establishing new connections between things, systems, and people use of absorbent, a new material, opens a world of IoT possibilities.

8.3.1 The Future—Cognitive Systems and the IoT

Gadgets along with computers, should not anything be said about cutting-edge new research on the verge of computerization, even though the IoT is poised for rapid growth in the next years? To what degree will the protection of the IoT today affect the future? Our understanding of the future of the IoT is greatly enhanced by intellectual frameworks and research.

Transmission of prepared material via information transports, IP systems, and even the Internet is made possible by an advanced transformation of cerebrum detected signals (by pneumoencephalography). BMI-related psychological study suggests that certain smart gadgets in the future will be inquisitive about whether they are guided by a person or another form of cerebrum. On the other hand, humans may be rendered hyper-aware by feeding their thoughts data from sensors located hundreds of kilometers away. To control the automaton, the pilot would use his hands in place of a joystick. Using just concept signals (controls) and input (feeling) given through an interchanges interface, all essential flying maneuvers and alterations are achievable. Let us imagine that a computational framework communicates the airplane's piton tube velocity via a computer to the pilot's BMI interface. The pilot "feels" the speed as if it were a wind on his skin. This may not be as far off as it looks.

As an example, consider the sort of IoT security that is necessary in psychological frameworks where the items are human brains and dynamic physical structures. Authenticating a human mind to a gadget or a device to the cerebral cortex is a difficult task. The BMI has a role to play in fostering untrustworthiness. When signs are mocked, destroyed, or their accessibility and timeliness are restricted, what would happen? It is easy to see that the IoT's apparent benefits pale in comparison to the implications of such future frameworks for mankind. They are all the same in terms of threats and hazards.

8.4 Security Engineering for IoT Development

Brains are generating new cognitive capabilities to deal with difficulties on a massive scale while IoT enhancements are testing individual boundaries by building new connections between things, frameworks, and individuals. Today's fast-paced technology industry prioritizes market-driven features over security design. As a result, toxic programmers have a wide range of opportunities to abuse the system. Evidence that cannot be denied and the evolution of utilitarian corporate requirements in an ideal work environment are part of a systematic strategy. Before they are made, tested, and transmitted, these requirements have been tried, developed, and resolved into engineering. This is how a cascade model that is faultless and error-free may work. Businesses will build IoT devices and frameworks that utilize a range of inventive techniques, because the world is not flawless.

Businesses and organizations of all sizes, both small and large, would rely heavily on the ostensible security of their suppliers' technology and programming. The following issues will be covered in this part as they pertain to IoT security building [3]. A safe IoT upgrading method is essential. Include security in the design process from the start. Consistency Consciousness Investigating IoT security frameworks already exist. Security policies and procedures are created. In order to support the IoT, security solutions and administrations must be chosen. Choosing a safe advancement strategy is not easy because there are few alternatives. A new layer is being revealed in the region today.

8.5 Building Security Into Design and Development

Ethical development of IoT products and platforms is the focus of this chapter. This guidance applies whether you are developing a single IoT item or coordinating and transmitting many IoT devices into a project framework. This must be done by focusing on accumulating risks on purpose, following security standards to the end, and maintaining a strong focus on data protection.

As a product developer or framework designer, it is easy to say that security must be considered from the start. But what does that entail? Construction teams have carefully assessed methods to enhance security from inception to end, based on this information. This aspect is missing from many of today's fast-paced coordinated improvement initiatives. It takes money and effort to achieve this level of rigor when businesses analyze the methods and equipment, they will utilize to fulfill their security goals. To be sure, the cost of these activities is small compared to the cost of having your product or business at the top of news feeds, taking a beating online or getting fined by an administration controller for net negligence that resulted in a major trade-off.

When you begin a change of events or reconciliation project, one of your first responsibilities is to determine your advancement philosophy and determine how to update it into a more security-conscious one. This section outlines a few suggestions for you to consider. When extras help both the item and framework groups, they are considered extras.

8.6 Security in Agile Developments

A development strategy that incorporates security must be considered from the start in order to ensure that all security, health, and protection requirements are considered and met during the events and updates of an IoT device or framework (by a framework, the mean an assortment of IoT gadgets, applications, and administrations that are incorporated to help a business work). A templated approach to development can be beneficial to any project type [4].

Dexterous methods will be used to develop many IoT products and frameworks, allowing for fast configuration, creation, and deployment of highlight sets. When it comes to the security mix, the statement lays out numerous requirements as the deadline nears: Produce functioning code on a frequent basis (typically within a month or two), with the preference being for shorter periods. In order to progress, it is essential to have working programming. The tight development deadlines associated with agile initiatives are at the heart of the problems that must be addressed in order to provide a coordinated and safe development process. Various security requirements must be satisfied before an object can be considered safe. Addressing these demands in a short development cycle is difficult. An increased focus on security also hinders communication of utilitarian customer tales in event of an unexpected change of circumstances.

Securing needs requires the same technique and thinking as other non-functional criteria such as unshakable quality, execution, adaptable comfort, movability, and accessibility. Client stories, according to some, must contain nonfunctional demands as part of the notion of doneness. Transformation of all security (and nonfunctional) requirements into imperatives does not scale effectively when the development team is working with a significant number of security requirements. In particular, the technique emphasizes the management of security needs and offers suggestions for arranging requirements in a way that reduces pressure on the development team during each cycle. Security criteria One-Time, Every Sprint, and Bucket guide Microsoft's approach. Each Sprint requirement is unique to each run and is assessed during run planning. The criteria are suitable for the safe execution of an undertaking and other needs that must be met from the beginning, for example, developing secure coding rules that can be followed during events and developing a list of suggested programs for non-traditional segments/libraries. Basic needs are those that can be carried out and satisfied throughout a project. By categorizing these requirements into basins, organizations may choose whether to include them in their planning.

8.7 Focusing on the IoT Device in Operation

Merchant goods as a service contribution, in which users pay for a set of benefits each month, are a fascinating aspect of the IoT. Costly clinical imaging frameworks are an example. Customers can rent IoT equipment, which is then tracked for billing reasons.

It is possible for customers to create and record changes in their IoT devices by connecting them to seller's cloud platform, which is connected to the seller's cloud infrastructure. Some of these items are periodically outsourced to an ODM that specializes in IoT. The OEM then incorporates these operational costs into the master supplier agreement between the two firms (MSA). The administration of IoT devices can also be assisted by some carriers, if this is done in the client's domain [5].

Solid development activities (DevOps) strategies and time are essential for operational IoT frameworks, given the need of integrating them into client operational frameworks, as well as the requirement to support robust and varied back-end foundations. DevOps combines agile development techniques such as Scrum or Kanban with a strong focus on activities.

8.8 Cryptographic Fundamentals for IoT Security Engineering

Individuals that create consumer or industrial IoT goods or incorporate IoT communications into their companies are the target audience of this chapter. Cryptographic security in IoT deployments and implementations is laid out for readers in this book. This section deviates from the rest of the book's focus on practical applications and recommendations to cover some of the more difficult underlying principles connected with applied cryptography and cryptographic implementations. Although many cryptographic implementation mistakes and deployment vulnerabilities are still being used by even security-conscious IT companies today, the authors believed it was necessary to share this history. Because of this, several previously uninterested sectors (such as manufacturers of household appliances) have begun connecting their goods to the internet and integrating IoT features into their products. Meanwhile, they commit several errors that might put their consumers at risk.

An in-depth examination of how cryptography is used to secure IoT communication and messaging protocols is presented along with recommendations for further cryptographic protections at different levels of the technological stack.

8.8.1 Types and Uses of Cryptographic Primitives in the IoT

It is amazing to see how quickly items are being sold as service contributions, where consumers pay a monthly subscription fee for certain privileges. Costly clinical imaging frameworks are an example. Renting out IoT devices to clients and tracking its usage for billing purposes distinguishes this firm [6].

It is possible for customers to create and record changes in their IoT devices by connecting them to seller's cloud platform, which is connected to the seller's cloud infrastructure. An ODM that works with the IoT framework may outsource such components from time to time. When most people think about cryptography, encryption comes to mind. It is well known that information is "mixed" to keep unauthorized parties from understanding it. All the IA goals stated above are partially or totally met by genuine cryptography. The use of cryptographic natives to achieve a larger, more sophisticated security purpose should only be done by security experts who understand applied cryptography and convention design. Security objectives may not be met due to even the tiniest error, which can lead to expensive vulnerabilities. The number of ways to weaken cryptographic security is greater than the number of ways to do business.

Cryptographic crude sorts fall into the accompanying classifications:

- Encryption using symmetry (and decoding).
- Asymmetric hashing is a type of hashing that is performed on a pair of marks created with digital technology.
- Symmetric: MAC is used to verify and legitimize information from its beginning.
- Asymmetric cryptography employs elliptic bend (EC) and number factorization (IFC). As a starting point for validation, these, like non-denial, give respectability, personality, and expertise.
- A random number's age: Most of the cryptography's assumption requires large quantities generated from high-entropy sources.

The use of cryptography in separation is uncommon at best. As opposed to this, it provides the fundamental security characteristics required by upper-layer communication and other protocol standards. Examples include Bluetooth, ZigBee, SSL/TLS, and other conventions (for instance, how to deal with a bombed message uprightness check).

Conditional charges are under the master supplier agreement between the two companies (MSA). Many IoT service providers, however, provide secondary administrations to their IoT device services. Operational IoT frameworks demand robust development tasks (DevOps) strategies and time due to their reach into client operational frameworks and the requirement to support powerful and adaptable back-end foundations. It is a combination of coordinated improvement efforts based on Scrum or Kanban with a strong task-focused approach to software development and operations.

8.8.1.1 Encryption and Decryption

Encryption is the most well-known cryptographic service; it is used to jumble or disguise data so that unauthorized parties cannot read or comprehend it. In other words, it is employed to secure information from eavesdroppers while enabling only the intended recipients to interpret it [7].

In Figure 8.2, cryptography methods are accessible on both an asymmetric and symmetric basis (explained shortly). To cipher—encrypt, the encryption method requires a cryptographic key and unprotected data. This ensures that no one can listen in on the conversation. When the data is

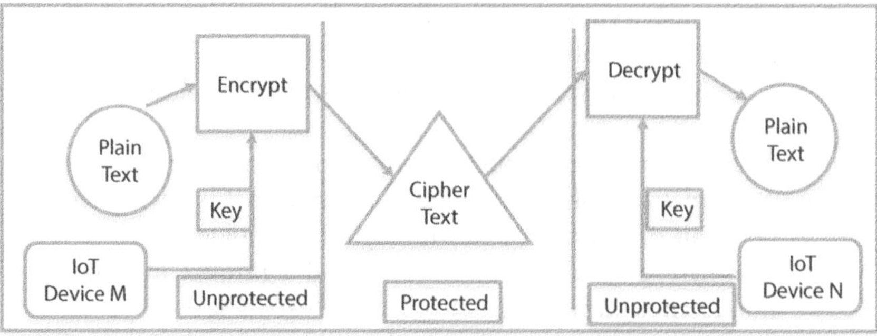

Figure 8.2 Encryption and decryption process.

needed, it is decoded by the receiving party using a special key. Unencrypted data is called plaintext; encrypted data is known as ciphertext. If the information is encrypted before it reaches IoT device B, the listener is at risk. A related topic is where encoding happens throughout the communication stack, and what protocol is utilized, based on the capabilities of the endpoints involved in communication. To protect communications, engineers were obliged to decide on which encryption method they would use, depending on the threat model they used. Considering that many encrypted protocols function solely point-to-point and must travel via several gateways, some of which are obviously hazardous, this is a high-risk industry.

To prevent data loss, sessions and apps must be encrypted from the beginning to the conclusion. Among the most prominent instances are the electricity sector and the vulnerable SCADA protocols employed there. One of the most popular safety upgrades is the construction of secure communication gateways (where recently extra encoding is performed). Others use end-to-end secured protocols to tunnel unsecure protocols through a secure tunnel. In system security designs, each encoding security technique should be taken into consideration, noting where plain-text data is stored (in storage or transit) and where it must be reincarnated (encrypted) into cipher-text. End-to-end encryption should be recommended wherever practicable. To put it another way, a secure-by-default posture must be reinforced all the time.

8.8.1.2 Symmetric Encryption

Simply said, symmetric encryption implies that both the sender (scrambled) and the recipient (unscrambled) utilize the same cryptographic key. The calculation, which can encode or decode depending on the mode, is a reversible activity, as seen in Figure 8.3.

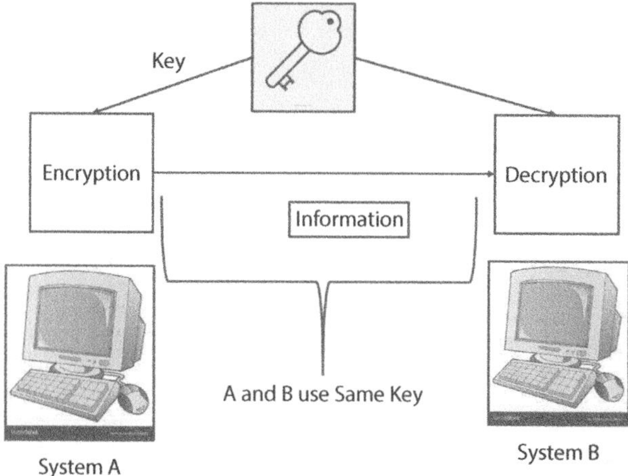

Figure 8.3 Symmetric encryption.

Several standards utilize an alternate symmetric key for each movement heading. Device A, for example, might encode to Device B in this manner by utilizing key X. Key X attends both meetings. The key Y, which is shared by both groups, may be used in the other direction (from B to A).

In addition to the cryptographic key and information processed by the figure, an introduction vector (IV) is periodically asked to help certain figure modes (clarified in a second). Figure modes are essentially various ways for bootstrapping the figure to work on successive chunks (obstructs) of plain-content and figure content information beyond the fundamental figure. The electronic codebook (ECB) is the fundamental figure, which works on a single square of plain-content or figures message at a time. Because repeated squares of indistinguishable plain content will have an indistinguishable figure content structure, jumbled information will be rendered impotent against catastrophic traffic inquiry, the ECB mode figure is employed without anyone else on occasion. There is no need for an IV in ECB mode; all that is necessary is the symmetric key and information to act with. In the former ECB, square figures may have worked in square tying modes and stream/counter modes, which were examined directly.

8.8.1.3 Asymmetric Encryption

Asymmetric cryptography essentially implies that two separate, paired keys, one public, and the other person, are used to encrypt and decode, respectively in Figure 8.4. IoT device A ciphers to IoT device B using IoT device B's public key in the image below. Device B, on the other hand,

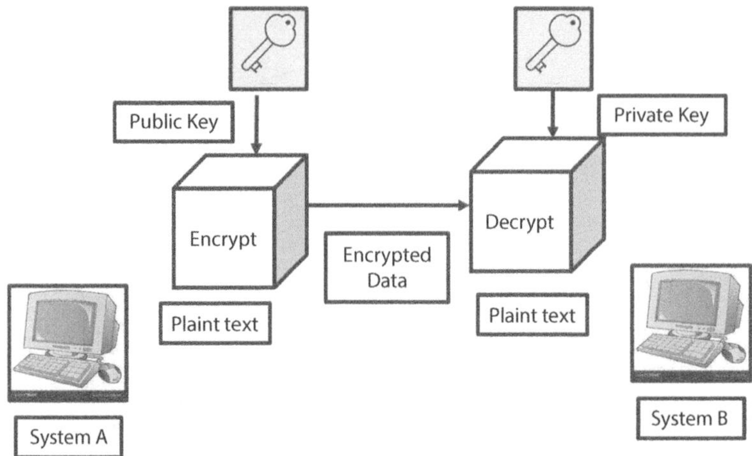

Figure 8.4 Asymmetric encryption.

encrypts data for device A using device A's public key. Personal keys for each device must be always kept secret, or else anybody or whatever with them will be able to decrypt and consider the data.

The most widely used asymmetric encryption technique nowadays is RSA (Rivest, Shamir, Adelman). It is an integer factorization algorithm that can encrypt and decode small amounts of data. The advantage of this method is that the traffic can only be decoded by one birthday party that possesses the corresponding RSA private key.

The drawback of uneven encryption (RSA) is that it can only encrypt up to the modulus length in question (1,024 bits, 2048 bits, and so on). Because of this issue, the most common use of RSA public key encryption is to encrypt and communicate other small keys (typically symmetric) or random values used as predecessors to cryptographic keys. Larger RSA modulus sizes (for better computational resilience against attack) are currently promoted with the aid of NIST.

8.8.1.4 Hashes

Cryptographic hashes are designed to represent a big message at random with a small, unique fingerprint. They can be used in several security tasks (the hash). They require the following qualities: They keep any information about the hashed data secret (this is named resistance to first pre-image attacks) They prevent two messages with completely different hash from sharing the same hash. They generate pricing that looks to be entirely arbitrary (hash).

8.8.1.5 Digital Signatures

A digital signature is a cryptographic feature that offers trustworthiness, validation, data beginning, and, in certain circumstances, non-renunciation security. They are intended to be unique to the underwriter, the person or device in charge of marking the message and who holds the marking key, like a hand-scribbled mark. The author of the mark in the accompanying graph may now accompany the message (now known as the marked message), allowing anybody with the necessary key to do the opposite of mark activity, known as signature check [8].

As a result, the verifiers should not trust the information or its source if the mark confirmation technique fails. Derivative marks, which are deviant in nature, and private keys that are typically not shared (and should never be disclosed) make them a valuable means of doing both substance and information verification, guaranteeing the respectability of information, and offering non-revocation capabilities. The following are examples of basic twisted advanced mark calculations:

- RSA
- DSA (digital signature algorithm)
- Elliptic curve DSA (ECDSA)

It is impossible for any organization to deny signing a message since digital signatures are produced using a single, private (unshared) key. As a result, the signature could only have come from the entity's private key. An array of cryptographic protocols employs asymmetric digital signatures. Examples include SSL/TLS/IPSEC/S/MIME networks, ZigBee networks, Connected Vehicle Systems (IEEE 1609.2), and many more.

8.8.1.6 Symmetric (MACS)

It is also possible to produce marks using symmetric cryptography. In the case of asymmetrical digital marks, D. MAC is a term that is occasionally used to describe symmetric marks. Because MACs are created using an asymmetric computation method, the same key is utilized to generate and validate them. MAC is often used to refer to both the computation and the final mark, thus keep that in mind when using the word [9].

This code is often generated by hash work or a symmetric figure in various scenarios. To protect both sender and receiver, MAC keys are utilized (as indicated in the adjacent outline) (verifier). Considering the possibility that the symmetric keys used to create MACs are shared, MACs generally do not claim to provide personality-based substance validation (nor can non-revocation be guaranteed), but they do provide enough check of cause (especially in momentary exchanges) to qualify as information starting point confirmation.

8.8.1.7 Random Number Generation

Numerical unpredictability is essential to cryptography since it is utilized in the creation of many cryptographic variables, including keys. While it is tough to compute or replicate huge, unexpected amounts (such as animal power), extremely deterministic quantities are not. They can be classed as either deterministic or non-deterministic RNGs (random number generators). As the name suggests, deterministic models are calculation-based and will consistently produce the same response for a single set of input data sources. Non-deterministic methodologies, alternatively, the RNG, generate arbitrary data, usually from relatively uncommon physical events such as circuit turbulence and other low-inclination sources (even semi-arbitrary hinders happening in working frameworks). It is no surprise that RNGs are among the most delicate components of a cryptographic device, given their effect on key security and sources.

Subverting a cryptographic device's RNG so that you can see the cryptographic keys it generates invalidates the device's security. It is a device that produces random data that may be used for a variety of applications including cryptographic keys, introduction vectors, padding, and more. They require seeds that must be very random and come from sources with high entropy levels in order to work properly. In the event of a seed or entropy source tradeoff, the RNG's yields will suffer, and cryptography will suffer as a result. This leads to data manipulation, mockery of encounters or even more terrible acts.

IoT RNGs must be seeded with high entropy sources, and the entropy sources must be completely protected from disclosure, alteration, or any other form of control, in order to be effective. The random clamor features of electrical circuits, for example, vary with temperature; therefore, it is sensible to set temperature boundaries from time to time and legitimately halt entropy gathering capacities that depend on circuit commotion when temperature limits are surpassed. In smart cards (for example, credit/charge swap chip cards), this component regulates the chip's temperature in order to avoid attacks on RNG.

During the design phase, a device's entropy quality should be assessed. There should be consideration given to the min-entropy characteristics, and the IoT setup should be flexible enough to avoid the NDRNG from being stuck and contributing to the RNG in a similar way. When developing the cryptographic architecture for an IoT device, it is important to have top-tier random number generation capabilities, even though it is not a commercial concern. RNG state, RNG data sources and RNG outputs are covered in this section, as well as extraordinary entropy production and entropy state insurance.

8.8.1.8 Cipher Suites

Combining one or more of the computing types to accomplish the most essential security features is the most enjoyable aspect of applied cryptography. In some communication protocols, these rule groupings are referred to as cipher suites. Depending on the current standard, a figure suite offers the specific structure of computations, possible key lengths, and applications for each.

8.9 Cloud Security for the IoT

A brief summary is provided in this section on cloud management and IoT's security. By using cloud administrations and security best practices, companies may work together and govern IoT enterprises that span several authorities and jurisdictions. AWS, Cisco (Fog Computing), and Microsoft Azure components were examined for their cloud and security contributions [10].

Security for IoT components that demand huge amounts of data is closely tied to the cloud and cloud security. On the agenda will be IoT data archive and disclosure frameworks along with best practices for these administrations' assurance. IoT features in the cloud need determining whether elements of security are under the client or cloud provider's purview. Topics covered in this section include:

Section 8.3 focuses on the cloud as it relates to and benefits IoT. As a result of IoT, they will also find new cloud-related requirements. On the way, they will identify and analyze IoT-related security threats both within and outside of the cloud, as well as cloud-based security policies, and look at additional contributions to this sector.

- Examining IoT contributions from cloud service providers (CSPs): They will investigate a couple of CSPs as well as their product/security-as-a-service management. The environment cloud computing is exemplified by Cisco's Fog Computing, Amazon's AWS, and Microsoft's Azure.

- Controls for cloud IoT security: An examination of the cloud's security capabilities to develop a solid IoT venture security plan.
- Creating a successful, all-encompassing IoT cloud security design: This section combines and matches available cloud security contributions to build a successful, all-encompassing IoT cloud security design.
- New cloud-enabled IoT calculation subheadings: Again, we are moving on from the cloud security debate to quickly investigate new processing standards that the cloud is keen to provide.

8.9.1 Asset/Record Organization

The capacity to track assets and inventory is one of the most critical components of a secure IoT. Device characteristics are included in this category. For corporate asset/inventory management, the cloud is a suitable solution, as it provides a view of all devices that have been registered and permitted to function inside the organization's limits.

8.9.2 Service Provisioning, Billing, and Entitlement Management

The fact that many IoT device suppliers would provide their products as a free bonus to consumers makes this a very interesting use case. Device operations need to be authorized (or denied) and payments depending on use must be set up. In addition to camera and sensor observing services (such as Drop Cam cloud recording), wearable observing, and following services (such as Fit Bit gadget administrations), there are a variety of additional services available.

8.9.3 Real-Rime Monitoring

Real-time monitoring is possible with cloud apps installed in the back-end of mission-critical capabilities such as crisis management, mechanical control, and manufacturing. It is becoming more commonplace for businesses to move to the cloud their mechanical control framework, mechanical observation, and other capacities in an effort to cut operational costs, improve data accessibility, and open up existing B2B and B2C administrations when feasible.

8.9.4 Sensor Coordination

Automated benefits agreements are made possible by machine-to-machine interactions. Over time, workflows will become more automated, removing individuals from the exchange circle in the meanwhile. Cloud computing will be crucial to the success of these automated procedures. Examples of cloud services that IoT devices can use to acquire the most current data, limitations, or information will be developed in the future.

8.9.5 Customer Intelligence and Marketing

One of the most important aspects of the IoT is the ability to customize displays for individual users. An IoT cloud that is primarily focused on smart devices and reference points has been created by salesforce. It is built on the cloud and is a contemporary, real-time event motor. Clients can use this framework to send salespeople warnings or notifications based on their activity. The notion of crisp neighborhood alerts is a good example. Customers are detected when they pass through a company or retail area using a few sensors at these occasions. Their purchase history, tastes, and other variables are examined once they have been identified, and material is given to them that is specifically customized to them. A hostile actor might utilize the following instrument or file against a client, which is interesting from a security perspective.

Another type of IoT customer insight is improvements in vitality proficiency that benefit the environment. Household appliances, for example, can transmit consumption data to cloud-based back-end frameworks as part of a smart framework approach. Device utilization can be balanced based on demand and cost. IoT devices and consumers can adapt to data from IoT devices, such as time and frequency of use, energy spent on the device, and current electrical display estimation, by changing use patterns to save energy expenditures and reduce environmental impact.

8.9.6 Information Sharing

As a result of the IoT, multiple parties can exchange data. An implanted rehabilitation device, for example, may communicate data to a therapeutic office, which may then transmit that data to a protection provider. Depending on the circumstances, the data might be stored with additional patient information. Cloud-based data exchange and interoperability services are required for effective IoT analytics. Wot.io focuses on middleware-layer information trade administrations for horde information sellers' sources and sinks because to the variations in IoT equipment stages, administrations, and information structures. Many IoT applications and accompanying protocols employ the publish/subscribe paradigm, which lends itself well to middleware systems that can translate between the different information languages. The availability of such services is essential for the development of information-based B2B, B2I, and B2C solutions.

8.9.7 Message Transport/Broadcast

A large-scale IoT message exchange administration may be built on top of the cloud because of its centralization, flexibility, and adaptability. This is because many cloud administrations utilize a combination of protocols like as HTTP and MQTT that may be used to broadcast and disseminate data as well as subscribe to and move it in several ways (centrally or at the organized edge). While there are a few exceptions, the security options given by cloud-based platforms need less cybersecurity professionals and can reduce on-premises security costs. VMs and systems in cloud-based IaaS administrations are more likely to be linked constantly and securely by default, leading in security scale economies that benefit client organizations, according to the study. First, this post will examine IoT commerce goods and features now available in the cloud, before diving into IoT cloud security.

8.10 Conclusion

Because of the characteristics of WSN devices and the needs of applications, low-power remote communications are utilized, and the functionalities supported must be carefully balanced against the restricted assets during application transfer. Even though numerous studies on security instruments for WSN situations currently exist, our objective is to examine how security may be treated as an empowering figure of the integration of low-power WSN with the Web, within the framework of its commitment to the IoT. The great promise of IoT brings with it a host of new challenges. This chapter focuses on security problems, among other challenges, and because IoT is built on the Web, security issues from the Web will also surface in IoT. The representation here clearly focuses on the security of the Web of Things in several scenarios. The extensive usage of the framework has exacerbated the security issues associated with the Web of Things (IoT).

References

1. Jing, Q., Vasilakos, A.V., Wan, J. *et al.*, Security of the Internet of Things: perspectives and challenges. *Wirel. Netw.*, 20, 2481–2501, 2014.
2. Zhao, K. and Ge, L., "A Survey on the Internet of Things Security". *2013 Ninth International Conference on Computational Intelligence and Security*, Leshan, pp. 663–667, 2013.
3. Deebak, B.D. and Al-Turjman, F., "A hybrid secure routing and monitoring mechanism in IoT-based wireless sensor networks". *Ad Hoc Netw.*, 97, 102022, 2020.
4. Santos-González, I., Rivero-García, A., Burmester, M., Munilla, J., Caballero-Gil, P., "Secure lightweight password authenticated key exchange for heterogeneous wireless sensor networks". *Inf. Syst.*, 88, 101423, 2020.
5. Wang, G., Lee, B., Ahn, J., Cho, G., "A UAV-assisted CH election framework for secure data collection in wireless sensor networks". *Future Gener. Comp. Sy.*, 102, 152–162, 2020.
6. Jha, S.K., Panigrahi, N., Gupta, A., "Security Threats for Time Synchronization Protocols in the Internet of Things", in: *Principles of Internet of Things (IoT) Ecosystem: Insight Paradigm*, pp. 495–517, Springer, Cham, 2020.
7. Aakanksha, T. and Gupta, B.B., "Secure Timestamp-Based Mutual Authentication Protocol for IoT Devices Using RFID Tags". *Int. J. Semant. Web Inf. Syst. (IJSWIS)*, 16, 3, 20–34, 2020.
8. Julie Golden, E. and Harold Robinson, Y., "Security and Privacy Issues in Wireless Sensor Networks", in: *IoT and Analytics for Agriculture*, pp. 187–210, Springer, Singapore, 2020.
9. Siddiqui, S.T., Alam, S., Ahmad, R., Shuaib, M., "Security Threats, Attacks, and Possible Countermeasures in Internet of Things", in: *Advances in Data and Information Sciences*, pp. 35–46, Springer, Singapore, 2020.
10. Das, S.K., Samanta, S., Dey, N., Kumar, R., *Design Frameworks for Wireless Networks*, Springer Nature Singapore Pte Ltd., Springer, 2020.

9

Xilinx FPGA and Xilinx IP Cores: A Boon to Curb Digital Crime

B. Khaleelu Rehman[1], G. Vallathan[1], Vetriveeran Rajamani[1] and Salauddin Mohammad[2*]

[1]*Department of ECE, Nalla Malla Reddy Engineering College, Hyderabad, India*
[2]*Department of ECE, J.B. Institute of Engineering and Technology, Hyderabad, India*

Abstract

The popularity of internet is increasing dramatically day by day, and the use of handheld devices is also increasing, like smartphone, smart watches, iPod, and smart tab. It is not only changing our life but also change the way of crime. To solve these types of problems, one must collect the data by digital forensic tools. The paper aims to target the Xilinx intellectual property (IP) cores and the methodology that allows in the easy way of implementing the IP cores and their functionalities and the interface with the recent Xilinx FPGAs. The proposed work is developed with Xilinx ISE 14.7 programming and the IP cores which are associated with it. VHDL programming style is used to describe the hardware and its functionality. An 8-bit down counter is designed using conventional programming and Xilinx IP core approach and implemented using Spartan-6 (xc6slx45t-3csg324) device. A 16-bit up counter and down counter is designed using the Xilinx IP core approach and implemented using Virtex-5 XC5VXT50T device. The square root is designed using conventional programming and the Xilinx IP core approach and implemented using the Virtex-5 XC5VXT50T device. The binary down counter design is verified using different Xilinx FPGAs and compared with the existing method. Simulation and analysis of multiplier with conventional programming and Xilinx IP core approach are verified and simulated.

Keywords: FPGA, VHDL, Xilinx IP, Spartan-6, Virtex-5 XC5VXT50T, square root

**Corresponding author*: afridi.1156@gmail.coms

Anita Gehlot, Rajesh Singh, Jaskaran Singh and Neeta Raj Sharma (eds.) Digital Forensics and Internet of Things: Impact and Challenges, (131–162) © 2022 Scrivener Publishing LLC

9.1 Introduction

Counters in digital electronics are having a variety of applications like timers and delays, system clocks, watches, alarms, clocks, memory addressing, frequency division, cycle controls, sequence controls, and protocols. The binary up counter [1] counts the number of events in the upward direction, for example, the N bit up counter counts the events from 0 to $2^N - 1$. Similarly, the down counter [2] counts the events in the $2^N - 1$ to 0. The square root is used to calculate the root of the particular value [3]. The binary down counter is designed using the conventional model and its RTL, simulation, and synthesis reports are tabulated below. The multiplier [4] circuit is used to multiply the two 8-bit numbers. Multiplicand and multiplier are multiplied, and the resultant is the product.

9.2 Literature Review

Many researchers used the counters for counting the number of events. A counter is one of the basic components of any digital system [5]. Cellular 1d automation technique is used for the counter and its area; a delay is optimized; Virtex-5, Spartan-3E, and Virtex-6 FPGA hardware kits are used to compare area and delay [6]. Systolic binary counter using cellular-based automation technology is used, and power delay product is analyzed [7]. The 4-bit unsigned binary counter is performed and analyzed with Xilinx ISE software [8]. A 64-bit synchronous up counter and up/down counter is performed, and the area is analyzed [9].

9.3 Proposed Work

In the era of digital design, the engineers choose the hardware description language for describing any complex logic function. For example, if the digital design engineer needs the counter, up counter, down counter, or an up/down counter for designing the counter each time they were doing the project, then it would be reinventing the wheel and wasting their time. Similarly, if the design engineer wants to re-code, then it continually and reuse the same code, it will be very difficult, and one has to end up wasting more time and money; one solution for the above problem is using the Xilinx intellectual property (IP) [10] cores. An IP is a piece of HDL code where the design engineers have already written to perform a specific task and hence saving the designer's time.

Figure 9.1 shows the Xilinx Counter [11] 11.0 IP core; to open the IP core, the following steps should be followed: open the Xilinx ISE or Xilinx Vivado [12] suite, then click file, then click New project under the project, give the name of the project, specify the device details, and then click IP (core generator and architecture wizard). As shown in Figure 9.1, many IP cores are available; it uses the basic elements under the basic elements. Binary counter is used in the design.

Figure 9.2 is the binary counter IP core. The IP core shown above has two halves. The left side has the IP symbol which is the prototype of the RTL but not exactly the RTL. The exact RTL can be observed after writing the HDL code and after instantiating the counter IP core. q[7:0] is the 8-bit counter output; "clk" is the clock input. One input and one output are enabled; all the remaining pins are disabled. "CE" is the clock enable. "SCLR" is the synchronous clear. "SSET" is the synchronous set. "SSIT" is the synchronous Init. All the inputs and outputs which are disabled are optional. The binary counter will have an up counter, down counter, and up/down counter. Up counter counts the events in the upward direction, for example, for a 4-bit counter, it will count "0000, 0001, 0010, ..., 1111" in the binary format. The example of a down counter is in the down direction, i.e., for 4-bit down counter; it will count "1111, 1110, 1101, ..., 0000". The up/down counter will count in an upward and downward direction with the help of 1 bit, i.e., switch in one case; it will act as an up counter for logic level high, and in another case, and it will act as a down counter for logic level low.

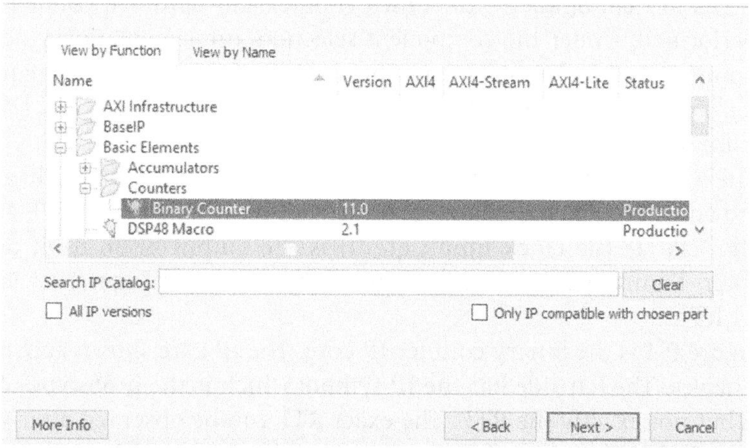

Figure 9.1 Xilinx counter IP core.

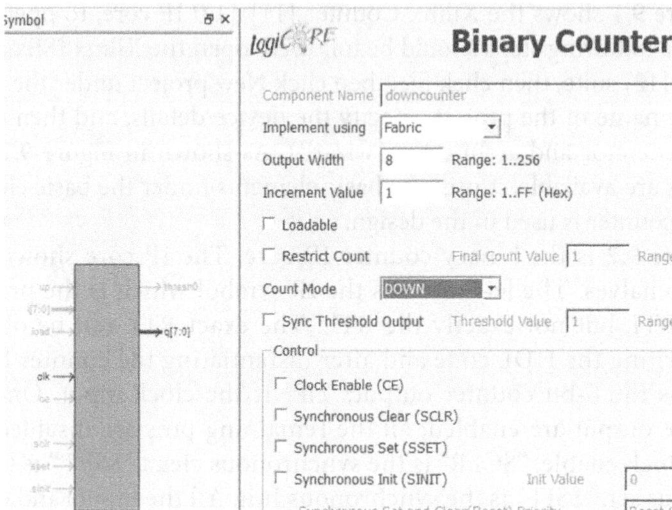

Figure 9.2 Binary counter IP core.

The right side has the drop-down menu count mode under the count mode; if the up/down counter is selected, then "up" will be enabled on the left side. It can count a minimum of 1 bit and a maximum of 256 bits, for example, if the output is 1 bit, then $2^1 = 2$. 2 events are counted 0 and 1.2^{256} is the maximum counter.

The increment value is used to increment the counter, for example, for the 4-bit counter; if the increment value is 2, then it will count the events after leaving one value, for example, 0, 2, 4, 6, …., 14 in unsigned decimals format. Similarly, the down counter and up/down counter will be performed. Under the component selection, implementation type has two options: one is Fabric and another is DSP; the 8-bit counter requires 8 look-up tables (LUTs), and 8 flip-flops (FFs) through Fabric, and DSP48 [13] uses one DSP.

The RTL schematic of the 8-bit down counter IP core block diagram is shown in Figure 9.3. Xilinx generates an .ngr file for the RTL schematic. "clk" is the clock input; q(7:0) is the output of an 8-bit down counter. Figure 9.2 is the prototype of the RTL, and Figure 9.3 is the exact RTL.

Figure 9.4 is the binary counter IP core. The IP core shown above has two halves. The left side has the IP symbol which is the prototype of the RTL but not exactly the RTL. The exact RTL can be observed after writing the HDL code and after instantiating the counter IP core. q[15:0] is the 16-bit counter output; "clk" is the clock input. "up" is 1 bit. Two

Figure 9.3 RTL schematic of 8-bit down counter IP core.

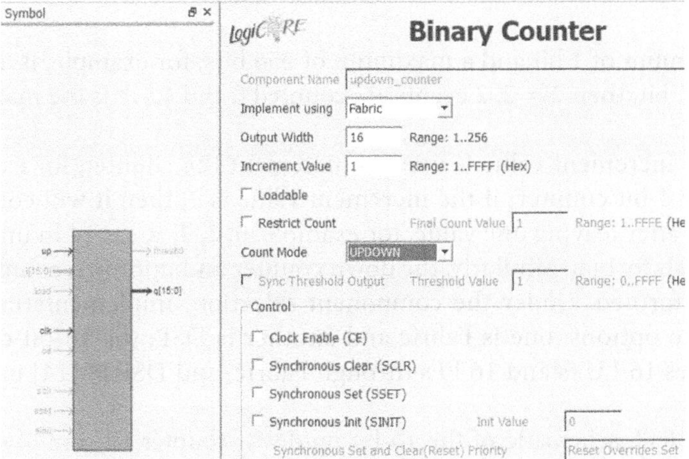

Figure 9.4 Binary counter IP core.

inputs and one output are enabled, and all the remaining pins are disabled. "CE" is the clock enable. "SCLR" is the synchronous clear. "SSET" is the synchronous set. "SSIT" is the synchronous Init. All the inputs and outputs which are disabled are optional. The binary counter will have an up counter, down counter, and up/down counter. Up counter counts the events in the upward direction, for example, for a 4-bit counter, it will count "0000, 0001, 0010, ..., 1111" in the binary format. The example of a down counter is in the down direction, i.e., for 4 bit down counter, it will count "1111, 1110, 1101, ..., 0000". The up/down counter will count in an upward and downward direction with the help of 1 bit, i.e., switch in one case; it will act as an up counter for logic level high, and in another case, it will act as a down counter for logic level low. The right side has the drop-down menu count mode under the count mode; if the up/down counter is selected, then "up" will be enabled on the left side. It can count

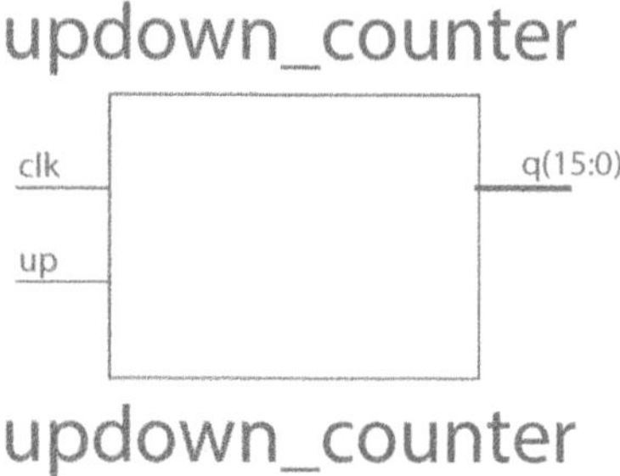

Figure 9.5 RTL schematic of 16-bit up/down counter IP core.

a minimum of 1 bit and a maximum of 256 bits, for example, if the output is 1 bit, then $2^1 = 2$. 2 events are counted 0 and 1.2^{256} is the maximum counter.

The increment value is used to increment the counter, for example, for the 4-bit counter; if the increment value is 2, then it will count the events after leaving one value, for example, 0, 2, 4, 6, …, 14 in unsigned decimals format. Similarly, the down counter and up/down counter will be performed. Under the component selection, implementation type has two options: one is Fabric and another is DSP; the 16-bit counter requires 16 LUTs and 16 FFs through Fabric, and DSP48 [14] uses one DSP.

The RTL schematic of the 16-bit up/down counter IP core block diagram is shown in Figure 9.5. Xilinx generates an .ngr file for the RTL schematic. "clk" is the clock input. "up" is 1-bit switch. q(15:0) is the output of 16-bit up/down counter. Figure 9.4 is the prototype of the RTL, and Figure 9.5 is the exact RTL.

9.4 Xilinx IP Core Square Root

Figure 9.6 shows the Xilinx Counter [15] 11.0 IP core; to open the IP core, the following steps should be followed: open the Xilinx ISE or Xilinx Vivado [16] suite, then click file, then click New project under the project, give the name of the project, specify the device details, and then click IP (core generator and architecture wizard). As shown in Figure 9.6, many IP cores are available; it uses the basic elements under the basic elements. Square root is used in the design.

Figure 9.7 is the square root IP core. The IP core shown below has two halves. The left side has the IP symbol which is the prototype of the RTL but

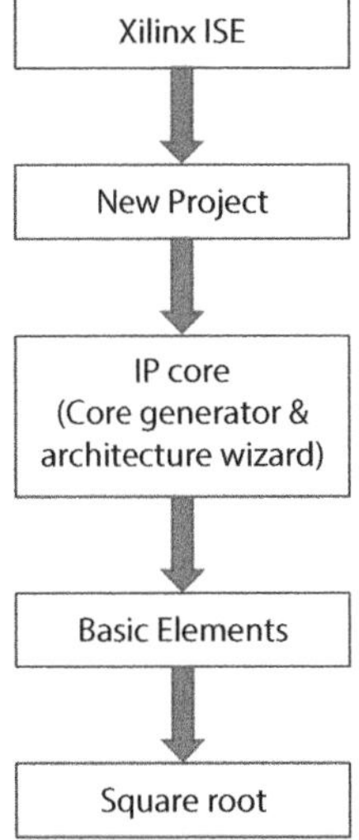

Figure 9.6 IP core generation wizard.

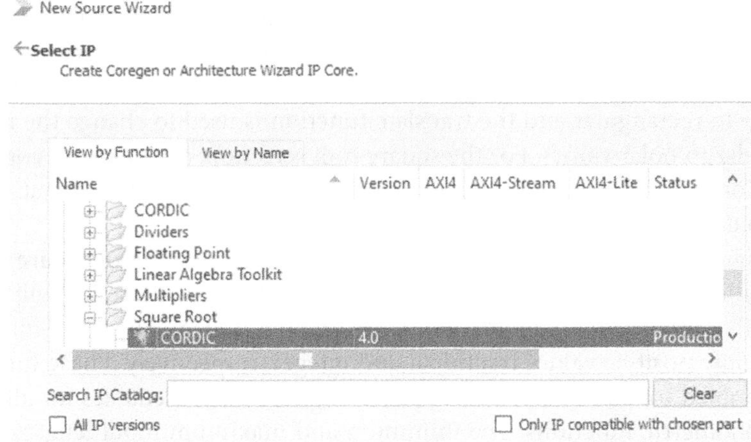

Figure 9.7 Xilinx square root IP core.

not exactly the RTL. The exact RTL can be observed after writing the HDL code and after instantiating the counter IP core. X_In[7:0] is the 8-bit input. X_out[4:0] is the output bits. "clk" is the clock input. From Figure 9.8, it can be observed that two inputs and one output are enabled; all the remaining pins are disabled. Under the functional selection, there are many inbuilt functions like Rotate, Translate, and Trignometric functions like sin and cos.

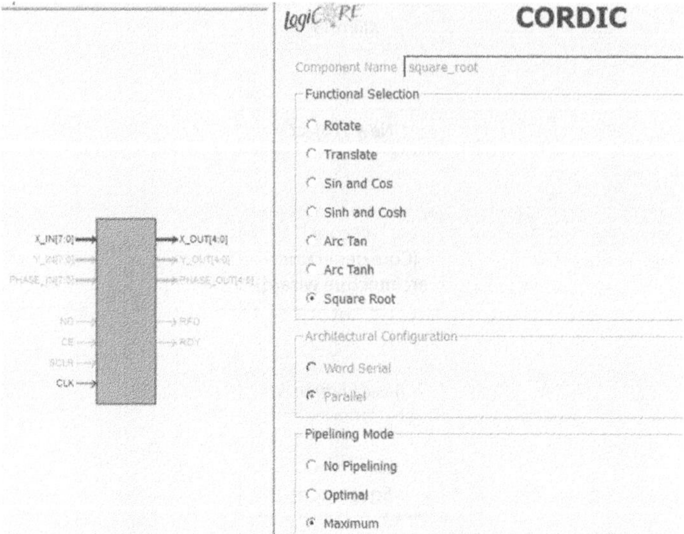

Figure 9.8 Square root IP core.

Trignometric hyperbolic functions are sinh and cosh. Inverse tan is represented as arc tan. The inverse hyperbolic function is represented as arc tanh and square root functions. Rotate function means the vector rotation from polar to rectangular and the translate function is used to change the rectangular to polar values. For the square root selection, architectural configuration remains disabled. A pipelining mode is selected. All the inputs and outputs which are disabled are optional.

Figure 9.9 shows the next page in the IP core generation of square root in which the selection of data format is given. The signed fraction will give positive and negative square roots. Unsigned fraction and unsigned integer will only positive values fractional and integer, respectively. Phase format is disabled for square root; this option of phase format enables for all the trigonometric functions. The minimum and maximum input lengths can be 8 to 48 bits. If the minimum input width is selected by default, then the 5 output width is selected. Figure 9.10 is the RTL view of the 8-bit square root with total of 13 input-output blocks (IOBs): 9 input pins and 4 output pins.

The RTL schematic of the 8-bit square root IP core block diagram is shown in Figure 9.11. Xilinx generates an .ngr file for the RTL schematic. "pclk" is the clock input; a(7:0) is the 8-bit input, and b(4:0) is the 5-bit output of square root. Figure 9.3 is the prototype of the RTL, and Figure 9.8 is the exact RTL. Table 9.1 shows the pin details of the 8-bit square root.

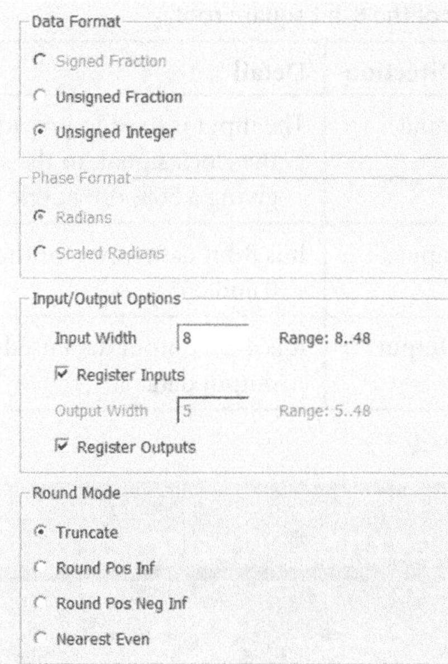

Figure 9.9 Square root IP core.

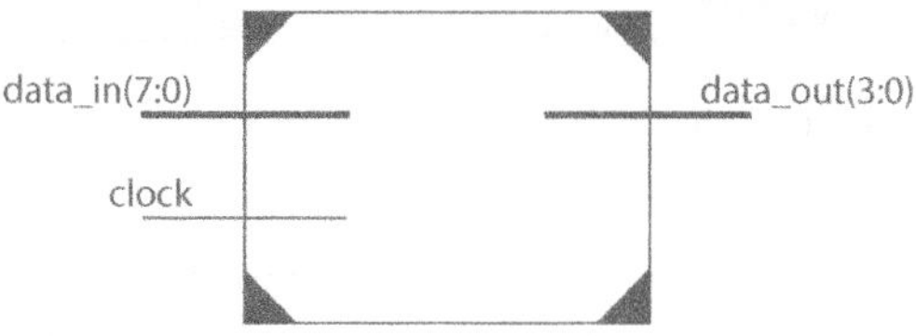

Figure 9.10 RTL view of 8-bit square root.

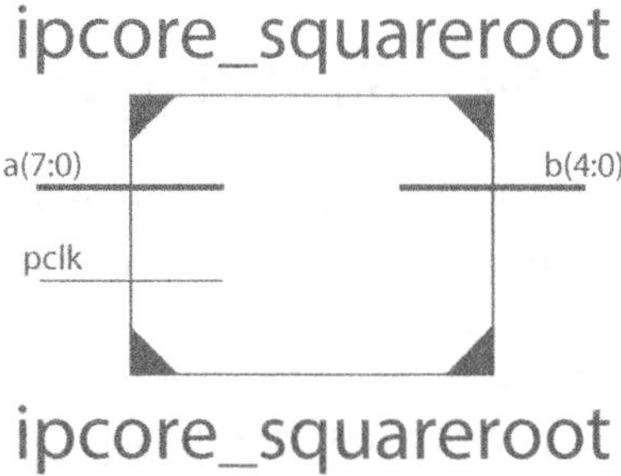

Figure 9.11 RTL view of 8-bit square root.

Table 9.1 Pin details of the 8-bit square root.

Pin	Direction	Detail
clk(1 bit)	Input	The input is used to provide the rising edge of the clock signal. In the simulation, we are giving a 50% duty cycle clock signal
Data_in(8 bits)	Input	It is 8-bit data input for the numbers between 0 and 255.
Data_out(3:0) (4 bit)	Output	It is 4-bit output data used to calculate the output data.

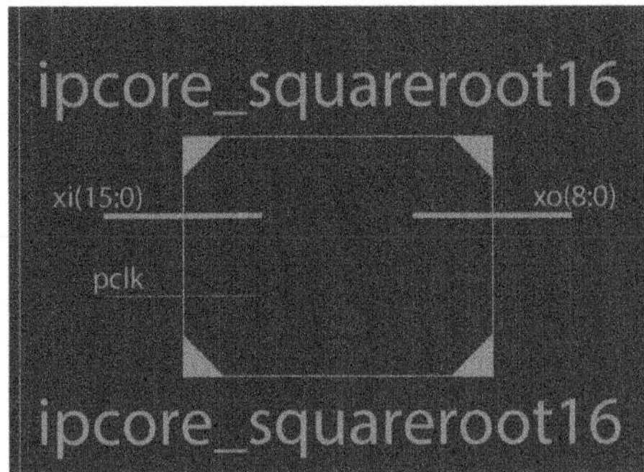

Figure 9.12 RTL view of 16-bit square root using IP core.

The RTL schematic of the 16-bit square root IP core block diagram is shown in Figure 9.12. Xilinx generates an .ngr file for the RTL schematic. "pclk" is the clock input; xi(15:0) is the 16-bit input, and xo(8:0) is the 9-bit output of square root. Figure 9.8 is the prototype of the RTL, and Figure 9.12 is the exact RTL.

9.5 RTL View of the 8-Bit Multiplier

Table 9.2 shows the pin details of the 8-bit multiplier and Table 9.3 shows the synthesis report of the 8-bit multiplication. The number of IOBs and DSP58Es are 24 and 1, respectively. In Figure 9.13, RTL view shows that a[7:0] is the 8-bit input and b[7:0] is the one more input and c[7:0] is the 8-bit output product; hence, in the synthesis report, total IOBs are 24. The maximum combinational path delay (MCPD) for the 8-bit multiplier circuit is 6.477 ns through which 5.906 ns for the logic and 0.571 ns for the

Table 9.2 Pin details of 8-bit multiplier.

Pin	Direction	Detail
a(7:0) (8 bit)	Input	It is the 8-bit input multiplicand.
b(7:0) (8 bits)	Input	It is an 8-bit input data multiplier.
c(7:0) (8 bits)	Output	It is an 8-bit output data product (product of multiplicand and multiplier).

Table 9.3 Synthesis report of 8-bit multiplier.

Hardware device utilization summary (estimated values): 8 bit	
Number of input-output blocks (IOBs)	24/240
Number of DSP48Es	1/48
MCPD	6.477 ns
Speed Grade	–2
REAL time to Xst completion	21.00 s
CPU time to Xst completion	21.15 s
Routing	0.571 ns

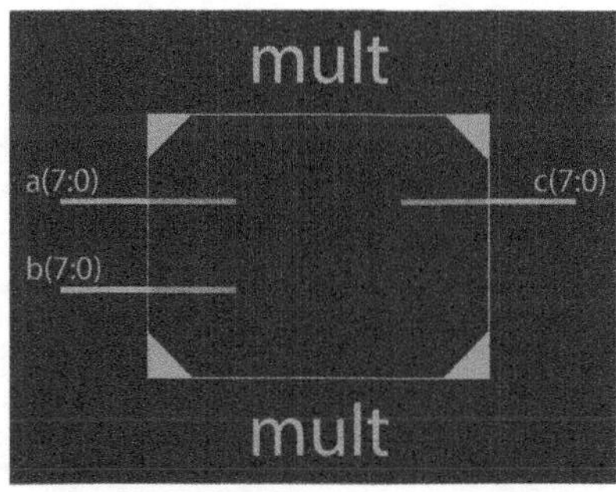

Figure 9.13 RTL view of 8-bit multiplier.

routing. Total REAL time to Xst (Xilinx Synthesis Technology) completion is 21.05 s and total CPU time to Xst completion is 21.15 s, and the speed grade is −2.

Figure 9.14 shows the ISIM simulation waveform of the 8-bit Multiplier. By default, Xilinx has the ISim simulator but the third-party simulator like ModelSim; the product of Mentor graphics [17] will also give the same simulation waveform.

One input from Figure 9.14 in the simulation is the input signal multiplicand a[7:0]. The hexadecimal format of the multiplicand is "14" and its decimal equivalent is "20", and its binary value is "00010100". The second input is the multiplier b[7:0]; its hexadecimal value is "0c"; its decimal value is "12". From Figure 9.14, it can be observed that the multiplication of the two 8-bit binary numbers. The result of the multiplicand and the multiplier is the product, i.e., c[7:0]; its value is "f0" in the hexadecimal and the decimal its value is 240. 20 * 12 = 240 in the decimal format.

Figure 9.15 shows the Xilinx multiplier [18] 11.2 IP core; to open the IP core, the following steps should be followed: open the Xilinx ISE or Xilinx Vivado suite, then click file, then click New project under the project, give the name of the project, specify the device details, and then click IP (core generator and architecture wizard). As shown in Figure 9.15, many IP cores are available; it uses the math functions: under the math functions, use multipliers, and under the multipliers, use multiplier 11.2.

Figure 9.16 is the binary multiplier IP core. The IP core shown above has two halves. The left side has the IP symbol which is the prototype of the RTL but not exactly the RTL. The exact RTL can be observed after writing the HDL code and after instantiating the counter IP core. A[7:0] is the 8-bit input multiplicand. "clk' is the clock input. B[7:0] is another input; multiplier[15:0] is the 16-bit output. Three inputs and one output are enabled;

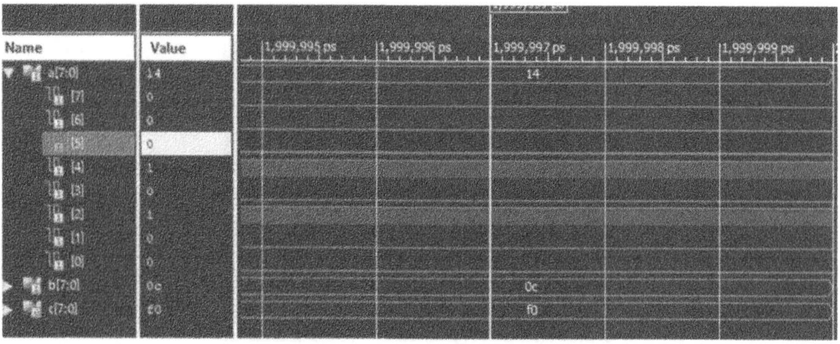

Figure 9.14 Simulation view of 8-bit multiplier.

New Source Wizard

Select IP
Create Coregen or Architecture Wizard IP Core.

View by Function | View by Name

Name	Version	AXI4	AXI4-Stream	AXI4-Lite	Status	Lice
Complex Multiplier	3.1				Production	
Complex Multiplier	5.0		AXI4-Stream			
Math Functions						
Multipliers						
Complex Multiplier	3.1				Production	
Complex Multiplier	5.0		AXI4-Stream			
Multiplier	11.2				Production	

Search IP Catalog: multipl   Clear

All IP versions   Only IP compatible with chosen part

More Info   < Back   Next >   Cancel

Figure 9.15 Xilinx multiplier IP core.

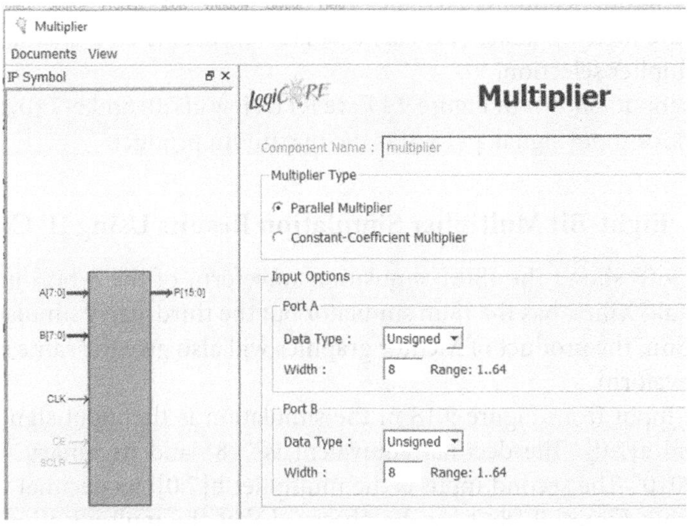

Figure 9.16 Multiplier IP core.

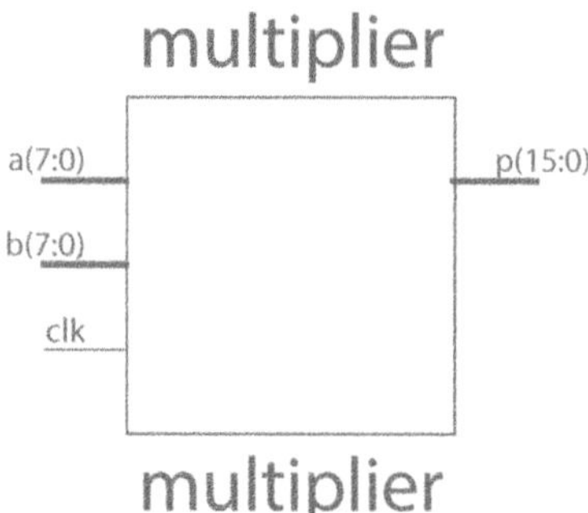

Figure 9.17 RTL schematic of 8-bit multiplier IP core.

all the remaining pins are disabled. "CE" is the clock enable. "SCLR" is the synchronous clear. All the inputs and outputs which are disabled are optional. The parallel multiplier type of multiplier is selected for the multiplication of two 8-bit numbers. The parallel multiplier takes the two inputs and multiplies its product with dedicated multiplier resources and maximum achievable clock frequency. The constant-coefficient multiplier takes the input data width and multiplies it with the constant user-defined value. The multipliers are constructed using block memory in conjunction with slices and distributed memory. The data type for both the inputs is set as unsigned numbers with the data width being 8 bits. The maximum input widths can be 64 bits. If the signed data type is selected, then negative number multiplication is possible. The hardware parameters used for the design are look-up tables (LUT6s) that are 72. Xtreme DSP slice 1 is used for multiplier selection.

Two inputs shown in Figure 9.17 are RTL view a(7:0) and b(7:0), and clk is the clock input signal. p(15:0) is the maximum product.

9.5.1 Eight-Bit Multiplier Simulation Results Using IP Core

Figure 9.18 shows the ISIM simulation waveform of the 8-bit multiplier By default, Xilinx has the ISim simulator but the third-party simulator like ModelSim; the product of Mentor graphics will also give the same simulation waveform.

One input from Figure 9.18 in the simulation is the input signal multiplicand a[7:0]. The decimal equivalent is "18" and its binary value is "00010010". The second input is the multiplier b[7:0]; its decimal value is "15". From Figure 9.18, it can be observed that the multiplication of the two 8-bit binary numbers. The result of the multiplicand and the multiplier

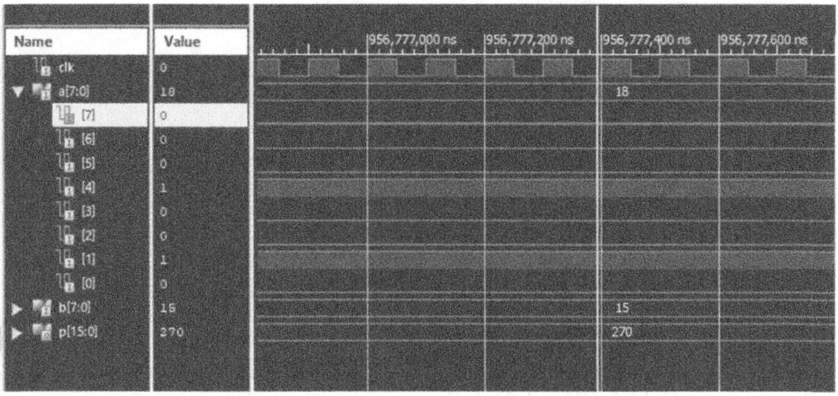

Figure 9.18 Eight-bit multiplier simulation using IP core.

is the product, i.e., p[15:0]; its value is "270" in the decimal. The decimal value of the product is 270. 18 * 15 = 270 in the decimal format.

9.6 RTL View of 8-Bit Down Counter

Xilinx generates an .ngr file for the RTL schematic. The RTL schematic of the 8-bit down counter is shown in Figure 9.19; the input clk and rst are the 1-bit data, and the output Q(7:0) is the 8-bit down counter.

The RTL schematic of the 8-bit down counter IP core block diagram is shown in Figure 9.20. Xilinx generates an .ngr file for the RTL schematic. "clk" is the clock input; q(7:0) is the output of an 8-bit down counter.

9.6.1 Eight-Bit Down Counter Simulation Results

The Xilinx ISim [3] waveform simulation is shown in Figure 9.21.

Step-1: Force reset = "1", then the counter output will be zero.

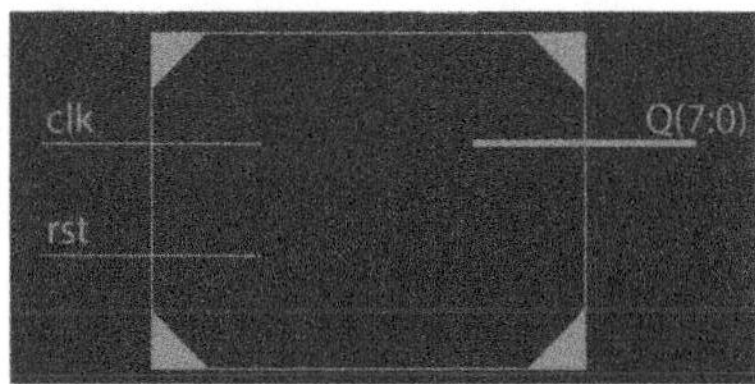

Figure 9.19 RTL view of 8-bit down counter.

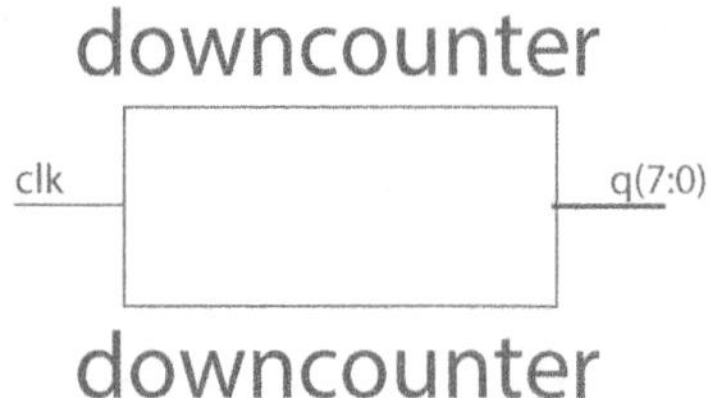

Figure 9.20 RTL schematic of 8-bit down counter IP core.

Table 9.4 Pin details of 8-bit up counter.

Pin	Direction	Detail
clk(1 bit)	Input	The input is used to provide the rising edge of the clock signal. In the simulation, we are giving a 50% duty cycle clock signal
rst(1 bit)	Input	The input used to keep all the output register contents as zero and synchronized with the clock signal
Q(7:0) (8 bit)	Output	It is 8-bit output down counter used to count the events in the downward direction

Figure 9.21 Eight-bit down the counter simulation.

Step 2: Force reset = "0", apply direct clk signal with a rising edge. One output q [7:0] is the counter value; the maximum value of the 8-bit down counter is $2^8 = 256$ in the unsigned decimal format [4], and in the binary format, its value is "11111111". From Figure 9.21, it can be observed that, after the counter reaches the maximum value, again, it starts at 0 and it continues 255, 254, 253, …, 210.

Table 9.5 shows the synthesis report of the 8-bit down counter. The number of slice registers, slice LUTs, fully used LUT-FF pairs, IOBs, and Buffer memories, respectively, are 8, 8, 0, 10, and 1. In Figure 9.22, RTL

Table 9.5 Synthesis report of 8-bit down counter.

Device utilization summary (estimated values)		
Logic utilization	**Used**	**Available**
Number of slice registers	8	54,576
Number of slice LUTs	8	27,288
Number of fully used LUT-FF pairs	0	16
Number of bonded IOBs	10	190
Number of BUFG/BUFGCTRLs	1	16

view shows that there is a 1-bit clock signal, 1-bit reset signal, and the 8-bit output down counter, and hence, in the synthesis report, total IOBs are 10. BUFG is a global clock signal. The MCPD for the 8-bit down counter circuit is 3.634 ns through which 3.018 ns for the logic and 0.616 ns for the routing. Total REAL time to Xst completion is 14.00 s, and total CPU time to Xst completion is 14.46 s. The maximum frequency is 544.292 MHz. The minimum period is 1.837 ns. The maximum output required time after clock pulse is 3.634 ns. The minimum input arrival time before the clock is 2.454 ns, and the speed grade is −3.

Figure 9.22 shows the ISIM simulation waveform of the 8-bit down counter. By default, Xilinx has the ISim simulator but the third-party simulator like ModelSim; the product of Mentor graphics will also give the same simulation waveform.

One input from Figure 9.22 in the simulation is "clk", i.e., clk is the clock pulse of the rising edge of the input signal, and output q[7:0] is the 8-bit down counter; the maximum value of the 8-bit down counter is $2^8 = 256$ in the unsigned decimal format, and in the binary format, its value is "11111111". From Figure 9.22, it can be observed that the binary value of the 248 is "11111000"; after the counter reaches the maximum value, again, it starts at 0 and it continues 255, 254, 253, …, 210.

Table 9.6 shows the synthesis report of the 8-bit down counter using Xilinx IP core. The number of slice registers, slice LUTs, and IOBs, respectively, are 4, 4, and 9. The MCPD for the 8-bit down counter circuit is 3.109 ns through which 2.791 ns for the logic and 0.310 ns for the routing. Total REAL time to Xst [19] completion is 11.00 , and total CPU time to Xst completion is 10.46 s. The maximum frequency is 600.232 MHz. The minimum period is 1.237 ns. The maximum output required time after clock

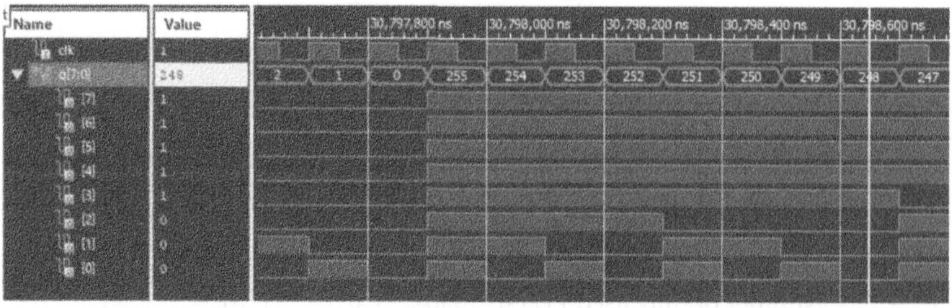

Figure 9.22 Eight-bit down counter simulation using IP core.

Table 9.6 Eight-bit down counter IP core synthesis report for Spartan-6 FPGA hardware.

Hardware device utilization summary: Spartan6		
Hardware parameters	**Used**	**Available**
Number of slice registers	4	54,576
Number of slice LUTs	4	27,288
Input-output blocks	9	17

pulse is 3.109 ns. The minimum input arrival time before the clock is 1.954 ns, and the speed grade is −3.

Figure 9.23 shows the 16-bit down counter simulation using IP core with one increment value. As discussed in Figure 9.2, there is an option of increment value; by default, the value will be "1"; for the above simulation,

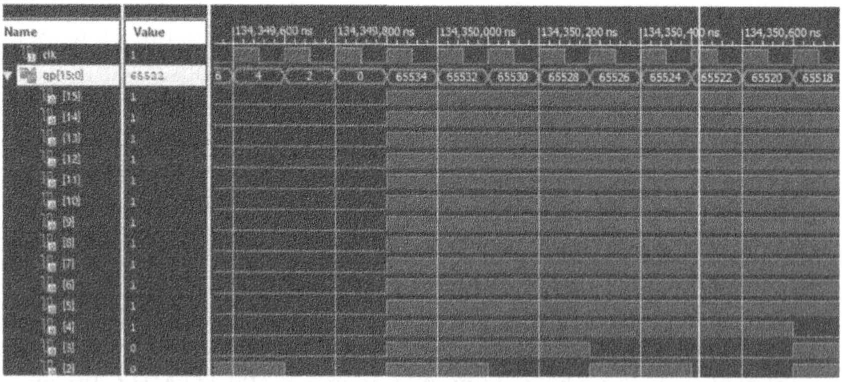

Figure 9.23 Sixteen- bit down counter simulation using IP core.

we changed the value of increment to "2" which means that it counts the value after leaving one value. Since it is the down counter, the values are 65534, 65532, 65530, ..., 6420 in the unsigned decimal format.

9.7 Up/Down Counter Simulation Results

Figure 9.24 shows the ISIM simulation waveform of the 16-bit up counter. By default, Xilinx has the ISim simulator but the third-party simulator like ModelSim [12]; the product of Mentor graphics will also give the same simulation waveform.

One input for Figure 9.24 in the simulation is "clk", i.e., clk is the clock pulse of the rising edge of the input signal. Up is the 1-bit signal; if "up" is high logic level, then the counter acts as an up counter, and output q[15:0] is the 16-bit up counter; the maximum value of the 16-bit up counter is 2^{16} = 65535 in the unsigned decimal format, and the binary format, its value is "1111111111111111". From Figure 9.24, it can be observed that, after the counter reaches the maximum value, again, it starts at 0 and it continues 0, 1, 2, ..., 65535. From the Figure 9.24 , it can be seen that the binary value of 65527 is "1111111111110111".

Figure 9.25 shows the ISIM simulation waveform of the 16-bit down counter using IP core. If "up" is low-level logic, then the counter acts as a down counter. From Figure 9.24, it can be observed that the hexadecimal value of the fff8 is "1111111111111000". After the counter reaches the maximum value, again, it starts at 0 and it continues ffff, fffe, fffd, ..., 0002,0001,0000 in the hexadecimal format.

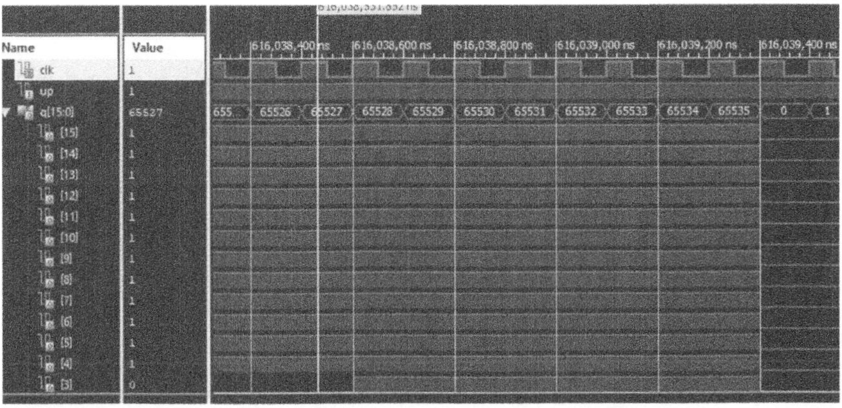

Figure 9.24 Sixteen-bit up a counter simulation using IP core.

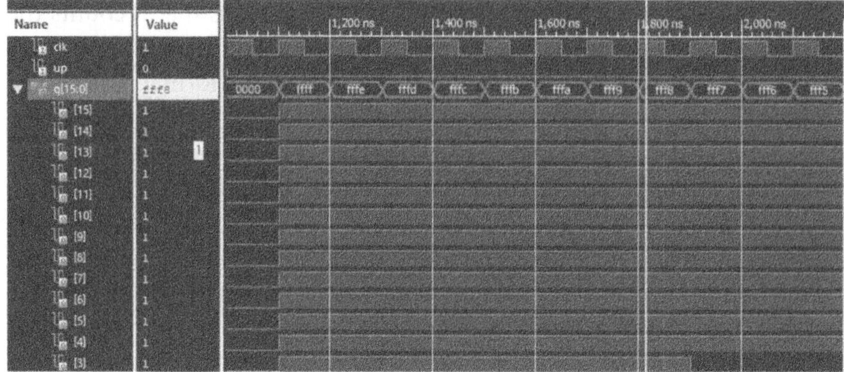

Figure 9.25 Sixteen-bit down counter simulation using IP core.

9.8 Square Root Simulation Results

Figure 9.26 is the simulation result of the 8-bit square root simulation; data_in[7:0] is the input data. The decimal format of the input data is "169" and the output data is "13" in the decimal format. The square root of the decimal number "169" is "13".

Figure 9.27 shows the ISIM simulation waveform of the 8-bit square root simulation using IP core. By default, Xilinx has the ISim simulator but the third-party simulator like ModelSim; the product of Mentor graphics [9] will also give the same simulation waveform.

One input from Figure 9.27 in the simulation is "pclk", i.e., "pclk" is the clock pulse of the rising edge of the input signal; a[7:0] is the 8-bit input

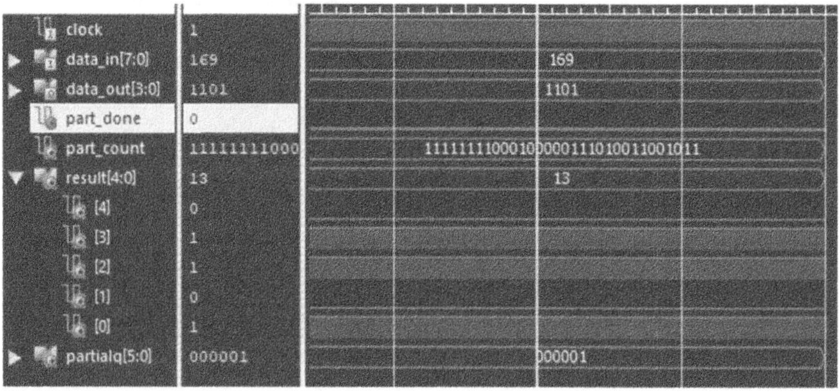

Figure 9.26 Eight-bit square root simulation.

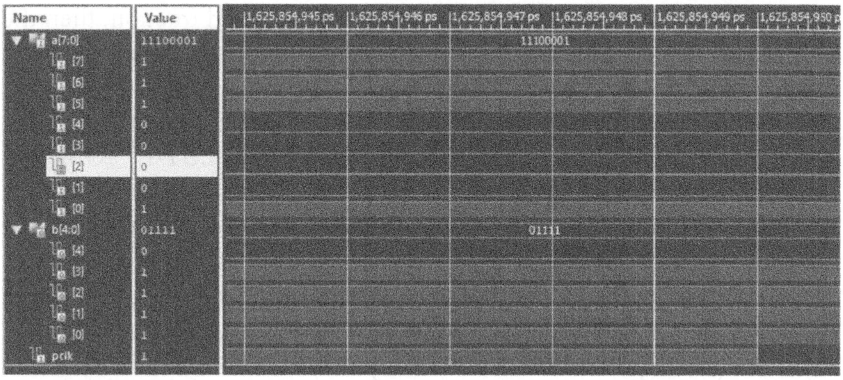

Figure 9.27 Eight-bit square root simulation using IP core.

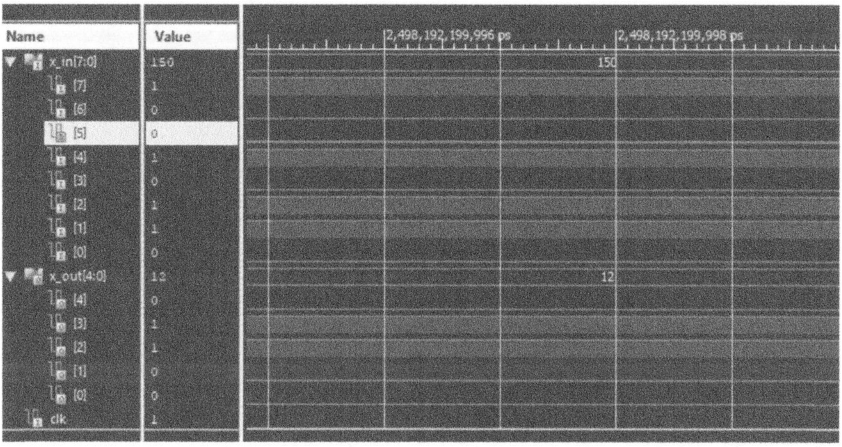

Figure 9.28 Square root simulation for a non-perfect square number using IP core.

width; "1110 0001" is the binary value; and its decimal value is 255; and b[4:0] is the 5-bit output width; its binary value is "01111"; and its decimal value is 15. From Figure 9.27, it can be observed that the square root of 255 is 15. The maximum integer square root for the 8-bit input data is 255.

One input from Figure 9.28 in the simulation is "clk", i.e., "clk" is the clock pulse of the rising edge of the input signal; x_in[7:0] is the 8-bit input width; "1001 0110" is the binary value; and its decimal value is 150; and x_out[4:0] is the 5-bit output width; its binary value is "01100"; and its decimal value is 12. From Figure 9.28, it can be observed that the square root of 150 is 12.25 (up to two decimals) but the output is 12 in the decimal format; this is because the data format in Figure 9.28 is selected as an integer. If the data format is selected as the unsigned fraction, then the output will be accurate. The maximum integer square root for the 8-bit input data is 255.

Table 9.7 shows the synthesis report of the 8-bit square root. The number of slice registers, Slice LUTs, Number of fully used LUT-FF, IOBs, and Buffer clock signals are, respectively, are 47, 50, 41, 13, and 1. The MCPD [20] for the 8-bit square root is 2.190 ns through which 1.770 ns for the logic and 0.421 ns for the routing. Total REAL time to Xst completion is 32.00 s, and total CPU time to Xst completion is 32.44 s. The maximum frequency is 456.527 MHz. The minimum period is 2.190 ns. The maximum output required time after clock pulse is 2.826 ns. The minimum input arrival time before the clock is 1.599 ns, and the speed grade is −2.

Table 9.8 shows the synthesis report of the 8-bit square root using Xilinx IP core. The number of slice registers, slice LUTs, number of fully used LUT-FF,

Table 9.7 Synthesis report of an 8-bit square root.

Device utilization summary (estimated values)		
Logic utilization	**Used**	**Available**
Number of slice registers	47	28,800
Number of slice LUTs	50	27,288
Number of fully used LUT-FF pairs	41	56
Number of bonded IOBs	13	480
Number of BUFG/BUFGCTRLs	1	32

Table 9.8 Synthesis report of 8-bit square root IP core.

Device utilization summary (estimated values)		
Logic utilization	**Used**	**Available**
Number of slice registers	37	28,800
Number of slice LUTs	38	27,288
Number of fully used LUT-FF pairs	14	61
Number of bonded IOBs	14	480
Number of BUFG/BUFGCTRLs	1	32

IOBs, and Buffer clock signals are, respectively, are 37, 38, 14, 14 and 1. The MCPD for the 8-bit square root IP core is 2.173 ns through which 1.196 ns for the logic, 0.977 ns for the routing. Total REAL time to Xst completion is 16.00 s and total CPU time to Xst completion is 15.32 s. The maximum frequency is 460.151 MHz. The minimum period is 2.173 ns. The maximum output required time after clock pulse is 2.826 ns. The minimum input arrival time before the clock is 1.274 ns, and the speed grade is −2.

Table 9.9 is the comparison of the 8-bit square root using the conventional approach and the IP core approach using 8 bits. From Table 9.9, it is clear that the IP core approach is the optimized results in terms of device utilization summary. The number of slice registers, number of slice LUTs, and number of fully used LUT-FF pairs are less.

The waveform of the 16-bit square root simulation using IP core is shown in Figure 9.29; one input x_in[15:0] is the 16-bit input. The

Table 9.9 Comparative table of conventional approach and IP core approach.

Hardware device utilization summary: Virtex-5		
Hardware parameters	**Conventional approach (8 Bit)**	**IP Core approach (8 Bit)**
Number of slice registers	47	37
Number of slice LUTs	50	38
Number of fully used LUT-FF pairs	41	14
Input-output blocks	13	14
Number of BUFGs	1	1

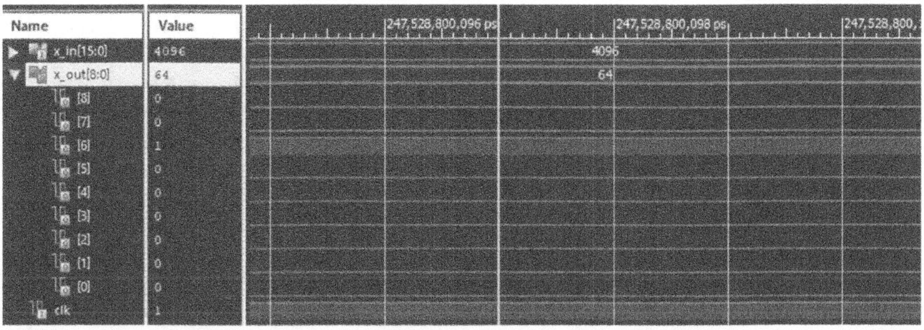

Figure 9.29 Sixteen-bit square root simulation using IP core.

maximum value for the 16-bit input is 65,536. x_in[15:0] = 4096 for the input data and the output data is x_out[8:0]=64. Clk is the clock pulse of the rising edge of the input signal. The square root of 4096 is 64.

9.9 Hardware Device Utilization Reports of Binary Down Counter

The hardware utilization summary of Spartan-3E Xilinx FPGAs using different lengths is shown in Table 9.10. Two different FPGAs are used for comparison Spartan-3E(xc3s500e-5fg320) and Spartan-6 (xc6slx45t-3csg324). The hardware parameters and the timing parameters are tested for the binary down counter, i.e., 8, 16, 32, 64, and 128-bit; up counter by using Xilinx IP core is verified: number of slices, number of LUTs, IOBs, maximum frequency, minimum period (ns) before clock pulse, and maximum period (ns) after clock pulse. The 2 FPGAs Spartan-3E and Spartan-6 work on 180-nm [21] and 60-nm technology.

Figure 9.30 compares the three hardware parameters, i.e., area (slices), slice LUTs, and the number of IOBs for 8, 16, 32, 64, and 128 bit using Xilinx IP core generator for the binary down counter.

The hardware utilization summary of Spartan-6 Xilinx FPGAs using different lengths is shown in Table 9.10. The hardware parameters and the timing parameters are tested for the binary down counter, i.e., 8, 16,

Table 9.10 Spartan-3E FPGA hardware device utilization summary of different lengths.

	Spartan-3E length (Bits)				
Hardware parameter	**8**	**16**	**32**	**64**	**128**
Number of slices	4	8	17	31	63
Number of slice LUTs	8	15	32	63	127
Number of bonded IOBs	9	17	33	65	129
Max frequency (MHz)	312	270	221	193	180
Minimum Period (ns)	2.18	3.69	4.52	5.12	5.32
Time after clock (ns) (maximum)	3.06	4.06	4.06	4.06	4.06

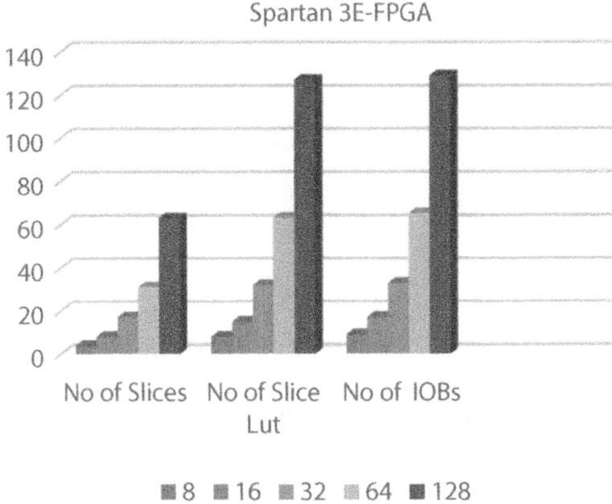

Figure 9.30 Graph of spartan-3E synthesis report.

Table 9.11 Spartan-6 FPGA hardware device utilization summary of different lengths.

Hardware parameter	SPARTAN-6 length (bits)				
	8	**16**	**32**	**64**	**128**
Number of Slices	8	16	32	64	128
Number of slice LUTs	7	15	31	63	127
Number of bonded IOBs	9	17	33	63	129
Max Frequency (MHz)	544	502	436	356	316
Minimum Period (ns)	1.83	1.18	2.29	3.12	3.22
Time after clock (ns) (maximum)	3.64	3.63	3.63	3.63	3.63

32, 64, and 128 bit; up counter by using Xilinx IP core is verified: number of slices, number of LUTs, IOBs, maximum frequency, minimum period (ns) before clock pulse, and maximum time period (ns) after clock pulse. Table 9.11 shows the synthesis report for different lengths using Spartan-6 FPFA.

Figure 9.31 compares the three hardware parameters, i.e., area (slices), slice LUTs, and number of IOBs for 8, 16, 32, 64, and 128 bit using Xilinx IP core generator for binary down counter.

The comparison of hardware utilization of different Xilinx FPGAs is shown in Table 9.12. Three different FPGAs are used for comparison

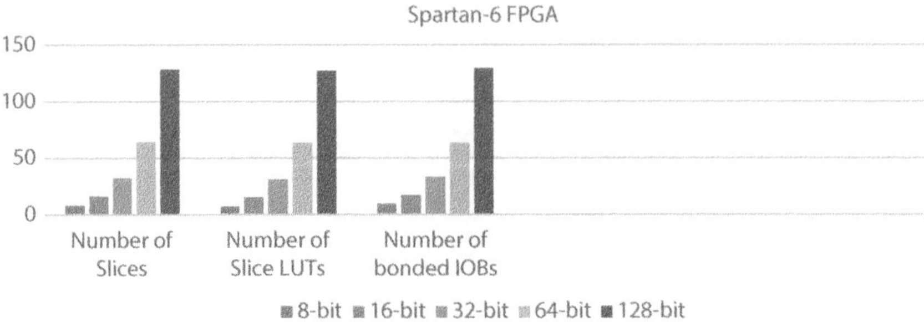

Figure 9.31 Graph of Spartan-6 synthesis report.

Spartan-3E [22] (xc3s500e-5fg320), Spartan-6 [23] (xc6slx45t-3csg324), and Virtex-5 [24] (xc5vlx50t-2ff1136).

The hardware parameters and the timing parameters are tested for the binary up/down counter i.e., 8, 16, 32, 64, and 128; up/down counter by using Xilinx IP core is verified: number of slices, number of LUTs, IOBs, maximum frequency, minimum time period (ns) before clock pulse, and maximum time period (ns) after clock pulse. The three FPGAs: Spartan-3E, Spartan-6, and Virtex-5, work on 180-, 60-, and 45-nm technology.

The hardware utilization summary of different Xilinx FPGAs comparisons is shown in Table 9.13. Three different FPGAs are used for comparison: Virtex-5 (xc5vlx50t-2ff1136), Spartan-6 (xc6slx45t-3csg324), and Zynq [25] (XC7Z010-clg400). The hardware parameters and the timing parameters are tested for the square root IP core for 8 and 16 bit: number of slices, number of LUTs, IOBs, maximum frequency, minimum time period (ns) before clock pulse, and maximum time period (ns) after clock pulse. The three FPGAs: Virtex-5, Spartan-6, and Zynq work on 45-, 60-, and 28-nm technology. Table 9.14 shows the synthesis report for comparing existing method. Table 9.15 shows the power calculations for binary updown counter.

9.10 Comparison of Proposed and Existing Work for Binary Up/Down Counter

The comparative analysis of the existing work with our work reveals that the hardware parameters utilization of our work is less in comparison to the work done by Christakis *et al.* (2016). The total number of slices occupied by the proposed design in Spartan-3E is optimal that is synthesized. The total power dissipation for the proposed design using Spartan-3E 16-bit up/down counter is 0.083W, and the existing work done by Pandey *et al.* [27] is 3.483W.

Table 9.12 Area and delay comparison with different FPGAs.

Hardware parameter	**Spartan-3E length (Bits)**					**Spartan-6 length (Bits)**					**Virtex-5 length (Bits)**				
	8	**16**	**32**	**64**	**128**	**8**	**16**	**32**	**64**	**128**	**8**	**16**	**32**	**64**	**128**
Number of slices	4	8	17	31	63	8	16	32	64	128	8	16	32	64	128
Number of slice LUTs	8	15	32	63	127	7	15	31	63	127	7	15	31	63	127
Number of bonded IOBs	10	18	34	66	130	10	18	34	64	130	10	18	34	66	130
Max frequency (MHz)	304	270	221	193	180	544	502	436	356	316	629	559	468	368	320
Minimum period (ns)	3.28	3.69	4.52	5.12	5.32	1.83	1.18	2.29	3.12	3.22	1.58	1.87	2.13	2.98	3.15
Time after clock (ns) (maximum)	4.16	4.16	4.16	4.16	4.16	3.92	3.92	3.92	3.92	3.92	3.21	3.21	3.21	3.21	3.21

Table 9.13 Area and delay comparison with different FPGAs.

Hardware parameters	Virtex-5 length (Bits)		Spartan-6 length (Bits)		Zynq length (Bits)	
	8	**16**	**8**	**16**	**8**	**16**
Number of slices	37	113/28800	42	113/54576	44	113/35200
Number of slice LUTs	38	63/28800	64	118/27288	66	118/17600
Number of Fully used-FFs	14	52/60	22	52/179	23	152/179
Number of bonded IOBs	14	26/480	14	26/190	14	26/100
Max Frequency (MHz)	460	364	259	224	453	474
Minimum Period (ns)	2.173	2.742	2.143	4.445	1.559	2.109
Min i/p arrival time before clock	2.826	1.274	2.534	2.083	0.789	0.344
Time after clock (ns) (maximum)	1.274	2.826	2.623	4.118	1.563	0.575

Table 9.14 Comparison with existing work.

Hardware parameters	**Spartan-3E length (Bits) (Area/slices)**				
	8	**16**	**32**	**64**	**128**
Proposed	4	8	17	31	63
Christakis, Christoforos *et al.* [26]	8	20	43	96	174

Table 9.15 Power calculation.

S. no.	**Voltage (V)**	**Total current (A)**	**Power (W)**
1	Vccint = 1.2	0.026	1.2 × 0.026 = 0.0312
2	Vccaux = 2.5	0.018	2.5 × 0.018 = 0.045
3	Vcco33 = 3.3	0.002	3.3 × 0.002 = 0.0006
4	----	-----	0.083 (total on chip power)

9.10.1 Power Analysis of Binary Up/Down Counter

The power report binary up/down counter-power report is shown in Figure 9.32 The total power occupied by the design is 0.083 W. The Xilinx generates a .pcf file to create the power report. To estimate the power dissipation, Xilinx X power analyzer software is required, and the input to the xpower analyzer is the .ncd file which means native circuit design. By adding the .ncd file to the xpower analyzer, it gives the power report of the design.

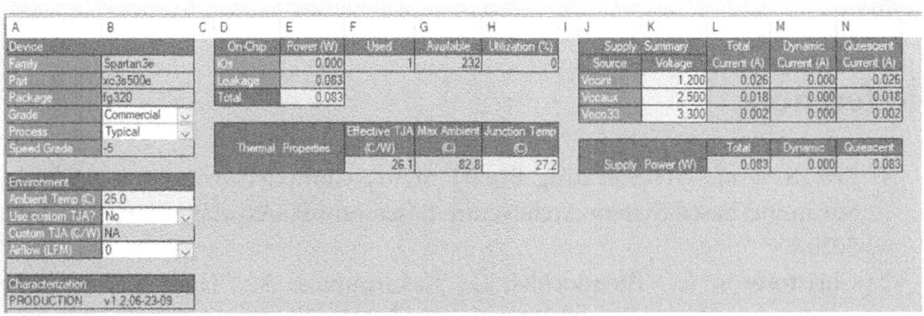

Figure 9.32 Sixteen-bit binary up/down counter-power report.

The power report of a 16-bit binary up/down counter is shown in Figure 9.32. The total power [12] occupied by the design is 0.083 W. Vccint is the source voltage with 1.2 Volts, and it has the quiescent current of 0.026 Amps. Vccaux is the voltage that corresponds to the clock input signal of the device. The Vccaux has a voltage of 2.5 Volts and 0.018 quiescent currents. Vcco33 has 3.3 Volts and 0.002 Amps of quiescent current.

9.11 Conclusion

In present years, there are more computer crime cases reported every day. The term hacking is no more. Therefore, the investigator showing how to collect any information of computer after an incident is becoming an important issue. Most of the digital forensics software is commercial version, has high cost, and just support English version which is the obstacle in using. One solution for this problem is using Asics and ICs that can be fabricated and tested the hardware using FPGAs. The VHDL implementation of 8-bit down counter using IP core generation and conventional approach is performed. Its device utilization summary, RTL view, simulation results, and power report have been tested with FPGA Spartan-6 (xc6slx45t-3csg324) device which works on 90-nm technology. Two different FPGAs are used for comparison: Spartan-3E (xc3s500e-5fg320) and Spartan-6 (xc6slx45t-3csg324). The design is verified using 8, 16, 32, 64, and 128 bit, respectively. Xilinx ISim is used for simulation analysis. Xilinx 14.7 is used for synthesis, place, and route. VHDL implementation of 16-bit up/down counter using IP core generation is performed. Its device utilization summary, RTL view, simulation results, and power report have been tested with different FPGAs. The comparative analysis of the proposed work with existing work is tabulated. Three different FPGAs are used for comparison: Spartan-3E (xc3s500e-5fg320), Spartan-6 (xc6slx45t-3csg324), and Virtex-5 (xc5vlx50t-2ff1136). The design is verified using 8, 16, 32, 64, and 128 bit, respectively. Xilinx ISim is used for simulation analysis. Xilinx 14.7 is used for synthesis, place, and route. The total power occupied by the design is 0.083 W.

References

1. Pilz, S. *et al.*, "Accelerating Binary String Comparisons with a Scalable, Streaming-Based System Architecture Based on FPGAs". *Algorithms*, 13, 2, 47, 2020.
2. Christoforos, C., Theodoridis, G., Kakarountas, A., "High-speed binary counter based on 1D Cellular Automata". *2016 5th International Conference on Modern Circuits and Systems Technologies (MOCAST)*, IEEE, 2016.

3. Lachowicz, S. and Hans-Joerg, P., "Fast evaluation of the square root and other nonlinear functions in FPGA". *4th IEEE International Symposium on Electronic Design, Test and Applications (delta 2008)*, IEEE, 2008.
4. Kumm, M., Abbas, S., Zipf, P., "An efficient softcore multiplier architecture for Xilinx FPGAs". *2015 IEEE 22nd Symposium on Computer Arithmetic*, IEEE, 2015.
5. Tenca, A.F. and Ercegovac, M.D., "Synchronous up/down binary counter for LUT FPGAs with counting frequency independent of counter size". *Proceedings of the 1997 ACM fifth international symposium on Field-programmable gate arrays*, 1997.
6. Christoforos, C., Theodoridis, G., Kakarountas, A., "High speed binary counter based on 1D Cellular Automata". *2016 5th International Conference on Modern Circuits and Systems Technologies (MOCAST)*, IEEE, 2016.
7. Chioktour, V., Spathoulas, G., Kakarountas, A., "Systolic Binary Counter using a Cellular Automaton-based Prescaler". *Proceedings of the 21st Pan-Hellenic Conference on Informatics*, 2017.
8. Pandey, B. and Pattanaik, M., "Low power VLSI circuit design with efficient HDL coding". *2013 International Conference on Communication Systems and Network Technologies*, IEEE, 2013.
9. Tenca, A.F. and Ercegovac, M.D., "Synchronous up/down binary counter for LUT FPGAs with counting frequency independent of counter size". *Proceedings of the 1997 ACM fifth international symposium on Field-programmable gate arrays*, 1997.
10. Ferrandi, F. *et al.*, "VHDL to FPGA automatic IP-Core generation: a case study on Xilinx design flow". *Proceedings 20th IEEE International Parallel & Distributed Processing Symposium*, IEEE, 2006.
11. Christoforos, C., Theodoridis, G., Kakarountas, A., "High speed binary counter based on 1d cellular automata". *2016 5th International Conference on Modern Circuits and Systems Technologies (MOCAST)*, IEEE, 2016.
12. https://www.xilinx.com/support/documentation/ip_documentation/counter_ds215.pdf
13. Chethan, K.H.B. and Kapre, N., "Hoplite-DSP: Harnessing the Xilinx DSP48 multiplexers to efficiently support NoCs on FPGAs". *2016 26th International Conference on Field Programmable Logic and Applications (FPL)*, IEEE, 2016.
14. Chethan, K.H.B. and Kapre, N., "Hoplite-DSP: Harnessing the Xilinx DSP48 multiplexers to efficiently support NoCs on FPGAs". *2016 26th International Conference on Field Programmable Logic and Applications (FPL)*, IEEE, 2016.
15. McGettigan, Edward S. "Loadable up-down counter with asynchronous reset". *U.S. Patent No. 6,157, 209*. 5 Dec. 2000.
16. Zamacola, R. *et al.*, "Impress: Automated tool for the implementation of highly flexible partial reconfigurable systems with Xilinx Vivado". *2018 International Conference on ReConFigurable Computing and FPGAs (ReConFig)*, IEEE, 2018.

17. Bhatti, M.K. *et al.*, "Curriculum design using mentor graphics higher education program (hep) for ASIC designing from synthesizable HDL to gdsii". *Proceedings of IEEE International Conference on Teaching, Assessment, and Learning for Engineering (TALE) 2012*, IEEE, 2012.
18. Walters, E.G., "Array multipliers for high throughput in Xilinx FPGAs with 6-input LUTs". *Computers*, 5, 4, 20, 2016.
19. Jin, S. *et al.*, "FPGA design and implementation of a real-time stereo vision system". *IEEE Trans. Circuits Syst. Video Technol.*, 20, 1, 15–26, 2009.
20. Paldurai, K. and Hariharan, K., "FPGA implementation of delay optimized single precision floating point multiplier". *2015 International Conference on Advanced Computing and Communication Systems*, IEEE, 2015.
21. Rauchenecker, A. and Ostermann, T., "Examination of different adder structures concerning di/dt in a 180nm technology". *2015 10th International Workshop on the Electromagnetic Compatibility of Integrated Circuits (EMC Compo)*, IEEE, 2015.
22. Kumar, S. and Sasamal, T.N., "Verilog Implementation of High-Speed Wallace Tree Multiplier", in: *Green Technology for Smart City and Society*, pp. 457–469, Springer, Singapore, 2021.
23. Fysikopoulos, E. *et al.*, "A Spartan 6 FPGA-based data acquisition system for dedicated imagers in nuclear medicine". *Meas. Sci. Technol.*, 23, 12, 125403, 2012.
24. Gupta, S. *et al.*, "CAD techniques for power optimization in Virtex-5 FPGAs". *2007 IEEE Custom Integrated Circuits Conference*, IEEE, 2007.
25. Mandal, H. *et al.*, "FPGA based low power hardware for quality access control of compressed gray scale image". *Microsyst. Technol.*, 22, 1–14, 2018.
26. Christoforos, C., Theodoridis, G., Kakarountas, A., "High speed binary counter based on 1D Cellular Automata". *2016 5th International Conference on Modern Circuits and Systems Technologies (MOCAST)*, IEEE, 2016.
27. Pandey, B. and Pattanaik, M., "Low power VLSI circuit design with efficient HDL coding". *2013 International Conference on Communication Systems and Network Technologies*, IEEE, 2013.

10

Human-Robot Interaction: An Artificial Cognition-Based Study for Criminal Investigations

Deepansha Adlakha and Dolly Sharma*

Department of Computer Science and Engineering, Amity School of Engineering and Technology, Amity University, Noida, Uttar Pradesh, India

Abstract

The alliance between humans and robots is becoming increasingly significant in our community. Accordingly, there is a thriving interest in the evolution of models that can strengthen and improve the interactions between humans and robots. A critical challenge in the human-robot interaction (HRI) is to furnish robots with cognitive and affective skills, by evolving architectures that allow them to establish compassionate relationships with users. Over the last few years, many models were formulated to face this challenge. This paper contributes a survey of the different cognitive structures and a brief discussion on most relevant architectures. In fact, it proposes a synopsis of the architectures present in literature concentrating on three aspects of HRI: the evolution of adaptive/acquirable behavioral models, the structure of cognitive architectures, and the skill to establish empathy with the companion. While summarizing the current progress in the cognitive architecture exploration, this survey interprets various strategies and ideas that have earlier been attempted and the comparative accomplishment in modeling the human cognitive capacities, later section of the paper states which aspects of cognitive behavior still require more research and thus can further interpret how cognitive science can lead to advancements in fields like digital forensics. In the end, we have discussed about the role of social robots, equipped with cognitive skills to fight the COVID-19 pandemic.

Keywords: Cognition, robots, architecture, skills, COVID-19

**Corresponding author*: dolly.azure@gmail.com

Anita Gehlot, Rajesh Singh, Jaskaran Singh and Neeta Raj Sharma (eds.) Digital Forensics and Internet of Things: Impact and Challenges, (163–198) © 2022 Scrivener Publishing LLC

10.1 Introduction

Owing to the intense pursuit of social life, human beings have brought into light several potentials that prompt them to make sense of supplementary agents to interpret, elucidate, and anticipate the behavior and harmonize interactions with them. Human beings can very well anthropomorphize things around them that led to the discovery of machines that acquire human characteristics but as well as emotional, susceptible, and interactive skills comparable to man. These skills are commonly subsumed following the caption: "social cognition". The tremendous progress in hardware execution, computer graphics, machine learning, and AI leads to the innovation of "social robot" which is entirely or partially an autonomous machine that co-builds value with humans over their social functionaries and is a rapidly evolving element of service industries. Robots consequently have proceeded from industrial perspectives (factories, etc.) to public and private services (e.g., retail, entertainment, hotels, and healthcare and homes). Two proposed ultimate conditions for social robots are: 1. the Turing Test to ascertain the robot's social skills and 2. Isaac Asimov's three laws of robotics to determine its social behavior [1].

The realm of social robotics is still blooming, and although considerable research has centered on aspects of designing human-like interaction for social robots, limited consideration so far has been given to the evolution process itself, which is normally achieved by programmers. However, this is a multidisciplinary process blending a technological understanding of hardware, software, cerebral knowledge of communication mechanisms, and domain-specific understandings of the application. The advancement of social robot applications meets not just the traditional hurdles of robotics which includes robot localization and action planning but faces many new difficulties particular to social robots, including different varieties of sensory data processing, dialog supervision, and the use of empirical design acquaintance during the interaction. The following section disuses the historical perspectives of the early robotics and the evolution of the social robots with advancements in the artificial intelligence (AI). Further, the control system of the social robots with human-aware planning architecture and knowledge model is discussed with a survey on the cognitive architecture and its taxonomies in various social robots. The concluding section encompasses the various challenges and the suggested solutions to bring about the successful human robot interaction.

10.1.1 Historical Background

Here is a brief survey of the sequence of events that have made contemporary human-robot interaction (HRI) feasible and had ultimately led to the development of "social robots". Developing the robots was the crucial first stage. Even though the social robots were primarily evolved in the late 20th century, we cannot ignore the fact that the idea of robot-like behavior and its significances have existed for centuries not only in theology and mythology but also in philosophy and fiction. The term "robot" emerged out of the Slavic word "robota" signifying "work" or "labor". The word "robot" occurs to have been used first in Capek's play Rossum's Universal Robots in the late 1920s. However, this was not the first specimen of a humanoid. Leonardo da Vinci illustrated a mechanical man shown in Figure 10.1 in the 1490s, scrutinized for feasibility in contemporary times [2]. Before the emergence of Vinci's humanoid, automated creatures appeared from ancient Egypt, China, and Greece. The Iliad also referred to as the golden maids behaved similarly to the real people [3]. Some ancient Chinese creation resembled like a human that when it blinked, it was unavoidable to take apart it to ascertain it to be an artificial creature. Some other robotic devices, like the wooden ox and flowing horse, was a one-wheeled cart with the two handles, which was an invention of Zhuge Liang [4], a renowned Chinese carpenter. Zhang Heng (78AD–139AD), an ancient scientist, also built an automated cart that can measure the distance traversed. Feasts

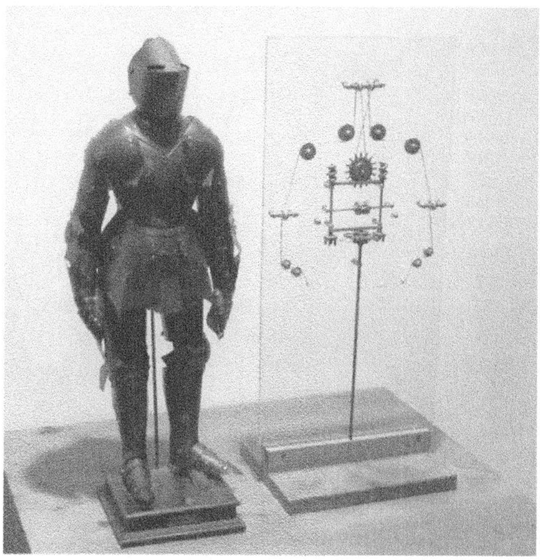

Figure 10.1 The Vinci's knight [6].

of automation continued into the Tang Dynasty (618AD–907AD) when a carpenter named Yang Wulian developed a humanoid having a resemblance to a monk, which is skilled for begging in place of the alms, clasping a copper bowl. It was also capable of bowing after receiving money and was aware of putting the money away when the bowl is full [5]. Robots have had a substantial existence in science, fiction, and literature, and this appears to be the designing platform for HRI.

In 1898, a radio-control boat was illustrated by Nicola Tesla and defined it as consisting of "a borrowed mind." Tesla theorized, "...you will witness a race of robots, mechanical workers which will be doing the laborious jobs of the humans." Some other prominent examples include: The Naval Research Laboratory developed an "Electric Dog" robot in 1923, as an

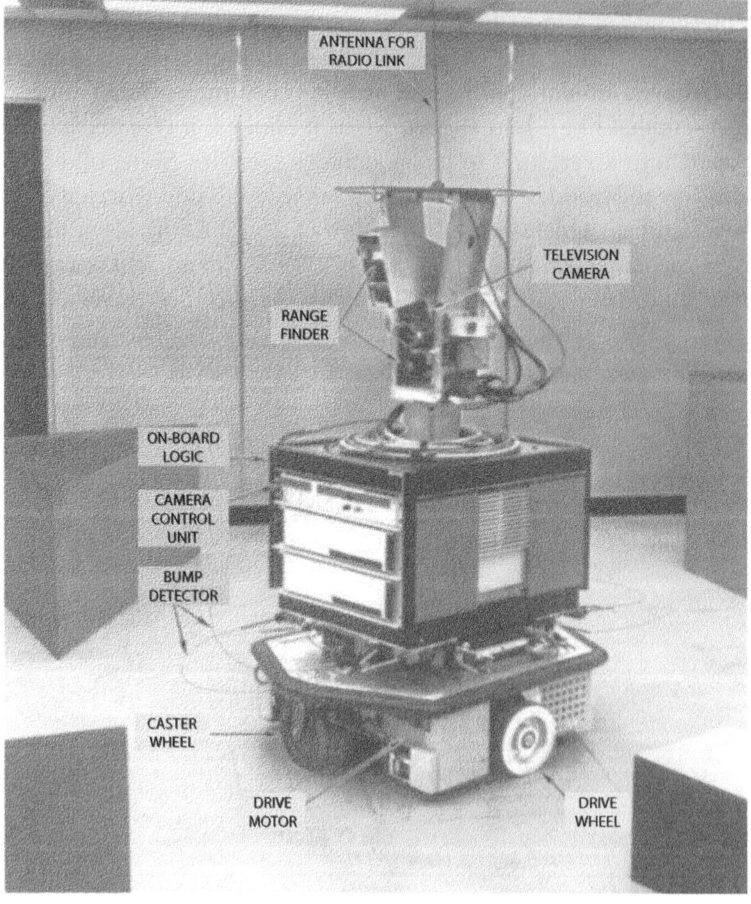

Figure 10.2 Shakey the robot [9].

endeavor to pilot the bombers in World War II are formulated to convey the impression of life. With the advancement in the technology, the skills of robots being operated remotely have evolved [7]. With the progressions in robotics, research in AI has endeavored to build up a fully autonomous robot. The most cited early autonomous robot shown in Figure 10.2 was "Shakey the robot", developed in 1966 with enough AI to navigate the blocks on its own with the help of TV Camera, a range detector, radio communication, and the drive wheels controlled by the motors [8].

Drawing conclusions from the earlier works in robotics the developers have given substantial attention on to paradigms for human robot interaction. These are the teleportation and supervisory control. In the former, a human being remotely monitors a moveable robot or a mechanical arm, while in the latter, a human control the behavior of the automated system and interferes if necessary. Every robotic system seems to have interaction even if it is a fully automated robot. In case of a teleported system, the interaction is quite evident while for an automated system, the interaction comprises of high-level surveillance with the human in order to set goals and with the robot to keep up the knowledge about the surroundings, its tasks, and about its constraints. This is done either by observing the environment or by the implicit communications. This forms the basis of HRI.

10.2 Methodology

10.2.1 Deliberative Architecture and Knowledge Model

Human beings are peers of social synergy. Various researchers, consequently, explore the design scope of anthropomorphic robots, seeking to enrich their inventions with components of deliberate agents. Consequently, robots are being implemented with appearances, speech perception, behavior, and other traits and abilities to make robot-human interaction more "human-like". Social robots can fundamentally be built in two ways. The first approach is to build a biologically inspired robot, ideas drawn from the natural mind; creators try to build robots that mentally reproduce rather mimic the social intellect found in humans. The second way is to build a functionally designed robot aimed at developing a robot that may be thought of as social robot irrespective of the fact that the inner design has no actual cognitive approach. Robots have restricted perceptual, choice-making, cognitive, and behavioral abilities in comparison to human beings. As with proficient operations, it is conceivable that robots turn out to be profoundly refined in defined areas of socialization, e.g., in an old age home. Conclusively, variations in design methodology imply that the assessment and success models virtually always differ from robot to robot. Therefore, it is difficult to draw a comparison between the robots outside of their domains. Here, we will be discussing about the biologically inspired design approach for developing a social robot.

10.2.1.1 Natural Mind

The fundamental aspect of natural mind is a sensation, indicating to the modeling of sensory information by the sensory network. Sensation analysis is done to know the insights of how human beings see, listen, taste, smell, and observe hap tics. The detecting of physical incentives and then transmitting that information to the brain is known as sensation [10]. This entire process can be split up in four steps as shown in Figure 10.3.

The sensory system with the help of the receptors such as the eye, ear, mouth, nose, and skin take up the stimuli and converts it into the pattern of the neural response, and thus, the process of sensory coding begins. This leads to the development of devices that work as the receptors for producing the artificial sensation. The next aspect of natural mind is the perception that is responsible for the brain's further refining, planning, and analysis of the sensory data. Perception is considered as the most complicated processing of the brain. Perception is either through vision, speech, auditory or haptic methods. The third feature is the emotions, which are perceived experiences marked by strong psychic activity, either by a certain amount of pleasure, thrill or sadness. Emotions are instantaneous, straightforward negative or positive acknowledgments of the incidents in the surroundings or inner thoughts. The last important aspect is learning, a relatively lasting shift in behavior, which arises from the experience. This shift in the state of a system is an outcome of the experience which is reflected in behavior. The psychical study provides the classification of four classes of learning: 1. non-associative, 2. active learning, 3. associative learning, and 4. observational learning. Non-associative learning is "a relatively permanent change in the strength of response to a single stimulus due to repeated exposure to that stimulus" [11]. Active learning arises when an individual gets control of its learning activity. Associative learning

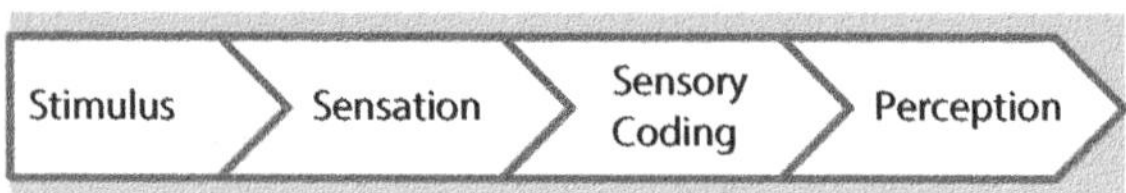

Figure 10.3 The sensory network.

is the means that allows a person or animal to learn the association among two stimuli. Observational learning refers to observing the behavior of others. Memory just like learning is another important aspect. Memory is the ability of the mind to encode, store, or retrieved. Usually, memory is interpreted to be an informational processing arrangement comprising of a sensory processor, short-term (or working) memory, and long-term memory (LTM). Sensory memory retains sensory data less than one second after an item is perceived. Short-term memory also referred to as the working memory enables recall for a duration of several seconds without repetition. LTM has the potential to store a large amount of data for a very long period. Consciousness, another important aspect is the ability to be aware of an object present outside or within it [12]. The awareness and explicit knowledge about all these aspects of the human natural brain help to design an artificial brain that makes a successful HRI and consequently an efficient social robot.

10.2.1.2 Prerequisites for Developing the Mind of the Social Robots

The following elements are required for developing the cognitive architecture aiming to build the mind of a social robot:

1. Imperative control architecture.
2. A distributed modular architecture for designing of a system with multiple conceptual and physical layers.
3. A deliberative reasoning high-level architecture
4. A pattern-matching engine prepared to supervise search and analysis procedure.
5. Spontaneous and easy-to-use behavior descriptive language.
6. A high-level reasoning system intended for extracting high-level social, emphatic and emotional parameter.
7. To easily direct and elaborate the data of varied categories an object-oriented data communication and storage system is required [13].

10.2.1.3 Robot Control Paradigms

It is essential to discuss the major paradigms employed for building robot control architecture. The three most established paradigms are hierarchical, reactive and hybrid deliberate paradigm. They are all distinguished by the relationship among these three primitives, i.e., SENSE, PLAN, and ACT, accompanied with the processing of sensory data by the system.

10.2.1.3.1 The Hierarchical Paradigm

Here in the hierarchical paradigm, the robot initially senses the surroundings to build a model, plans its subsequent actions to achieve a certain goal, and carries out the primary directive. This progression of activities is repeated in a loop wherein the goal may or may not have been changed.

10.2.1.3.2 The Reactive Paradigm

According to this paradigm, the system is segregated into "task-achieving behaviors" which operate in parallel and are independent of any other behavior. This system helped to develop robot control paradigms with a better link between judgment and action, i.e., SENSE and ACT components, and eliminated the PLAN component.

10.2.1.3.3 The Hybrid Deliberate/Reactive Paradigm

Since the reactive paradigm omitted planning or any of the scheming functions, as an outcome, the robot with this sort of the control architecture failed to opt for the best behavior to fulfill a task or follow the thespian on the basis of some particular criteria. Therefore, at the commencement of the 1990s, AI robotics attempted to reintroduce the PLAN component without disturbing the accomplishment of the reactive behavioral control, which was assumed the appropriate way to perform low-level control.

10.3 Architecture Models for Robots

In the mid-1980s, Rodney Brooks provoked an interest in the field of autonomous machines by introducing the Subsumption architecture [14]. The AI community then believed that a controller for an autonomous portable robot should be disintegrated into three working components: a system for sensing, planning, and executing [15]. The sense-plan-act (SPA) strategy had two notable architectural peculiarities. Firstly, the flow of information is unidirectional as well as linear and secondly, the intelligence lies in the hand of a programmer or the planner instead of the execution system. These shortcomings lead to the emergence of Subsumption, which is the most recognized departure from the SPA. Subsumption is rather considered as an endeavor to make SPA efficient by implementing some constraints. It arrived at a climax with the emergence of Herbert, which was developed to search for and recover soda cans in an office [16]. But this failed to reach the goal because it lacked the mechanism for dealing with the complexities. While on the other hand Tooth and the RockyIII were extremely reliable,

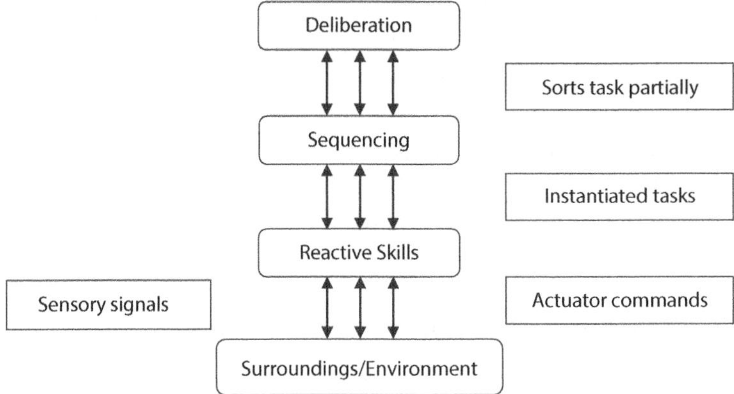

Figure 10.4 3T architecture.

operating without any failures [17]. This is because they worked on the principles of computational abstraction, unlike the Subsumption theory that suppresses the results of the lower levels. This model too had some shortcomings—it was not feasible to alter the task they executed without editing their control programs.

The three researchers (Connell, Gat, and Bonasso) [17] came up with a solution that led to the emergence of the three-layered architecture as shown in Figure 10.4 which consists of three components:

i. A reactive feedback control mechanism.
ii. A reactive plan execution mechanism.
iii. A mechanism for carrying out three deliberative computations.

10.4 Cognitive Architecture

Cognitive architectures have been a significant topic of study in the GAI, which began in the 1950s intending to design programs that can think about problems over various domains, generate insights, and adjust to new circumstances. Thus, the ultimate aim of the study in cognitive architectures is to create a human-like mind, which will help enables effective HRI.

According to Russel and Norvig [18], AI can be apprehended in four approaches: like-humans thinking, analytical thinking, human-like behavior, and reasonable behavior. Still there lies many uncertainties and to overcome them many researchers have presented their studies, the most notable one is the Sun's objectives for cognitive architectures [19]. Sun's objectives are comprehensive and cover ecological, cognitive, and bio-evolutionary synergy. Executing a reduced set of abilities in a single architecture is a substantial undertaking. This objective of AGI is achieved by the architecture like the SOAR, LIDA, ACT-R, SiMA [20], NARS, SIGMA [21], ARCADIA, STAR, and FORR. Some of the others are designed for particular applications such as the ARDIS [22] for the visual examination or MusicCog for understanding and creating music.

10.4.1 Taxonomy of Cognitive Architectures

Analyses of cognitive architectures suggest various skills, properties, and examination norms, including the recognition, choice-making, understanding, prediction, planning, performing, interacting, comprehending, goal setting, adaptability, generalization, autonomy, reasoning, as well as meta-cognition. A comparison has been drawn on the various architecture models present so far on the basis of the taxonomies, memory type, various modalities and learnings in the Table 10.1. A more comprehensive assemblage of architectures is done on the basis of the representation type and data processing they enforce. As shown in Figure 10.5 the three primary classes of cognitive architecture are symbolic architecture (cognitivist), emergent architecture (connectionist), and the hybrid architecture [18].

10.4.1.1 Symbolic Architectures

Symbolic architectures represent data making use of symbols which can be altered using a predefined instruct set. These instructions can be carried out as if-then rules applied to the symbols depicting the existences understood about the world. Examples of such architectures are ACT-R, SOAR, and many others. Being a natural and instinctive representation of information, symbolic manipulation stays relatively common. Regardless

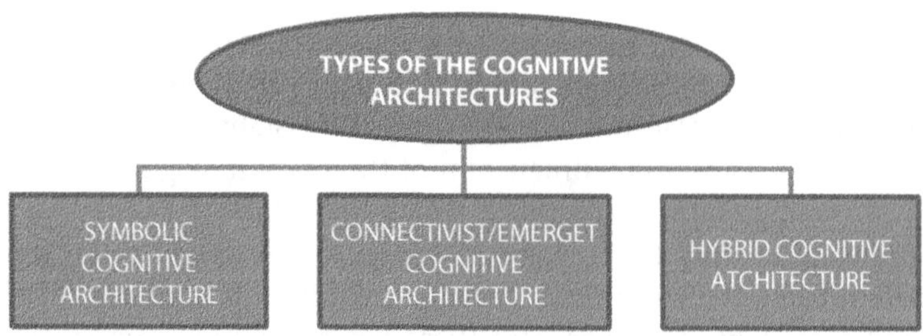

Figure 10.5 Types of the cognitive architectures.

of the fact that the design of a symbolic architecture is the most appropriate for planning, understanding, and reasoning, it is not efficient enough to handle the flexibility and adaptive skills that are prerequisites to survive in a transforming environment as well as for the perceptual processes.

10.4.1.2 The Emergent or the Connectionist Architecture

The emergent or the connectionist architecture unravels the adaptability and learning/grasping problems by creating massive similar replicas, identical to neural systems in which the data progression is carried out by the propagation of signals from the input nodes. Consequently, the arising system lacks the transparency of data, since information does not occur in the form of symbolic elements and is rather dispersed throughout the entire system. As a result of these justifications, logical conception in a conventional sense serves to be troublesome in the connectionists.

10.4.1.3 The Hybrid Architecture

As neither of the paradigms is competent in dealing with all crucial facets of social cognition, the hybrid architectures endeavor to incorporate aspects of both symbolic connectionist architectures. These hybrid architectures become the priority while choosing architecture to meet all the essential demands for successful HRI. Generally, there are no constraints for how the hybridization of the architectures is carried out and many probabilities have been scrutinized. Other than the representation, one can evaluate whether the architectural model is single- module or multi-module and also if the system is heterogeneous or homogeneous, further on the basis of granularity of hybridization the architecture can be coarse-grained or fine-grained, the symbolic as well as the sub-symbolic elements, and classifications of memory classes and learning techniques.

10.4.2 Cognitive Skills

10.4.2.1 Emotions

Emotions form an indispensable part of human behavior, interaction, and social communication. Emotion's impact cognitive processes, including the analytical and decision-making process. Emotions also supervise actions and cast dialogues. Emotions are multiplex aspects and oftentimes tightly linked to social connection. There are three theories to describe emotions. According to the first theory, emotions are described in the form of discrete categories i.e., sadness or happiness [23]. While in the second theory, emotions are categorized based on scales (e.g., arousal and valence) [24] and the third theory acknowledges the importance of both the scales as well as the categories of the first approach [25].

10.4.2.1.1 Artificial Emotions in Social Robots

Artificial emotions are customarily represented as transitory states (correlated with anger, anxiety, happiness, etc.) that impact cognitive skills. Artificial emotions are applied in social agents for various purposes. The prime intention, undoubtedly, lies in the fact that emotions help conduct convincing interaction between humans and the robot. It can also give feedback to the humans indicating the robot's inner situation, goals as well its intentions. Ultimately, artificial emotions can serve to be the control mechanisms, managing behavior, and revealing how the robot is influenced by and adapts to, different factors over time. For example, in CoJACK, confidence and panic emotions result to plan modification. Consequently, plans that face a threat are more efficient when confidence is high, but lower efficiency when fear is high [26]. Other examples where decision-making is influenced by stress are MAMID, CHREST, DUAL, ACT-R, DIARC, and CELTS.

10.4.2.1.2 Speech Emotion Recognition

Speech is a profoundly efficient means of delivering emotion. The fundamental parameters that direct the emotions of speech are volume, pitch variations, and rhythm. The three fundamental steps of this system are audio segmentation, feature extraction and processing, and emotion analysis. Based on the nature of the transform among the original feature range and the compressed representations, dimensionality compression methods can be categorized as linear and nonlinear.

10.4.2.1.3 Facial Expression

The human face showcases an individual's motives, which makes it easy to predict the behavior and understanding others. It improves verbal communication by indicating the attitude of the speaker toward the message being delivered. These expressions are not human-like and exhibit some design challenges. For instance, instant variations among expressions manage to be abrupt, occur quickly and immediately, unlike the way it happens in humans. Sparky's face has a degree of freedom 4 that comprises of the eyebrows, eyelid, and mouth (lips) which represent an assemblage of discrete, primary emotions. Félix is developed utilizing the LEGO

Figure 10.6 Kismet's facial expressions [28].

MindstormsTMrobotic development kit. Feelix's face too has a degree of freedom 4 with two eyebrows along with two lips, intended to represent six different facial expressions, i.e., anger, grief, anxiety, joy, surprise, and neutral along with many combinations. Kismet's face comprises of fifteen regulators, which work in combinations to reveal a specific emotion. Kismet's emotions are produced utilizing an "affect space". Kismet is capable to express emotions like anger, joy, sadness, anxiety, surprise, and distrust as shown in Figure 10.6 [27].

Conceivably, the most naturalistic robotic faces are the ones created at the Science University of Tokyo. These faces are precisely intended to be exactly like humans and include features like the hair, teeth, and a wrapping silicone skin cover. Infinite control points operated underneath the "skin" give a broad spectrum of facial gestures and humanistic expression. Vikia, with the help of computer graphics, has a 3D face of a woman who has many degrees of freedom is capable of generating different facial expressions.

10.4.2.2 Dialogue for Socially Interactive Communication

Dialogue is a mutual means of conversation. It includes the sharing of knowledge like the information in the form of symbols and texts and control links linking two (or more) individuals. Humans make use of many para-linguistic clues including the facial expressions and various gestures to manage the flow of dialogues. These clues have also determined to be useful for managing human-robot dialogues, which is essential considering the prevailing performance of the robot's perception restricts the pace of preceding the human-robot dialogues. To make the communication possible and effective, grounding of the symbols is necessary. If the representations vary, then data exchange or learning will be required before communication can proceed. The three fundamental dialogue types by which human-robot communication is feasible are as follows.

10.4.2.2.1 Low-Level or Pre-Linguistic Dialogue

It is basically communication etiquette, stimulated by the society of insects, that does not require high level data exchanges among the sensors and the actuators. Billiard and Dautenhahn report several trials where an autonomous movable robot was grounded in an artificial protolanguage [7]. Language learning is achieved from various spatiotemporal connections over the robot's sensor and the actuators. Steels have considered the opinion that communication is bootstrapped in the learning process of social robots and that the sense of the communication is totally situation dependent [29].

10.4.2.2.2 Non-Verbal Dialogue

The various non-verbal forms of communication include body language, various gestures, and other physical movements. Considering most social robots to have somewhat crude inclination to recognize and deliver the speech, the non-verbal can prove to be a successful alternative. Non-verbal communication is generally characterized into some of the discrete, but humanly interrelated forms—kinesics, proxemics, haptics, and chronemics [29].

10.4.2.2.2.1 Kinesics

It is described as non-verbal interaction by body actions, positioning, facial emotions, as well as gestures. These movements can be classified into arm gesticulations, body and head actions, gaze cues, and facial expressions.

Arm Gesticulations: These are typically represented by notable actions of the limb such that it creates an expression of consciousness or oratory. They are also utilized in deictic communication, i.e., for pointing, iconic, i.e., representative of articles and activities, metaphoric, i.e., representative of theoretical notions.

Body and Head Movements: Body movements display static as well as the dynamic behaviors of the body while head movements are linked with distinct communication purposes which include the apparent semantic implications of nodding as well as shaking during the communication.

Eye Gaze: The proximity of task-relevant robot gaze can improve the performance of the user for different tasks. The gaze is a useful reference in handover businesses, pointing users to harmonize the robot's gaze, and decreasing accomplishment time. These can even sometimes exert negative social impacts. So care should be taken while designing.

10.4.2.2.2.2 Proxemics

Proxemics concerns the understanding and utility of space specifically, the distances among different articles, agencies, and oneself. Space is categorized within four proxemic stretches: public for the distance more than 12 feet; social for the distance lying in the range of 4–12 feet; personal for the distance lying in the range of 1.5–4 feet; and intimate for the distances between the range of 0–1.5 feet.

10.4.2.2.2.3 Haptic

In 1965, Austin issued the term Haptic Communication which refers to communication with physical interactions. It is still an emerging field where harmless robot physical actions such as handshaking, and gentle touch have been reviewed, and precisely the impact of these interactions on the people.

10.4.2.2.2.4 Multimodal Non-Verbal Interaction

Multimodal non-verbal forms have proved to be powerful influencers of users' cognitive structures. In customary, multimodal representations of non-verbal interaction have confirmed to have greater emotional acceptance rates in comparison to the uni-modal non-verbal interaction. Concerning task execution, the application of multimodal behaviors resulted in advances in reaction rate and completion rate for primary cooperative searching chores, along with memory recognition, at the minimum for children [29].

10.4.2.2.3 Natural Language Processing

Natural language processing (NLP) is a comprehensive interdisciplinary area that reflects a perception of written or vocalized language. In cognitive science, multiple features of NLP have been recognized which includes the low-level audible perception, syntactical analyzing, and semantics to the communication in confined domains. There are a very a smaller number of robots with low-level auditory understandings. Examples include designs established on Adaptive Resonance Theory (ART) (such as The ARTPHONE, the ARTSTREAM, and ARTWORD) [18], which have been adopted to create perceptual methods concerned with speech assortment, auditory stream segregation, source dissociation and assimilation of phonics. Contrarily, most maximum study in NLP is linked to studying aspects of the syntactical and semantic processing of data in the written form. Some notable examples constitute epanaphora analysis (Polyscheme, NARS, and DIARC), acquiring passive voice in English (NARS), and word sense clarification (SemSoar and WordNet). NL-Soar, considered to be the earliest models for NLP, was a combination of syntactical knowledge and semantics of simplistic directions for the quick rationalizing while performing a task. A recent design (presently employed in Soar) is intelligent enough of understanding directions, interrogations, syntax as well as semantics both in English and Spanish. In prevailing, multiple existing NLP models are restricted in their field of application as well as in terms of the syntactical formations that can be interpreted by them. Contemporary architectures, such as DIARC, intend at establishing more naturalistic requests like can you bring me something good to read? Though, it is still an interesting topic of research for the researchers.

10.4.2.3 Memory in Social Robots

Memory is a critical component of any cognitive architecture. Therefore, almost all the architectures covered in this survey have memory systems for storing the intervening outcomes of computations, facilitating learning, and adapting to the transforming environment. Considering the cognitive architectures, memory is interpreted in the context of its time duration (short-term memory and memory) and category (procedural memory, declarative memory, semantic memory, etc.).

10.4.2.3.1 Sensory Memory in Robots

The objective of sensory memory is to hoard the incoming data forms the sensors and pre-process it prior to transferring Information to further memory systems. The extinction rate for the data in sensory system is supposed to be in fractions of milliseconds (EPIC and LIDA [27]) for optical data and extended for auditory information (MusiCog). Further, architectures enforcing this memory system constitute the Soar, Sigma, ACT-R, CHARISMA, CLARION, ICARUS, and Pogamut.

10.4.2.3.2 Working Memory in Robots

Working memory is described as an apparatus for the provisional storehouse of information associated with the prevailing or ongoing task and the world model. Precise recognition of working memory varies chiefly in what data is being filed, how it is expressed, accessed, and sustained. Although we do not have any obvious constraints on the potential that working memory possesses, new objectives or new tangible data normally overwrite the existing content. This ordered report of the efficient working memory can be unearthed in multiple illustrative architectures (3T [17], ATLANTIS [17], Homer, IMPRINT, and MIDCA). As, by description, working memory can be described as a moderately small volatile storage, for anatomical reality, its capability should be confined. But there exists no accord in what manner this should be performed. The extent of this memory can rise extensively without some added restrictions. To counter immense growth, a limit can be set for the total collection of data in the memory. While the latest information comes, the previous or numerous useless pieces would be eliminated to dodge overcrowding. Items that are not being employed for some time would also be rejected. The duration can range within 4–9 seconds (EPIC) to 5 seconds (MIDAS and CERA-CRANIUM) to tens of seconds (LIDA [30]).

10.4.2.3.3 Long Term Memory in Robots

LTM conserves a considerable quantity of data for a quite prolonged time. Conventionally, it is classified to be a procedural memory with implicit knowledge, for example, motor abilities and everyday actions as well as a declarative memory, that consists of explicit knowledge which is also further categorized into semantic and the episodic memory. The procedural memory includes information on how to make things prepared in the work area. Semantic memory stock details regarding the things and connections among them. Episodic memory is responsible for storing precise instances of past happenings. These have an advantage that they can be reused in the future if an alike circumstance awakes (MAX, OMAR, iCub, and Ymir).

10.4.2.3.4 Global Memory in Robots

Irrespective of the indication for the discrete memory systems, there still exist architectures that do not possess separate distinctions for varying kinds of information or short-term memory and the LTM, and rather, apply a centralized arrangement for storing whole data in the order. For example, CORTEX and RoboCog have adopted a unified, vibrant multi-graph gadget that can express both sensitive data and high-level representations illustrating the position of the automaton and the surroundings.

10.4.2.4 Learning

Learning refers to the aptitude of a plan in order to develop its production over a period of time. Eventually, each type of learning is built around experience. Example, it is possible for a system to gather facts and practices from the perceived events or from events of its individual operations. The kind of learning and its recognition rely on numerous determinants, for example, configuration criterion (e.g. physiological and psychical), application situation, data arrangements, and various algorithms adopted for executing the architecture, etc. Learning is split into declarative knowledge or explicit knowledge acquisition and the non-declarative that comprises perceptual, procedural, associative, and non-associative sorts of learning.

10.4.2.4.1 Perceptual Learning

Perceptual learning refers to the structures which actively alter the form in which sensitive data is tackled or in what way patterns are studied on-line. This sort of learning has been repeatedly presented to gain implicit knowledge regarding the circumstances, such as spatial maps (RCS, AIS, and MicroPsi), clustering visual features (HTM, BECCA, and Leabra) or discovering relationships between percepts.

10.4.2.4.2 Declarative Learning

Declarative learning is a compilation of truths regarding the universe and multiple connections established within them. In numerous biotical motivated systems, uncorking new theories normally takes the mode of acquiring the similarity between the optical peculiarities of the thing and the name it has (iCub, Leabra, MACsi, Novamente, CoSy, and DIARC).

10.4.2.4.3 Procedural Learning

Procedural knowledge leads to acquiring numerous skills, which occurs continuously through repetition until an automatic skill is generated.

The most manageable means of accomplishing so is by acquiring designs of problems that have already been cracked and are used as a reference for later purposes. This sort of learning is somewhat limited and additional processing of gathered expertise is required to develop productivity and versatility.

10.4.2.5 Perception

Nevertheless, of its layout and objective, an intelligent agent cannot have existence in solitude and needs an intake of information to generate any behavioral skills. Perception is determined as a manner that transforms raw information into the internal representation of the system in order to achieve the cognitive tasks [31]. Counting on the inception and properties of the input received several sensory systems are defined. For illustration, the five senses that are sight, hearing, smell, taste, and touch.

10.4.2.5.1 Visual-Based Perception Means

Visual cues have been widely adopted in social intelligent agents to accomplish semantic perception task that involves face identification as well as recognition, human tracking, and classification of face expressions and gesticulations. The reason of this being so much in use is that most of the information exchange between humans takes place with the help of the vision. Encouraged by this concept, a large number of these social agents make use of visible signals to accomplish human-like understanding. Based on the type of the cameras, optical signals comprise of 2D-based signals and the 3D-based signals. 3D visual signals are generally received by Kinect [32] or the stereo camera. One of the finest examples is Bumblebee and has turned out to be a significant modality in the artificial perception newly.

10.4.2.5.2 Audio-Based Perception Means

Audio plays another major role in many of the social robots to carry out semantical reasoning tasks, which includes the speaker's location, speech identification, sound event categorization, and emotion distinction. In this article, we would not define auditory features for recognizing the speech as a variety of software are available for this purpose such as the IBM's Via voice and Dragon Naturally Speaking are used directly in the intelligent agents [18].

Table 10.1 Compares the various architectures on the basis of the taxonomies, memory type, various modalities and learning mechanisms.

Name of the architectural model	Type of architecture	Various modalities								Types of memory						Types of learnings					
		V	D	P	O	A	T	S	M	Se	w	s	p	e	g	Del	Per	Pro	Ass	NA	Pri
ARCADIA	Hybrid	✓								✓	✓					-					
CELTS	Hybrid	✓									✓	✓	✓	✓				✓			
MLECOG	Hybrid	✓								-									✓		✓
BECCA	Emergent	✓		✓							✓	✓	✓	✓			✓	✓			
RoboCog	Hybrid	✓		✓	✓	✓	✓		✓		✓	✓	✓		✓			✓			
CORTEX	Hybrid	✓			✓	✓			✓		✓	✓	✓		✓			✓			
MusiCog	Symbolic		✓		✓					✓	✓	✓	✓			✓				✓	
CSE	Hybrid	✓	✓			✓			✓		✓		✓					✓	✓		
CHARISMA	Hybrid	✓		✓						✓	✓	✓	✓	✓		✓			✓		
SAL	Hybrid	✓									✓	✓	✓			✓					
MIDCA	Hybrid	✓									✓	✓	✓	✓		-					
DSO	Hybrid	✓			✓						✓	✓	✓			✓			✓		✓

(Continued)

Table 10.1 Compares the various architectures on the basis of the taxonomies, memory type, various modalities and learning mechanisms. (*Continued*)

Name of the architectural model	Type of architecture	Various modalities								Types of memory						Types of learnings					
		V	D	P	O	A	T	S	M	Se	w	s	p	e	g	Del	Per	Pro	Ass	NA	Pri
MACSi	Hybrid	✓		✓		✓			✓		✓	✓	✓			✓	✓	✓			
STAR	Hybrid	✓									✓		✓			-					
ASMO	Hybrid	✓				✓	✓				✓	✓	✓	✓	✓				✓	✓	
Xapagy	Hybrid	✓	✓								✓	✓		✓		✓					
CERA-CRANIUM	Hybrid	✓		✓	✓		✓		✓		✓	✓	✓			-					
SPA	Emergent	✓									✓	✓	✓	✓		✓		✓	✓		✓
CogPrime	Emergent	✓	✓	✓		✓					✓	✓	✓	✓	✓	✓		✓			
Sigma	Hybrid	✓				✓				✓	✓	✓	✓	✓					✓		
ARDIS	Hybrid	✓								-						-					
Pogamut	Hybrid	✓		✓						✓	✓		✓	✓		✓				✓	
DiPRA	Hybrid	✓		✓							✓	✓	✓		✓			✓	✓		
DIARC	Hybrid	✓	✓	✓	✓	✓	✓		✓	-						✓		✓			

(*Continued*)

Table 10.1 Compares the various architectures on the basis of the taxonomies, memory type, various modalities and learning mechanisms. (*Continued*)

Name of the architectural model	Type of architecture	Various modalities								Types of memory						Types of learnings					
		V	D	P	O	A	T	S	M	Se	w	s	p	e	g	Del	Per	Pro	Ass	NA	Pri
LIDA	Hybrid	✓	✓						✓	✓	✓	✓	✓	✓			✓	✓	✓	✓	✓
HTM	Emergent		✓									✓				✓			✓		✓
CARACAS	Hybrid	✓		✓	✓				✓	-								✓	✓		
GMU- BICA	Hybrid	✓									✓	✓	✓	✓		✓		✓	✓		
ADAPT	Hybrid	✓									✓	✓	✓					✓			
ARAS/SiMA	Hybrid	✓									✓	✓	✓								✓
CoJACK	Hybrid	✓		✓							✓	✓	✓					✓	✓		
iCub	Hybrid	✓		✓			✓		✓	-						✓	✓	✓	✓	✓	
Kismet	Hybrid			✓		✓			✓		✓		✓							✓	
IMPRINT	Symbolic		✓								✓		✓			-					
MAMID	Symbolic		✓								✓	✓	✓	✓		-					
CLARION	Hybrid	✓	✓		✓					✓	✓	✓	✓	✓		✓		✓	✓		✓

(*Continued*)

Table 10.1 Compares the various architectures on the basis of the taxonomies, memory type, various modalities and learning mechanisms. (*Continued*)

Name of the architectural model	Type of architecture	Various modalities								Types of memory						Types of learnings					
		V	D	P	O	A	T	S	M	Se	w	s	p	e	g	Del	Per	Pro	Ass	NA	Pri
EPIC	Symbolic	✓		✓		✓	✓		✓	✓	✓	✓	✓			-					
FORR	Hybrid	✓	✓	✓	✓	✓					✓	✓	✓					✓	✓		
DUAL	Hybrid	✓	✓								✓	✓	✓	✓							✓
Naps	Hybrid		✓								✓	✓	✓	✓	✓	✓		✓	✓		✓
Soar	Hybrid	✓	✓	✓	✓				✓	✓	✓	✓	✓	✓		✓		✓	✓		
CAPS	Hybrid		✓								✓	✓	✓			-					
ACT-R	Hybrid	✓				✓				✓	✓	✓	✓	✓		✓		✓	✓		✓
ART	Emergent	✓	✓		✓				✓		✓		✓	✓	✓	✓	✓	✓	✓	✓	✓
SHRUTI	Emergent	✓	✓			✓				✓	✓		✓	✓		✓					✓
Subsumption	Emergent	✓		✓	✓		✓		✓	-						-					
Leabra	Symbolic	✓		✓						✓	✓		✓	✓			✓		✓		✓
GLAIR	Hybrid	✓	✓	✓	✓	✓	✓	✓	✓		✓	✓	✓	✓				✓	✓		

(*Continued*)

Table 10.1 Compares the various architectures on the basis of the taxonomies, memory type, various modalities and learning mechanisms. (*Continued*)

Name of the architectural model	Type of architecture	Various modalities								Types of memory						Types of learnings					
		V	D	P	O	A	T	S	M	Se	w	s	p	e	g	Del	Per	Pro	Ass	NA	Pri
3T	Hybrid	✓	✓	✓	✓	✓	✓		✓		✓		✓	✓							
Prodigy	Symbolic	✓	✓	✓	✓		✓		✓		✓	✓	✓	✓							
BBD	Emergent	✓		✓	✓	✓	✓		✓			✓	✓	✓		✓	✓	✓	✓		
ISAC	Hybrid	✓		✓	✓	✓			✓		✓	✓	✓	✓					✓		
ATLANTIS	Hybrid	✓			✓						✓	✓	✓			-					
✓	**Present**																				
	Absent																				

For the modalities: V, vision; D, Symbolic input; P, proprioception; O, other sensors; A, audition; T, touch; S, smell; M, multi-modal.

For the type of memory: Se, sensory memory; w, working memory; s, semantic memory; p, procedural memory; e, episodic memory; g, global memory.

For the learning mechanism: Del, deliberative learning; Per, perceptual learning; Pro, procedural learning; Ass, associative learning; NA, non-associative learning; Pri, priming.

10.5 Challenges in the Existing Social Robots and the Future Scopes

10.5.1 Sensors Technology

A significant characteristic of HRI is the way in which robots are somehow able to get the expectations and feelings of the person who is using them. They do this by the means of common clues (i.e., physique and body activities, face utterance, skull and eye exposure, and the sort of voice). Sensors fiddle a crucial part as they play a vital role in determining these signals, which are accordingly refined in the automaton. A problem associated to sensors is that it has a high possibility of facing data obtainment delays, hence an undertaking for the upcoming time might be to formulate detectors which can prove to be accountable and usable in the reality situations. Further, the automaton should possess a multi sensing device to attain varied types of cues. To accomplish this objective, microphones, 2D as well as 3D sensors, cameras detecting heat signatures, leap gesture, Myo, and detectors which can even perceive faces could be assembled to establish a network that provides a comprehensive sensor content to the automaton. Every gadget could have the ability to enclose a distinct region. Microphones could be essential for conversation, Myo to obtain IMU and EMG-related information, face-trackers would prove useful to find the head pose and looks, vision detectors to obtain the cloud information, thermal devices to perceive items in shady backgrounds, along with the leap signals which could prove useful in tracking and measuring the situation of the hand of the robot.

10.5.2 Understanding and Learning from the Operator

An additional skill which ought to be properly evaluated is the region of understanding. The central trouble of perception is none other than acquiring a dependable real-time detecting and understanding network [33]. With the means of this paper, the scholar exhibit that people's tendencies and awareness change time to time and a reasonable network must have the potential of adjusting in every situation to these alterations and should possess the ability to acquire from the person using the system. To attain this hindmost capability, improved understanding-based methods must be employed to fulfill user's desires, by enhancing the working of the automaton. Further, future labors should observe and deal with the feelings as humans have the capability to change their feelings quite regularly. This issue is among the major problems of HRI as the automaton must acquire an acquisition to handle the real time idealistic evolutions and it is relatively hard to achieve this because of uncertainties in the process of data obtainment. Next constraint regarding this field is the uncertainties or distinctions between feelings and efforts and this trouble needs to be conquered to get a robot which is far more reactive [15]. Another factor is that the modifications in the client's portrayal should be rapidly perceived to adjust behavior of the user automatically without any delay. An undertaking that could prove to be intriguing to research more concerningly in the coming time is the odds for the automaton to attain problematic abilities comprehended from their user (i.e., for rinsing clothes). It is also required that the automaton must be capable of altering the interior prototype by learning various tasks from their user, employing the understanding from the exhibiting method. Also, it is not at all irrelevant to emphasize the significance to boost the quantity of non-verbal activities and infuse parameters evaluated in the research, to formulate the automaton less infected and flexible in context to the user's choice and his requirements.

10.5.3 Architectural Design

Taking the architecture layout into consideration, interchangeable and additionally adaptable architectures must be developed, in our future: automatons should be skilled to, for instance, automatically respond to an impulsive circumstance and a detailed danger examination protocol should be conducted in the layout stage to precisely address the impulsive problems. Behavioral stability, anticipation, and recurrence should be examined as they occur to be the basic necessities in the layout of humanly helpful automatons in varied conditions, as for teenagers suffering from autism. Dealing with them expects a detailed topic examination, leveled on the modern tradition and on comprehensive inquiry. An apparent strategy could be the intention of memorizing from exhibition to educate the automaton with some abilities to attain promising results. Also, an interdisciplinary procedure should be urged to formulate and evolve responsible and satisfactory behavioral prototypes. Psychological factors along with biological, and physiological among, are regions of mastery, these should be component of the growth cycle as they can assist to enhance the HRI familiarity. Creative behavioral prototypes for helpful automatons could be created by reaping motivation from the analyses of human social prototypes or from the analysis of a certain bodily apparatus. By this way, future examination will keep in mind the manual protection (of the automaton and the people in the surroundings) as well as psychological, physical, and social aspects of human beings. It is crucial to emphasize that the automaton could be applicable in the surroundings for which the robot was initially formulated (i.e., personal residence, infirmary, and residential section of the society) as well as for humans with distinct categories of residual capacities. We can express it in simple words by just saying that, the automaton must be skilled to alter to the diversity and distinct traditional and civil contexts. At last, a prototype of an automaton should possess a cloud architectonic to maintain the offload exhaustive duties in the cloud, also to permit an enormous proportion of information, to permit dealt information, and avoid misplacing input during the time of connection flaws.

10.5.4 Testing Phase

The merit to examine automaton in comparison with the actual operators is truly amazing, as emphasized by the relation between sheets in presence or absence of the testing rounds. Especially, handful of researches emphasizes on the significance of experimenting the presented prototype as a crucial effort for forthcoming analysis. The major problem in some scenarios is that the automatons which attained a job in the simulation stage do not normally attain victory in the testing level. This is why that experimenting the nature of the automaton in an actual world is of utmost significance so that we can uncover decent parameters which operate for the testing level. Furthermore, the design must be assessed using real automatons that communicate with the person using it in vibrant domains (i.e., colleges, trades, and infirmaries). At the end, one more constraint can be easily recognized in many articles in the unavailability of a proper database (i.e., biological powers or sensitive condition of the operator). A database also plays a vital role in the collection of information.

10.5.5 Credible, Legitimate, and Social Aspects

Future exploration feat should comprise the credible intentions of formulating automatons which can easily interface with human beings and the information obtained must be properly compiled to safeguard secrecy. Considering legitimate and civic aspects, some experimentations emphasized that the automaton should be skilled to adapt its parameters for varied situations which possess unique requirements, so that it is able to fulfill real user proposals. In the end, the origin of an ordinance for civic automatons, for example, the robot developed to be used as drones nowadays, could prove to be a significant effort toward having the likelihood to operate an automaton in congested areas [34].

10.5.6 Automation in Digital Forensics

Digital forensics is a growing field in computing that frequently necessitates the intelligent analysis of large quantities of complex data. AI can aid in the automation of some processes and the faster identification of content or perspectives that might otherwise take investigators long time to discover. However, all of the work on integrating AI to digital forensics is still in its early stages and it can be classified into two parts: where AI is used to aid automate a specific portion of the forensic process which involves looking for a specific file type and where AI is being used to assist the expert in their task.

The use of intelligent agents in digital forensics investigation lists a set of components at different phases of the investigation project lifecycle: collecting digital evidence, preserving digital evidence, analyzing digital evidence, and presenting that evidence.

Detecting such anomalies necessitates the use of a wide range of AI techniques. Knowledge-based systems designed here can be used to seize a legal expert's knowledge of the legal principles and to detect suspicious behavior. Neural networks could also be equipped to classify unusual behavior and can even model the behavior of various users so that unusual use patterns for the presently logged in user can be indicated. Data mining and machine learning methods can be integrated into our system to detect behavior patterns and flag outliers. In order to catch pace with evolving trends in the digital forensics arena, it is possible to create systems that continually learn and improve system performance in conjunction with big data analytics along with high-performance computing platforms [35].

10.6 Conclusion

Social robots equipped with the artificial cognition have a great scope in the future because of its capabilities to serve the mankind in domestic as well as the commercial chores from hospitals, old age homes, hotels, kinder gardens, and laboratories to the manufacturing industries. These can prove to be the best coworkers for the humans even at the time of disasters when the human beings even with the maximum potential fail to succeed. An outburst of COVID-19 has turned out to be a pandemic and has affected almost all the continents and has been disturbing the life of people in every possible way. The proliferation and immensely meshed economies make it pretty obvious that all the countries will suffer a direct or indirect impact of the coronavirus outbreak [36]. This outbreak leads to the increased interests of people in the domains of AI and the humanoids. This seems to be the only way to compact this pandemic from further spreading. What makes social automata so thriving to fight against the coronavirus? In the conditions to be socially distant from one another, robots would prove to be of greater assistance to survive in the circumstances created by the COVID-19. Researchers state that the principal domains where automata could serve are healthcare, supply lines, and surveillance, that involves the identification of the infected person and assuring that these infected people follow the complete social isolation without any violation. Besides the medical province, social robots are also capable of keeping up with the economy by serving as an additional labor in the factories and other areas of development. At the time of the 2015 Ebola virus outbreak, workshops were conducted to help robots deal with the pandemics by the White House Office of Science and Technology Policy and the NSF [36]. However, after the pandemic was decreased, the study focused on other aspects, which led to very limited advancement in the solutions at the time the other pandemic broke in. Consequently, the fact remains unclear about the number of help robots will be able to contribute to humans during such bursts like the COVID-19.

The various utilizations of social robots during the time of pandemics are as follows [37]:

i. Robots have been successfully disinfecting the wards of the hospital autonomously; an independent mechanical machine is capable of disinfecting as well as sanitizing the contaminated regions without any assistance from the humans. This robot makes use of the UVC lights and an automated base [38].
ii. Automata can be of great use in delivering medicines, blood tests, and meals and also serve in the general hospital chores. In Spain, the TIAGo Base robot as shown in Figure 10.7 is capable enough to deliver the food and carrying objects which include vaccinations (medicines) and the samples of the tests inside the hospital premises [39]. Robot's aid keeps physicians safe of corona virus.
iii. In Italy, a humanoid nurse, TOMMY assists physicians as well as the nurses within a clinic in Lombardi, in order to observe requisite signals of devices present inside rooms, and enable corona virus victims to convey messages to physicians as shown in Figure 10.8 [41]. In Spain too, Robotnik, a portable humanoid base, is capable of serving as intermediate to get the patient's situation.

Figure 10.7 The TIAGo-based robot [40].

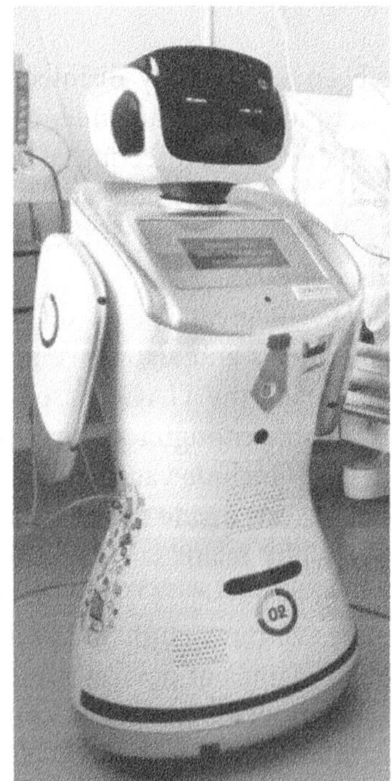

Figure 10.8 TOMMY—the nurse [42].

Figure 10.9 A four-legged robot spot in Singapore to comply to the rules of social distancing.

iv. Spain intends to extend a squadron of automata that will advance the corona virus testing by equipping automatic machines enabling them to perform 80,000 inspections in a day. Certain robots are also being developed that would be capable of performing many tests at the same point of time or simultaneously.

v. In Spain, automata are reprogrammed to generate a large quantity of masks.

vi. In Spain, the Center for AAT is producing aerial automata in order to sterilize logistics spaces.

    Germany too does not lack behind, and thus, the Pepper robot is employed in the supermarket to prompt people on sticking to the rules associated with social distancing.

vii. In Greece, too, throughout the closing of institutions, EdumotivaLab convinces how kids can continue studying to use and to program automata at the house.

viii. In Singapore, where corporate authorizations are employing Boston dynamic's four-legged automata to evoke park visitors to maintain a sustained distance while underlining the rules of social distancing as shown in Figure 10.9 [43].

Bots in South Korea are utilized to measure the temperature and for distributing hand sanitizers.

10.7 Robots in Future Pandemics

Positively, COVID-19 will stimulate the enactment of existing automata and their evolution to new domains; however, it may also lead to the formation or development of the new robots. Laboratory and logistics computerization is appearing to be a disregarded possibility. Automating and advancing the sluggish COVID-19 inspection processing which is reliant on the small laboratories needs to be the prime objective, and this automation will consequently eliminate any of the setbacks that are presently faced in some parts of the USA and other countries suffering from this pandemic. If the administration and enterprise have subsequently acquired and worked upon the drawbacks and in capabilities of the previous crashes, the more worldly automata will be developed and modified in order to assist the physicians and the nurses at the time of any further such pandemic [44].

Funding (information that explains whether and by whom the research was supported)
Declarations
Conflicts of interest/Competing interests
None
Availability of data and material
None
Code availability
None
Authors' contributions (optional: please review the submission guidelines from the journal whether statements are mandatory)

References

1. Skinner, K., Mataric, M.J., Feil-Seifer, D., "Benchmarks for evaluating socially assistive robotics,". *Psychol. Benchmarks Human-Robot Interaction*, 8, 423–439, October 2007.
2. Moran, M.E., "The da Vinci Robot,". *J. Endourol.*, 20, 986–990, 2006.
3. Maspero, G., *Manual of Egyptian Archaeology and Guide to the Study of Antiquities in Egypt*, Cambridge University Press, London, 2010.

4. Woods, M. and Woods, M.B., *Ancient Transportation Technology: From Oars to Elephants, Twenty-First Century Books*, p. 96, Lerner Publishing, Minneapolis, 2010.
5. Mani, M. and Hemal, A.K. (Eds.), *Robotics in Genitourinary Surgery*, 2 Ed, Springer, New York City, 2018.
6. Möller, P.B.E., 2005. [Online]. https://upload.wikimedia.org/wikipedia/commons/4/45/Leonardo-Robot3.jpg
7. Schultz, A.C. and Goodrich, M.A., *Human-Robot Interaction: A Survey*, Now Publications, 2008.
8. Perry, T., *"SRI's Pioneering Mobile Robot Shakey Honored as IEEE Milestone,"*, IEEE Spectrum, New York City, New York, 2017.
9. S. International, 1972. [Online]. https://upload.wikimedia.org/wikipedia/commons/thumb/0/0c/SRI_Shakey_with_callouts.jpg/375px-SRI_Shakey_with_callouts.jpg
10. Heatherton, T.F., Halpern, D., Gazzaniga, M., *Psychological science*, Fifth Ed, W.W. Norton, New York, 2016.
11. Types of learning, Britannica, Australia, 2015.
12. James, P. and Steger, M.B., "Globalization and global consciousness: Levels of connectivity,", in: *Global Culture: Consciousness and Connectivity*, Robertson, R. and Buhari, D. (Eds.), 2016.
13. Breazeal, C., "Emotion and sociable humanoid robots," *International Journal of Human-Computer Studies*, 59, 1, 119–155, Academic Press, Inc., USA, 2003.
14. Brooks, R.A., "A robust layered control system for a mobile robot," *IEEE Journal of Robotics and Automation*, 2, 1, 14–23, IEEE, 1985.
15. Mazzei, D., Cisternino, A., Cominelli, L., Lazzeri, N., "Designing the Mind of a Social Robot," *Applied Sciences*, 8, 2, 302, MDPI, Switzerland, 2018.
16. Brooks, R.A., Connell, J., Ning, P., *Massachusetts Institute of Technology Artificial Intelligence Laboratory*, MIT Libraries, 1988. [Online]. Available: https://dspace.mit.edu/handle/1721.1/6483.
17. Gat, E., *"On Three-Layer Architecture,"* Artificial Intelligence and Mobile Robots, 2, 1622–1627, AAAI Press, 1998.
18. Tsotsos, J.K. and Kotseruba, I., "A Review of 40 Years in Cognitive Architecture Research Core Cognitive Abilities and Practical Applications,". *Artif. Intell. Rev.*, *53*, 17–94, 2018.
19. Sun, R., "Memory systems within a cognitive architecture,". *New Ideas Psychol.*, 30, 227–240, 2012.
20. Wendt, A., Kollmann, S., Friedrich, G., Jakubec, M., Schaat, S., *"Interdisciplinary Development and Evaluation of Cognitive Architectures Exemplified with the SiMA Approach,"*, 2015.
21. Rosenbloom, P.S., Marsella, S.C., Pynadath, D.V., *"Reinforcement Learning for Adaptive Theory of Mind,"*, 2014.
22. Zamorano, M.R., Garcia.-Alegre, M.C., Guinea, D., Gomez, D.M., *"ARDIS: Knowledge-based dynamic architecture for real-time,"*, 2009.

23. Kidd, C., Thomaz, A.L., Hoffman, G., Breazeal, C., *"Effects of Nonverbal Communication on Efficiency and Robustness of Human-Robot,"*, IEEE, 2005.
24. Hart, J., Kim, E., Scassellati, B., Bainbridge, W.A., "The effect of presence on human-robot interaction,". *17th IEEE International Symposium on Robot and Human Interactive communication*, 2008.
25. Drury, J. and Yanco, H.A., *"Where Am I? Acquiring Situation Awareness Using a Remote Robot Platform,"*, IEEE, 2004.
26. Kase, S.E., Bittner, J.L., Ritter, F.E., Evertsz, R., Pedrotti, M., Busetta, P., "CoJACK: A high-level cognitive architecture with demonstrations of moderators, variability, and implications for situation awareness," *Biologically Inspired Cognitive Architectures*, 1, 2–13, Elsevier, Amsterdam, 2012.
27. Breazeal, C., "Believability and readability of robot faces,", in: *Proceedings of the Eighth International Symposium on Intelligent Robotic Systems*, 2000.
28. Benedic, P. T. B. J. C., 2005. [Online]. https://upload.wikimedia.org/wikipedia/commons/thumb/2/27/Kismet-IMG_6007-gradient.jpg/330px-Kismet-IMG_6007-gradient.jpg
29. Nourbakhsh, I., Dautenhahn, K., Fong, T., *"A Survey of Socially Interactive Robots: Concepts, Design, and Applications,"* Elsevier, Amsterdam, 2002.
30. Baars, B.J., D'Mello, S.K., Franklin, S., Ramamurthy, U., "LIDA: A working model of cognition,", in: *Proceedings of the 7th International Conference on Cognitive Modeling*, 2006.
31. Hommel, B. and Zmigrod, S., "Feature Integration across Multimodal Perception and Action: A Review," *Multi Sensory Research*, 26, 2013, 143–157, Brill, Netherlands, 2013.
32. Ang, M.H., Poo, A.N., Yan, H., "A Survey on Perception Methods for Human–Robot Interaction,". *Int. J. Soc. Robot.*, 6, 85–119, 4 July 2013.
33. Scassellati, B. and Admoni, H., "Nonverbal Behavior Modeling for Socially Assistive Robots,". *2014 AAAI Fall Symposium*, 2014.
34. Fiorini, L., Acerbi, G., Sorrentino, A., Mancioppi, G., Nocentini, O., "A Survey of Behavioral Models for Social Robots," *Robotics*, 8, 3, 54, MDPI, Switzerland, 9 July 2019.
35. Mitchell, D.F., "The Use of Artificial Intelligence in Digital Forensics: An Introduction," *Digital Evidence and Electronic Signature Law Review*, 7, 35–47, Pario Communication Limited, Bedfordshire, 2007.
36. Nelson, B.J., Murphy, R.R., Choset, H., Christensen, H., Collins, S.H., Yang, G.-Z., "Combating COVID-19—The role of robotics in managing public health and infectious diseases,". *Robots Soc.*, 5, 25 March 2020.
37. euRobotics, *"10 ways robots fight against the COVID-19 pandemic,"*, vol. 30, p. 4, euRobotics, Brussels, 2020, [Online]. Available: https://www.eu-robotics.net/eurobotics/newsroom/press/robots-against-covid-19.html.
38. Demaitre, E., *"UVD Robots responds to surging demand during COVID-19 crisis,"*, The Robot Report, March 2020. [Online].
39. *"COVID-19 and our robots: ready to help fight coronavirus in hospitals,"*, Pal Robotics, Barcelona, Spain, March 2020, [Online]. Available: http://blog.

pal-robotics.com/covid-19-and-our-robots-ready-to-help-fight-coronavirus-in-hospitals/.

40. Pal Robotics, April 2020. [Online]. https://sp-ao.shortpixel.ai/client/to_webp,q_glossy,ret_img,w_450/https://pal-robotics.com/wp-content/uploads/2020/01/ARI-humanoid-robot.jpg
41. *"Tommy, a Robot Nurse Helps Italy Doctors Safe from Coronavirus,"*, Tempo, Indonesia, 2020, [Online]. Available: https://en.tempo.co/photo/79449/tommy-a-robot-nurse-helps-italy-doctors-safe-from-coronavirus.
42. Scalzo, R.L., April 2020. [Online]. https://www.reuters.com/article/us-health-coronavirus-italy-robots-idUSKBN21J67Y
43. Bengali, S., *"Singapore enforces social distancing — with a robot dog,"*, Los Angeles Times, California, 13 May 2020, [Online]. Available: https://www.latimes.com/world-nation/story/2020-05-13/coronavirus-singapores-robot-dog-enforces-social-distancing.
44. Mehta, T., Gehlot, A., Sharma, D., "Design and Development of android-based BOT for medicine and food distribution to patients,", in: *Advances in Intelligent Systems and Computing*, vol. 479, pp. 537–543, Springer Singapore, Singapore, 2016.

11

VANET: An IoT Forensic-Based Model for Maintaining Chain of Custody

Manoj Sindhwani[1], Charanjeet Singh[1]* and Rajeshwar Singh[2]

[1]*Lovely Professional University, Phagwara, India*
[2]*Doaba Group of Colleges, Nawanshar, India*

Abstract

VANET itself presents the intelligent features including intelligent vehicles which are capable to go for adaptive decisions for communication between the two parties, i.e., the sender and the receiver. This concept is known as Internet of Vehicles (IOV) which is gaining popularity in emerging fields of technology. The major challenge faced can be the reaching of message to the destination in such peculiar and harsh traffic conditions with constrained mobility parameters. Various techniques have been developed in the recent years for the clustering of vehicular nodes but stability of the cluster is still a major concern. The clusters may integrate with other clusters if needed because other nodes may leave the cluster so if one node is left, then it may join other cluster as a cluster member. Hence, the increased lifetime of cluster, cluster head, and cluster members can enhance the stability for maintaining a predictable performance. In earlier researches, papers are considerably focused on the security issues, energy and storage capacity in the network, density-based algorithms, and comparison of algorithm with VANET, but it is required to primarily focus on intelligent transportation system connecting the vehicular communication with Internet of Things (IOT) and forensics. The significant part of this work is to stress upon the improved QoS parameters using the concept of routing protocols and IOV with forensic science for investigation purposes. The data collected from the sensors in the vehicle is used for the forensic activities and applications. This work relates the IOT forensic with vehicular ad hoc networks which is the need for various safety and security parameters.

***Keywords*:** Intelligent clustering, Internet of Things, forensics, IOT forensics, clustering, VANET

**Corresponding author*: rcharanjeet@gmail.com

Anita Gehlot, Rajesh Singh, Jaskaran Singh and Neeta Raj Sharma (eds.) Digital Forensics and Internet of Things: Impact and Challenges, (199–210) © 2022 Scrivener Publishing LLC

11.1 Introduction

VANETs present a largest real-time application but lacks security, scalability, efficient routing, and clustering protocols. Clustering in vehicular ad hoc networks has its sole hand in dividing the various groups of vehicles [1, 2] according to a specific set of rules as shown in Figure 11.1. For every cluster, a leader is required which is termed as a cluster head (CH) whose function is application specific. A CH acts as a mediator between the cluster and network. It provides the opportunity to reduce transmission overheads in V2V communication and also provides the provision of back up cluster in the absence of the CH till the time new CH is not elected. It also provides the advantage to dynamically set the parameters, and provision of wireless resource saving is also dispensed.

According to its operational area, the concept of clustering has scope of study as follows:

- It can be used in VANET [3, 4] for channel access management.
- Greatly be brought into common usage for traffic safety hence giving instructions to drivers regarding collision avoidance or need of cooperative driver (autodriving).
- It can provide way out for the management of frequent disconnections, hidden node problems, and mobility prediction with the clustering of the vehicles.

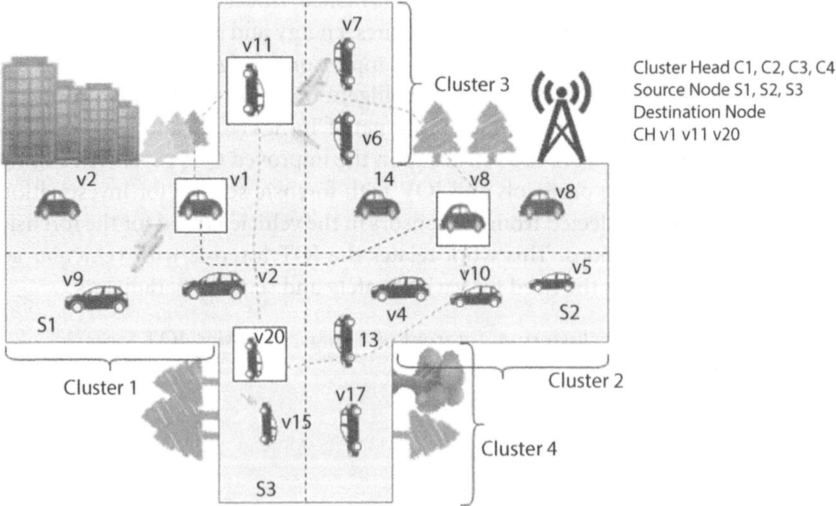

Figure 11.1 Clustering in VANET.

Table 11.1 Node description.

Nodes	Description
UN	• Vehicle belongs to none of the cluster • Initial state of the vehicles
CH	• Cluster leader communications with members in its cluster • One CH (primary) in one cluster at a time
CM	• One-hop neighbor of CH • Nodes in the cluster that communicate with CH • Performs inter cluster communication • Member nodes also assigned as gateways which are located at the edge of the cluster (GW)
CH_t	• Temporary cluster head • Mitigated after CH is finally elected

More usage of specific routing protocols for VANETs will lead to better QoS. Table 11.1 describes the node description of various parameters in clustering techniques.

The number of hops to the cluster members (CM) from the CHs can be determined as single-hop or multi-hop where maximum of the clustering algorithms [5] employ the single-hop clusters in which the distance between CM and CH is just one hop where it is easy to reduce or mitigate the issue of packet loss where the vehicle is made aware of the one hop away vehicle information.

11.2 Cluster Performance Parameters

Neighborhood discovery stands for the discovery of the nodes in a vehicular network to form the cluster. Initially, the willing node will enter the network and to be a part of the vehicular network. Availability announcement will be made by the broadcasting of periodic message being active or passive clustering [6, 7]. A database stores information regarding the neighboring nodes.

Cluster head selection is choosing a leader among all. The fittest of all wins the race to be a leader termed as a CH. When all the data is gathered in the database, then the CH is chosen on the bases of various parameters like mobility matrices, speed, velocity, relative and distance. The CMs are affiliated. Affiliation will be awarded to the CM and CH.

Announcement is done to know about the neighbors and affiliation process. *Maintenance* allows the maintenance process for the CHs as well as CMs. It enables the CH to manage a cluster and merging of the cluster and still maintains the network clusters. The nodes also periodically look for the links with the associated CH. The strongest CM can be turned out to a CH in case no CH is present.

11.3 Routing Protocols in VANET

The CBRP protocol used is outperforming all other conventional protocols such as AODV and DSDV in our comparison work. The CBR protocol is a cluster-based protocol which partitions the coverage area geographically into grids in order to transmit the data packets in an efficient way. Every grid comprises of clusters.

11.3.1 Performance Metrics

Packet Delivery Ratio (PDR): The ratio of received packets by the destination and the generated packets by the source is termed to be the packet delivery ratio.

$$PDR = \frac{Number\ of\ packets\ received}{Number\ of\ packets\ sent}$$

Throughput: It is the rate of successful message delivery over a communication channel. We have calculated the aggregate throughput of AODV, DSDV, and the CBRP [8] in which throughput is the combined sum of all data rates being delivered to all the nodes.

$$Throughput = \frac{Total\ Number\ of\ received\ byte}{Total\ no.\ of\ transmissions}$$

Normalized Routing Load (NRL): It is the number of transmitted routing packets for each data packet that has been delivered at destination.

Delay: Delay indicates the amount of time taken by the packets to reach to destination from the source.

$$Delay = \frac{\sum(arrival\ time - send\ time)}{no.\ of\ connections}$$

A vehicular ad hoc network comprises of nodes (source and destination vehicles), clusters, and CHs. Supposedly, it will choose the one which will be closest to the grid as the CH. One vehicle transfers data packets to the other vehicle which is the CH of another cluster. Similarly in every transmission the nodes will transmit the data packets to CH vehicles [9, 10]. An optimal CH is selected to route the packets to the final destined node.

The total number of nodes taken and the search for the fittest CH goes on in every cluster.

- According to the CBRP, the communication network has been partition into four parts, each making a cluster of seven nodes.
- The Source node S1 will transmit the packets with the help of CH of C1. C1 will interact with cluster C2 to route the packet to the destination node D1, i.e., v4
- Similarly, inter-cluster and intra-cluster communication can take place. This protocol will result in reduced OH. Furthermore, CH selection algorithm can be understood as given below.

11.3.2 Proposed Cluster Head Selection Algorithm

Cluster Head Selection Algorithm:

1. Begin;
2. CH (V_2)→ Broadcast INI
3. INI → (G, Loc)
4. If (V_1→ unable to receive INI)
   Wait till (T_1)
5. Then (Broadcast REQ)
   Wait till (T_2)
6. If (No Response)
7. Assignment of self as CH // CH leaves grid
8. CH (V_2)→ Broadcast LEAVE
9. LEAVE→ G
10. $V_{1,}$ $V_{2,\ldots,}$ $V_{n\rightarrow}$ REQ;
11. Select new CH;
12. End;

Clustering algorithms are a boon for the issues existing in routing protocols which leads to better cluster lifetime and stability. The studied algorithms are clubbed in Table 11.2 which illustrates various parameters such as follows:

- Metrics
- Clustering parameter
- Algorithm base
- Issues resolved
- Clustering
- Evaluation parameters
- Roadside scenario
- Vehicle speed
- Cluster stability
- Efficiency

Where road clustering provides a better end-to-end delay [11, 12], the static geographical-based clustering algorithm provides throughput improvement. Though scalability is always a big concern in VANETs which is achieved in content-based clustering, decentralized clustering is required more scalability in the network which is still a big challenge to overcome.

After the achievement of best clustering algorithm, the further work has been carried out with the *routing protocols* such as AODV, DSDV, and CBRP, which uses the clustering technique to overcome issues in routing. Since VANET is itself a subset of MANET, so MANET routing protocols does not suits for VANETs due to high dynamicity and mobility. A routing protocol is helpful in the management of information exchange by

Table 11.2 General comparison of AODV and DSDV.

AODV	DSDV
Reactive Protocol	Proactive Protocol
Better performance for large number of nodes	Better performance for small number of nodes
On demand route establishment	Packet OH requirement
More preferred over DSDV in case of real-time traffic	Not as preferred

establishing a route and making decisions of data forwarding, route maintenance and recover of failed routes.

The three routing protocols [13, 14] have been implemented and the performance has been compared on the bases of the following:

- Throughput
- PDF
- Delay
- Normalised routing load

The output conclusion that we get after the simulation of the protocols is as follows:

AODV is the routing protocol of wireless ad hoc networks which set up a route to the desired destination on demand and uses unicast and multi cast routing. AODV itself is an alteration of in DSDV. Since a number of challenges occur while routing the packets for which CBRP comes out to be a better part which outperforms AODV and DSDV. It geographically divides the area into the grid where a CH is to be selected per cluster.

11.4 Internet of Vehicles

The IOT is applicable now in mostly all smart technologies, including the smart vehicles gaining popularity in today's networks. IOT-based VANET contributes more in smart and secure communications called Internet of Vehicles (IOV). IOV uses a real-time data communication with major vehicular applications to improve security and privacy in the network. IOV supports all the technologies like navigation systems, sensor networks, and mobile communication. The motive of IOV is to connect multiple vehicles with users and offers a secure communication [15]. But still, there are some challenges and issues like reliability, dynamic topology, variable network load, and poor network connectivity. Major of the applications in IOV is in field of telecommunication and their functionality is divided into various classes like safety, navigation, information and infotainment, and remote telemetric.

Figure 11.2 represents the concept of IOV. IOV is the future of VANET and a new technique of route selection [16, 17] in vehicular networks. IOV can be boon to reduce mishap on roads and to resolve various security issues and delays transmission. The vehicles can pass the priority information in the network so as to earn security and the application can be to reduce the time delay [18] in medical help. IOV can also help in emergency systems like giving

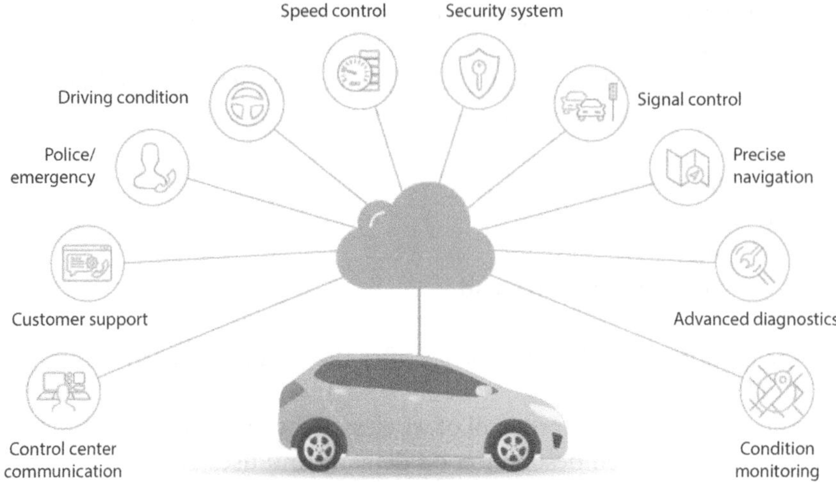

Figure 11.2 Internet of vehicles.

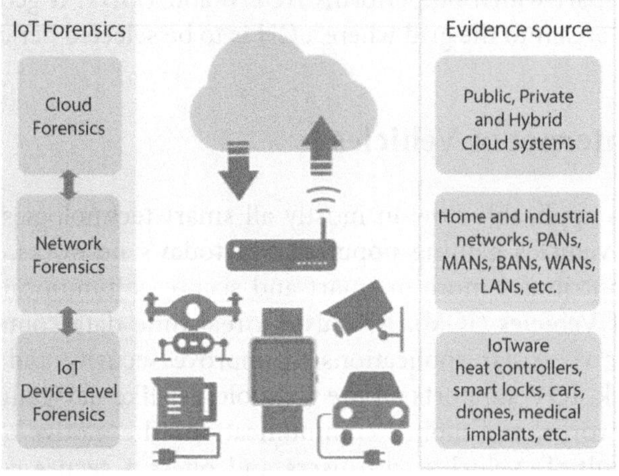

Figure 11.3 Components of the IoT forensics.

path to ambulances. So, considering this approach, IOV will be implemented to validate QoS parameters like throughput, packet transfer, and delay. The important components of the IoT forensics are shown in Figure 11.3.

11.5 IoT Forensic in Vehicular Ad Hoc Networks

New vehicles today contain electronic components and the control units which process the data collected by the sensors in the vehicles [19].

Also, the important data collected can be used for forensic purposes. So, the main focus is to deal with forensics of various problem areas and safety risks to make vehicular communication more preferable. From the viewpoint of forensic discipline, the vehicle creates lot of data as digital evidence. So, an intelligent vehicle connected with IOT-based network is a subject of forensic investigation [20]. In vehicle ad hoc networks, various parameters can be used for forensic purposes like vehicle's identity, behavior of driver/vehicle, vehicle geographical locations, and all the digital activities inside the vehicle. However, the dynamic topology of the vehicular networks sometimes loses the data collected in communication with other vehicles, and it also affects the information used in forensics. But the major issue is the security and safety parameters which can be improved by analysing of the data collected.

11.6 Conclusion

This work to date has primarily focused on the study of various clustering techniques algorithms and routing protocols, out of which the AODV DSDV and CBR routing protocols are compared and the clustering algorithms are compared to find the best suitable of all. Also, the stability algorithms stood to be more useful and more required in the dynamically unpredictable environment as in the prime objective. Stability and mobility are major concern. Furthermore, the IOV is also introduced to improve various QoS parameters like throughput, packet rate, and delay. IOV is the emerging technology in the field of vehicular communication. This research presented the overview of clustering in VANET, routing protocols, and IOV in the network. Such factors lead to motivation for such work, and hence, the QoS can be improved. Vehicle digital forensics is the new and emerging technology in latest fields of inventions. The data analysis and information collected is important for forensic applications, and new forensics methods and technologies can be implemented for better investigation.

References

1. Zhou, H., Wang, H., Chen, X., Li, X., Xu, S., Data offloading techniques through vehicular ad hoc networks: A survey. *IEEE Access*, 6, 65250–65259, 2018.
2. Abdel-Halim, I.T. and Fahmy, H.M.A., Prediction-based protocols for vehicular Ad Hoc Networks: Survey and taxonomy. *Comput. Netw.*, 130, 34–50, 2018.

3. Lu, Z., Qu, G., Liu, Z., A survey on recent advances in vehicular network security, trust, and privacy. *IEEE Trans. Intell. Transp. Syst.*, 20, 2, 760–776, 2018.
4. Tripp-Barba, C., Zaldívar-Colado, A., Urquiza-Aguiar, L., Aguilar-Calderón, J.A., Survey on routing protocols for vehicular ad hoc networks based on multimetrics. *Electronics*, 8, 10, 1177, 2019.
5. Cooper, C., Franklin, D., Ros, M., Safaei, F., Abolhasan, M., A comparative survey of VANET clustering techniques. *IEEE Commun. Surv. Tut.*, 19, 1, 657–681, 2016.
6. Yang, P., Wang, J., Zhang, Y., Tang, Z., Song, S., Clustering algorithm in VANETs: A survey, in: *2015 IEEE 9th international conference on anti-counterfeiting, security, and identification (ASID)*, IEEE, pp. 166–170, 2015, September.
7. Dhasian, H.R. and Balasubramanian, P., Survey of data aggregation techniques using soft computing in wireless sensor networks. *IET Inf. Secur.*, 7, 4, 336–342, 2013.
8. Katiyar, A., Singh, D., Yadav, R.S., State of the art approach to clustering protocols in vanet: a survey. *Wirel. Netw.*, 26, 7, 5307–5336, 2020.
9. Hande, R.S. and Muddana, A., Comprehensive survey on clustering-based efficient data dissemination algorithms for VANET, in: *2016 International Conference on Signal Processing, Communication, Power and Embedded System (SCOPES)*, IEEE, pp. 629–632, 2016, October.
10. Hamdi, M.M., Audah, L., Rashid, S.A., Mohammed, A.H., Alani, S., Mustafa, A.S., A review of applications, characteristics and challenges in vehicular ad hoc networks (VANETs), in: *2020 International Congress on Human-Computer Interaction, Optimization and Robotic Applications (HORA)*, IEEE, pp. 1–7, 2020, June.
11. Kennedy, J. and Eberhart, R., Particle swarm optimization, in: *Proceedings of ICNN'95-international conference on neural networks*, vol. 4, IEEE, pp. 1942–1948, 1995, November.
12. Bao, X., Li, H., Zhao, G., Chang, L., Zhou, J., Li, Y., Efficient clustering V2V routing based on PSO in VANETs. *Measurement*, 152, 107306, 2020.
13. Morissette, L. and Chartier, S., The k-means clustering technique: General considerations and implementation in Mathematica. *Tutorials Quant. Methods Psychol.*, 9, 1, 15–24, 2013.
14. Elhoseny, M. and Shankar, K., Energy efficient optimal routing for communication in VANETs via clustering model, in: *Emerging Technologies for Connected Internet of Vehicles and Intelligent Transportation System Networks*, pp. 1–14, Springer, Cham, 2020.
15. Ramalingam, M. and Thangarajan, R., Mutated k-means algorithm for dynamic clustering to perform effective and intelligent broadcasting in medical surveillance using selective reliable broadcast protocol in VANET. *Comput. Commun.*, 150, 563–568, 2020.

16. Khan, Z. and Fan, P., A novel triple cluster based routing protocol (TCRP) for VANETs, in: *2016 IEEE 83rd vehicular technology conference (VTC Spring)*, IEEE, pp. 1–5, 2016, May.
17. Zhang, G.P., Neural Networks for Classification: A Survey. *IEEE Trans. Syst. Man. Cybern. C. Appl. Rev.*, 30, 4, 451–462, 2000.
18. Bagherlou, H. and Ghaffari, A., A routing protocol for vehicular ad hoc networks using simulated annealing algorithm and neural networks. *J. Supercomput.*, 74, 6, 2528–2552, 2018.
19. Rak, R. and Kopencova, D., Actual Issues of Modern Digital Vehicle Forensic. *Internet Things Cloud Computing*, 8, 1, 12–16, 2020.
20. Bates, E.A., "*Digital Vehicle Forensics*", abforensics [online]. [cit, 2019-11-17], 2019. Available at. https://abforensics.com/wp-content/uploads/2019/02/INTERPOL-4N6-PULSE-IssueIV-BATES.pdf.

12

Cognitive Radio Networks: A Merit for Teleforensics

Yogita Thareja*, **Kamal Kumar Sharma**† **and Parulpreet Singh**

SEEE, Lovely Professional University, Phagwara, India

Abstract

An intellectual radio (cognitive radio) is a radio that can be altered and planned intensely to use the best remote diverts in its area to avoid client obstruction and stop up. A particularly radio subsequently recognizes available coordinates in remote range and, by then, properly changes its transmission or social event boundaries to allow logically synchronous far-off exchanges in a range band at one region. This exploration examines and discloses a clever way to deal with incorporation of the sensor hubs studies or information to sink, utilizing authorized way entrepreneurially. From different examinations, the specialists discovered extremely awful usages of range. To address it, psychological radio organization is acquainted all together with access the unique range. The range detecting issue is perhaps the most provoking issues in psychological radio frameworks to identify the accessible recurrence groups. In this chapter, we will consider different explorations which have been completed for further developing channel use proportion, QoS, and successful range the executives, for example, range detecting, dynamic range access, and allotment. EHNs (Energy Harvesting Cognitive Radio Networks) are needed to further develop energy usefulness by gathering energy of RF and inexhaustible sources. EHN is applied to CR innovation, and this EHCRN (Energy reaping psychological radio) is needed to utilize both essentialness and electromagnetic range viably.

***Keywords*:** Cognitive radio, wireless sensor network, intellectual radio, psychological radio, spectrum sensing, clustering, energy harvesting cognitive radio networks

**Corresponding author*: parulpreet.23367@lpu.co.in

†*Corresponding author*: kamal.23342@lpu.co.in

Anita Gehlot, Rajesh Singh, Jaskaran Singh and Neeta Raj Sharma (eds.) Digital Forensics and Internet of Things: Impact and Challenges, (211–226) © 2022 Scrivener Publishing LLC

12.1 Introduction

WSNs measure conditions like temperature, sound, wind, mugginess climate checking, frontline reconnaissance, medical care frameworks, submerged observation, and some more. Remote sensor organizing is a rising advancement that has a wide degree of potential applications. Such a structure generally contains countless passed on centers that sort out themselves into a multi-bounce far off framework. Every center point has in any occasion one sensor, inserted processors, and low-control radios and is generally battery-worked. According to the WSN engineering, it might comprise of many sensor hubs which are conveyed arbitrarily in the observing sensor field. Source hub and base station are the two parts of WSNs for information assortment. The source hubs send information to base station with the assistance of single or multi-bounce information transmission plot. Then, at that point, the sink hub sends the information to the ideal area with the assistance of the correspondence channel to achieve the observing application task. WSNs move in modern logical and clinical (ISM) recurrence band whose recurrence is relegated as 2.4 GHz by Federal Communications (FCC) guidelines. Tremendous development and multiplication of remote correspondence have driven toward the smooth and dependable correspondence among numerous gadgets. Thus, the interest for remote gadgets is expanding quickly with a pace of 30% to 40% consistently [1]. Verifiably, radio-gear has exclusively been utilized as simple specialized gadget. The utilization of radio correspondence hardware expands as various associations and organizations [2]. The usefulness here is generally short-range gadgets have extended to incorporate private call, information correspondence, and universal locator. A significant number of these gadgets additionally incorporate with cell phones, which conveys Push-to-Talk (PTT) benefits that make it conceivable to arrangement associations between clients utilizing a cell phone. Truth be told, these gadgets can be utilized to interface clients just utilizing cell phones. Until this point in time, there is little exploration on the computerized follows in current radio correspondence hardware. Indeed, it is expanding. The broadened number of remote gadgets working in the ISM band makes hindrance among dissimilar remote applications which are using this band. Additionally, the expanded number of remote gadgets advances the range shortage issues in view of the accessibility of restricted assets. Moreover, framework throughput relies upon the utilization of the channel [3]. In this way, obstruction, channel usage, and range the board stay testing issues in remote correspondence. Wireless sensor network (WSN) which comprises of sensors, sink hubs, web, and end client application which is additionally called base station. All are associated in bidirectional way that implies that sensors can send information to sink hub and sink hub is associated through web and web may offer support to end client application and base station. Similarly, end client application which is additionally called base station may send information to the web and sink hub is associated through web and afterward back to the sensor.

12.1.1 Integration of WSN with Psychological Radio

As of late, psychological radio scheme developed a promising answer for moderate issues of spectrum resource scarcity by enhancing the use of available resource. Cognitive radio (CR) network (CRN) engineering involves primary (essential) and secondary (optional) clients. The primary users (PUs) are the favored clients and are allowed to get to spectrum all the time, while secondary users (SUs) is permitted to access the spectrum opportunistically. At whatever point, the PU that is PU range is underutilized, the optional clients can get to it. This procedure assists with improving range usage and relieves the issue of congestion of unlicensed band [4]. In CRNs (CR networks), SUs (auxiliary clients) are not permitted to make any interference to PUs. When PU instates any correspondence on a similar channel where SUs is conveying, SUs must clear the channel to keep up the no-obstruction worldview. The CR correspondence strategies are received in different sorts of existing innovations like machine-to-machine systems, body area networks, and WSNs.

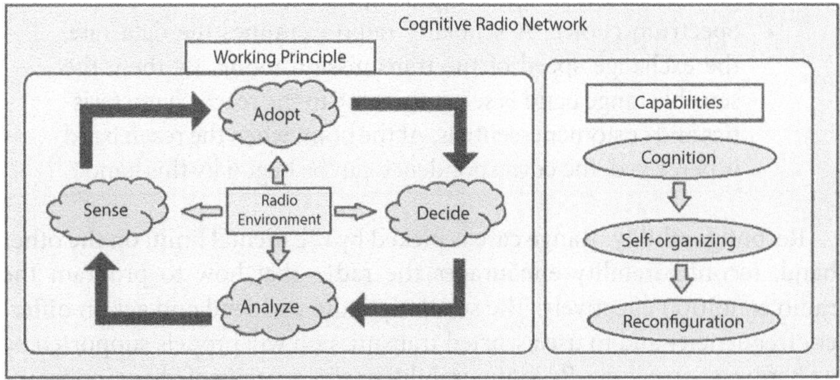

Figure 12.1 Cognitive radio network.

Unlike the conventional WSNs, the CRSNs operate on licensed band and opportunistically sense the spectrum to achieve the channel state information. A psychological radio (CR) is a radio that can be changed and planned continuously to use the best remote occupies in its district to avoid customer hindrance and blockage. The psychological procedure is the path closer to knowing through notoriety, organizing, addressing, acting, and often spotless and refreshing with a foundation set apart by utilizing becoming more acquainted with. Figure 12.1 depicts the network of CR.

12.1.2 Characteristics of Cognitive Radio

Scholarly limit which is intellectual limit is the limit of the radio development to identify the information from its current circumstance. In this, there are some intricate systems that are needed to get the common and spatial assortment in the radio condition instead of simply be recognized by checking the force and avoid deterrent to various customers. By this limit, the unused reach can be perceived at a specific time and region. However, the best reach and reasonable working limits can be picked. The mental limit engages nonstop participation with its current circumstance to choose sensible correspondence limits and adjust to the powerful radio climate. The three phases of cognitive cycle under this order are as follows:

- Spectrum distinguishing: A scholarly radio recognizes the available reach gatherings, takes their information, and by then distinguishes the range openings or void areas.
- Spectrum examination: The reach openings that are distinguished by the range recognizing are evaluated.
- Spectrum choice: A scholarly radio examines the data rate, the exchange speed of the transmission mode. By then, the sensible range band is select agreeing to the reach characteristics and customer essentials. At the point when the reach band is perceived, the correspondence can be begun by this band.

Reconfigurability: Range care is picked by the mental limit; on the other hand, reconfigurability encourages the radio that how to program the radio condition effectively. The scholarly radio can send and get on different frequencies and to use assorted transmission will propels supported by its hardware structure. Reconfigurability is the capacity of changing working limits for the transmission on the fly without any modifications on the hardware fragments.

There is a scholarly plan for predominant, which has versatile remote organization protocol running from simple to complex mix of exceptionally selected. The arrangement gives speedy RF checking limit, a deft RF handset working over an extent of repeat gatherings, an item described radio modem fit for supporting a variety of waveforms including OFDM and DSSS/QPSK, a group dealing with engine for show and coordinating convenience, and an all-around helpful processor for execution of reach conduct techniques and calculations. Here, there is a necessity for baseband and orchestrate processor board which would interface to the RF front-end and license continuously reconfigurable programming and hardware utilization of various far off associations supporting individual data speeds of 50 Mb/s and a biggest all out data speed of 100 Mb/s. There is a blend of DSP and FPGA squares alongside their vital memories. By using DSPs, there is an issue with programming these contraptions. Two channels are moreover supported by the straightforward front-end; one is used for assessment; what is more, another is used for data, which has information transmissions selectable in 1-MHz increments.

The fundamental customers (PU) save the choice to utilize the collection whenever assistant customers (SU) can use the grouping precisely when PU is not utilizing it [3]. With scholarly radio in WSN organizing, the probability of center point bits of knowledge development resembles the openness of void supported channels [4]. In reality, a WSN contained sensor center points equipped with mental radio may benefit by the cutoff benefits of the striking features of dynamic reach get to [5].

Spectrum hole (SH) is characterized as a band that can be used by unlicensed clients, which is a fundamental asset for psychological radio which is also called CR frameworks. The greater part of existing commitments distinguishes SHs by detecting whether an essential sign is available or missing and afterward attempt to get to them with the goal that the CR and essential clients utilize the range band either at various schedule openings or in various geographic locales. Transfers or directional transfers for CR clients to abuse new range opportunity are called spatial SH. It can give higher range effectiveness by conjunction of essential and CR clients at a similar locale, time, and range band. Specifically, whenever the range chance of an immediate connection from a CR transmitter to a CR beneficiary does not show up, and in any case set up the correspondence through circuitous connections, i.e., other CR clients go about as hand-off stations to help the correspondence by utilizing other spatial areas. Besides, the fruitful correspondence probabilities of CR clients show that the range productivity can be extensively improved. Full duplex of CRNs is explained in Figure 12.2.

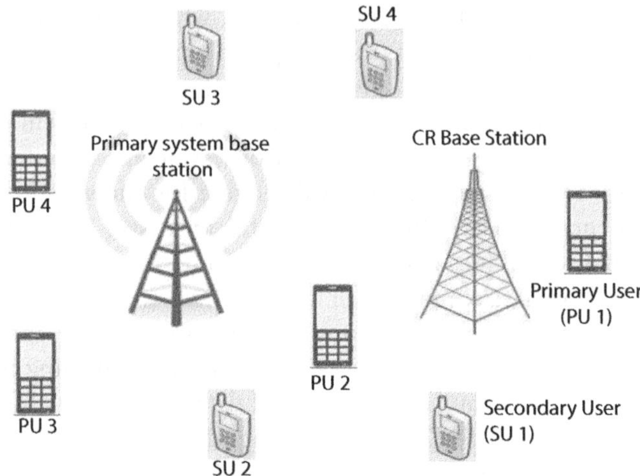

Figure 12.2 Cognitive radio cellular network (full duplex).

Similar to CRN, PUs have direct access to the spectrum, whereas SUs are allowed to access the spectrum opportunistically. On the other hand, CRSN adopts the general limitations of conventional WSNs such as energy consumption, and network lifetime. Moreover, the spectrum sensing is also considered as a crucial aspect in implementation of CRSNs. The SS has impact on energy consumption because more amounts of SUs for sensing will require more energy. Hence, current research progresses are focused on efficient approach for spectrum sensing. Similarly, routing and resource allocation is a challenging task in CRSNs. By taking the advantage of spectrum utilization rule of FCC and advancements of networking technology, the combined WSN and CR can mitigate the challenging issues such as spectrum utilization, resource allocation.

12.2 Contribution of Work

This section presents a brief discussion about recent trends and techniques in the field of WSN, CR, and CRSNs. Spectrum sensing is a most important task of CR which has a significant impact on network lifetime when combined with WSN. Various researches have been carried out for effective spectrum management such as sensing of spectrum, dynamic spectrum access, channel allocation, and access. Moreover, resource management and energy aware routing schemes are also presented. As discussed, the greater number of sensing node requires more energy which can lead toward the degraded network lifetime. Game theory-based schemes are also adopted for spectrum allocation and management. Later, spectrum allocation problem is formulated [7]. Similar to this, Abdalzaher *et al.* [6] used Stackelberg game approach to improve the security in CRSNs. Clustering is also known as an important part of routing in these networks. Under clustering organization, the passageway to the framework is through the cluster head (CH) that adds up to members of the cluster which demonstrate of the point lies in framework [8]. There are numerous methodologies in regard to grouping with varied application in designing. Be that as it may, larger part of the researchers despite everything embraces the underlying distributed work on cluster formation through transformation of systems from flat to CH. Most strategies have considered arrangement of CHs first reliant premise and a while later various hubs change as requirements be. The CN that connects clusters naturally becomes passage [9].

Today, noteworthy increment in the applications is that utilization these groups realizes the conjunction issue. Thus, WSN needs extra abilities to battle the obstruction brought about by different applications [10]. As of late, psychological methods have been utilized in remote systems to dodge the impediments forced by ordinary WSNs. Psychological radio which is CR is a contender for the up and coming+ age of wireless correspondences framework. The intellectual method is the way toward observation and arranging. The sensor in wireless networks (WSN) can be made to work in unlicensed groups. Be that as it may, to work in authorized range, the channels must be rented that costly and have arrangement limits. In opposite, unlicensed groups (ISM) are allowed to utilize; however, the headway in remote innovation brings about appeal for ISM groups [11-19]. Along these lines, it has become a test for WSN to work in unlicensed groups for basic. The current remote systems administration worldview comprises of the availability of numerous heterogeneous gadgets through connections working under unique situations. Henceforth, including intellectual radio abilities in WSNs through CR helped remote system that will permit sensor hubs to use the upsides of dynamic range get to. With the utilization of intellectual radio in WSN steering, the likelihood of hub information conveyance is corresponding to the accessibility of empty or vacant authorized channels [20-25]. Full duplex antenna with secondary base station is explained in Figure 12.3.

Most importantly, a psychological radio empowered sensor system will be sent where we characterized different norm boundaries, for example, hub limit, channel, data transfer capacity accessible, and transmission capacity utilization by every hub, power prerequisites, number of authorized and

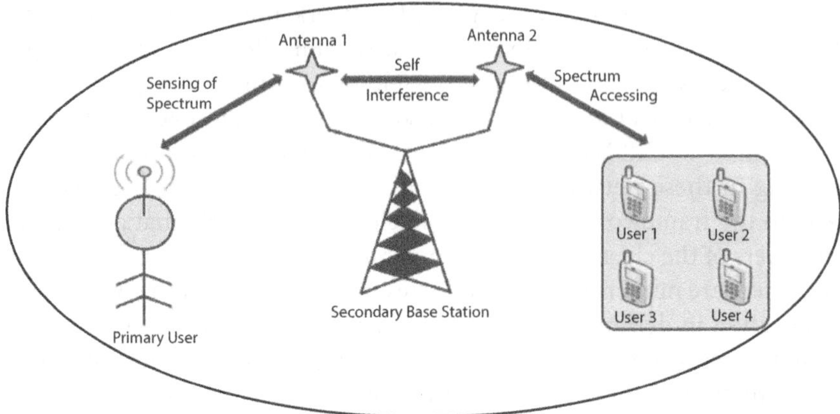

Figure 12.3 Secondary base station with full duplex antenna.

unlicensed clients, and so forth [26-29]. The total procedure can be isolated into following stages:

(a) Clustering: In this stage, we perform CH and group part or individuals or member determination dependent on their data transfer capacity accessibility like bandwidth and channel data.
(b) In the following stage, the improvement of routing protocol which thinks about obstruction, energy utilization, and data transmission necessities.
(c) Once the routing path is obtained, ideal asset assignment plot dependent on the detecting limit, i.e., sensing capacity of the hubs.
(d) Finally, multi-jump helpful game hypothesis model will be created to relieve the obstruction and to improve the general correspondence execution by improving the bundle or packet conveyance or delivery.

12.2.1 Push-to-Talk

It administrates are progressively the communication among different sorts of gadgets and radio preplacement. There are diverse mobile telephone programs designed specifically for that reason. One illustration of this is the WAVE Communicator software from Motorola, which utilizes their "WAVE Work Group Communications Solution". This makes it feasible to straightforwardly convey among two-way radios and smartphones.

Some cellular phones have a unique PTT button, a soft-button at the screen, or reassigns a contemporary seize, e.g., using the quantity down to move about as a PTT button. This makes radiocommunication hardware extra famous among companies that need bunch correspondence places of work which might be independent of public correspondence frameworks inside the occasion of a blackout of this public basis [30-35].

12.2.2 Digital Forensic–Radio Communication Equipment

Versatile and portable two-way radio can incorporate configuration records that display the dynamic settings of the radio. These setting experiments be downloaded from the radio and stored as a "code plug" [36, 37]. This code attachment could then be able to be dissected with the aid of stacking it into the Customer Program Software (CPS) software, programming furnished with the aid of the system dealer for configuring, perusing, and writing information to/from the advanced radio gear, e.g., settings including frequencies, speak corporations, contacts, strength yield, and keylock [38-40]. The radio may also have furthermore placed away name logs and message logs that is probably essential for an exam. The way radio is probably outfitted with a digital camera and potential media, which can include facts to be explored. Frequently elaborations, as an example, are mote speaker/receiver or Bluetooth gadgets are connected to flexible two-way radios for PTT programs. The less complicated variations of these a long way off speaker/mouthpiece gadgets does no longer contain important advanced follows. The in addition developed model test comprises a camera, voice recorder, and potential media. Re-bit PTT catches are likewise on hand in the business middle [51]. These are little fastens that associate by means of Bluetooth to a smart telephone or a way radio. These gadgets do not include tons virtual forensic proof but while these devices are skilled at a criminal offense scene it thoroughly might be a sign that a manner radio or a PTT management is blanketed [41-44].

The presentation of a clustering protocol as far as offering great outcomes with energy management, packet delivery or more all expansion of system lifetime relies upon an efficient methodology toward formation of viable clusters. In any case, with the development of the systems that will undoubtedly cover huge topographical regions, formation of powerful clusters will in general be hard [45-48]. Along these lines, the huge topographical zones and the spontaneous hub conveyance remains against successful clustering systems; it turns into a test when it is considered in cooperative communications. The various researches are explained below in a table with objectives, advantages and disadvantages.

12.2.3 Energy Harvesting Network

Energy harvesting community (EHN) is a trending subject matter a few of the current researches; EH-CRN is going through huge demanding situations associated with technical design. Bhowmick makes use of non-RF strength harvesting as a supplementary of energy harvesting from RF signal of PU motivated by using the work done in, Static sources, for example, TV towers and radio towers, emanate moderately consistent power with time though unique RF sources such as Wi-Fi frameworks and cell phones transmit fluctuating force with time. The energy putting away component might be single stage or two phases where the subsequent stage goes about as a reinforcement arrangement which is utilized when the energy put away in first stage got devoured [49-51].

Energy being collected from the ambient and RF sources utilized legitimately to give power to the wireless nodes with no storage. The harvesting system gathers the energy from the available sources with the help of harvesting antennas. These harvesting antennas might be intended to work either on a singly frequency or on different frequencies so that the gathering framework can collect energy from a solitary RF energy source or from multiple RF energy sources separately. After this, the harvesting energy is converted into electrical energy and this electrical energy is provided to wireless nodes and the nodes uses this energy for playing out its tasks. Another way is storage of energy component which convert electrical energy in case the energy is greater than the energy consumption of the wireless node and this stored energy can be used in future.

12.2.4 Challenges with the Use of Clusters in Cognitive Radio Networks

Majority of protocols of clustering has been explored in the network of wireless sensor which figured the equivalent conventions may reach out to agreeable interchanges in CR. The area displays a portion of the difficulties associated with the protocols (clustering) whenever they executed in CR agreeable interchanges. The presentation of a clustering protocol offering great outcomes regarding energy management, packet conveyance, or more all expansion of system lifetime depends on an efficient methodology toward making of useful clusters. Be that as it may, with the development of the systems that will undoubtedly cover huge land zones, making of intense clusters will, in general, be hard. The made clusters performs beneath standard. Along these lines, the huge land zones and the spontaneous nodes dispersion remains effective in the procedures of clustering, it turns into a test when considered in helping correspondences in CRNs. The key idea of the cognitive network's nodes in the network is portrayed as being heterogeneous. Along these lines, a few nodes have low abilities while others are progressed. This perspective confuses the clustering protocols that accept consistency of the considerable number of nodes. The uniform groups' creation relies upon the even conveyance of nodes in the framework, with all intents and purposes impossible. It very well may be suggested that uniform clusters arrangement is forgotten particularly for cognitive network's nodes in the network. Other challenges incorporate the intermittent irregular changes of the CHs likewise, the assumption that nodes remain at one circumstance in the system. The ratio of utilization of channel needs to be improved further with better result. The false detection probability needs to be reduced further to get better results. There should be universal routing protocol metric which includes all routing protocol for the better result.

12.3 Conclusion and Future Scope

In this study research, a singular way to cope with comprises the sensor nodes with cognitive nodes to route sensor statistics to sink using legal entrepreneur. The traumatic situations of the subsequent era IoT networks live in reducing the overall community latency and increasing throughput without sacrificing reliability. One feasible possibility is coexistence of networks running on amazing frequencies. However, records' bandwidth support and spectrum availability are the foremost annoying situations. Therefore, CRNs are the satisfactory available technology to cater to these sorts of traumatic conditions for the co-lifestyles of IoT, WSN, 5G, and beyond-5G networks The outcome is that law implementation automatic professionals have to inspect advanced radio hardware. There are techniques of getting the facts from this hardware; besides, it is predicated upon the benevolent of system if and how this should be feasible. Genera is shifting toward included gadgets, so it is not out of the normal that extra regularly radio correspondence hardware joined with smart telephones may be skilled at crime places.

Acknowledgement

We are grateful to Vivekananda Institute of Professional Studies, Delhi, India, for providing us infrastructure and laboratories to finish our research.

References

1. Ali, A., Abbas, L. *et al.*, "Hybrid fuzzy logic scheme for efficient channel utilization in cognitive radio networks". *IEEE Access*, 7, 24463–24476, 2019.
2. Ali, A. *et al.*, "RaptorQ-based efficient multimedia transmission over cooperative cellular cognitive radio networks,". *IEEE Trans. Veh. Technol.*, 67, 8, 7275–7289, Aug. 2018.
3. So, J. and Srikant, R., "Improving channel utilization via cooperative spectrum sensing with opportunistic feedback in cognitive radio networks". *IEEE Commun. Lett.*, 19, 6, 1065–1068, 2015.
4. Wyglinski, A.M. *et al.*, *"Cognitive Radio Communications and Networks: Principles and Practice"*, Academic Press, USA, 2009.
5. Zhang, D. *et al.*, "Energy-harvesting-aided spectrum sensing and data transmission in heterogeneous cognitive radio sensor network". *IEEE Trans. Veh. Technol.*, 66, 1, 831–843, 2016.
6. Abdalzaher, M.S., Seddik, K., Muta, O., Using Stackelberg game to enhance cognitive radio sensor networks security. *IET Commun.*, 11, 9, 1503–1511, 2017.
7. Zeng, B., Zhang, C., Hu, P., Wang, S., "Spectrum sharing based on a Bertrand game in cognitive radio sensor networks". *Sensors*, 17, 1, 101, 2017.
8. Byun, S.S. and Gil, J.M., "Fair Dynamic spectrum allocation using modified game theory for resource constrained cognitive wireless sensor networks". *Symmetry*, 9, 5, 73, 2017.
9. Sucasas, V. *et al.*, "A survey on clustering techniques for cooperative wireless networks". *Ad Hoc Netw.*, 47, 53–81, 2016.
10. Lindsey, S. and Raghavendra, C.S., "PEGASIS: Power-efficient gathering in sensor information systems", in: *Proceedings, IEEE aerospace conference*, vol. 3, IEEE, pp. 3–3, 2002.
11. Veyseh, M., Wei, B., Mir, N.F., "An energy-efficient decentralized clustering protocol for wireless sensor networks", in: *Proc. 5th WSEAS Int. Conf. Telecommun. Informat*, pp. 293–298, 2006, May.
12. Xu, J., Jin, N. *et al.*, "Improvement of LEACH protocol for WSN", in: *2012 9th International Conference on Fuzzy Systems and Knowledge Discovery*, IEEE, pp. 2174–2177, 2012, May.
13. Kumar, D., Aseri, T.C., Patel, R.B., "EEHC: Energy efficient heterogeneous clustered scheme for wireless sensor networks". *Comput. Commun.*, 32, 4, 662–667, 2009.
14. Dabas, P. and Gupta, N., "LEACH and its Improved Versions-A Survey". *Int. J. Sci. Eng. Res.*, 6, 184–188, 2015.
15. Joshi, G.P. and Kim, S.W., "A survey on node clustering in cognitive radio wireless sensor networks". *Sensors*, 16, 1465, 2016.
16. Tang, S., Trautman, A., Nguyen, H., "On Energy-Based Quality of Detection (QoD) for Cognitive Radio Sensor Networks,". *Int. J. Wirel. Inf. Netw.*, 23, 3, 214–221, Jun. 2016.

17. Whig, P. and Ahmad, S.N., "Simulation of Linear Dynamic Macro Model of Photo Catalytic Sensor in SPICE", in: *Compel, the International Journal of Computation and Mathematics in Electrical and Electronic Engineering*, vol. 33, 2014.
18. Byun, S.S. *et al.*, "Fair Dynamic spectrum allocation using modified game theory for resource-constrained cognitive wireless sensor networks". *Symmetry*, 9, 5, 73, 2017.
19. Byu, S.S. and Gil, J.M., "Fair Dynamic spectrum allocation using modified game theory for resource constrained cognitive wireless sensor networks". *Symmetry*, 9, 5, 73, 2017.
20. Liu, A., Chen, W., Liu, X., "Delay optimal opportunistic pipeline routing scheme for cognitive radio sensor networks". *Int. J. Distrib. Sens. Netw.*, 14, 4, 1550147718772532, 2018.
21. Zheng, M., Chen, S., Liang, W., Song, M., "NSAC: A Novel Clustering Protocol in Cognitive Radio Sensor Networks for Internet of Things". *IEEE Internet Things J.*, 6, 3, 5864–5865, 2019.
22. Idoudi, H., Mabrouk, O., Minet, P., Saidane, L.A., "Cluster-based scheduling for cognitive radio sensor networks". *J. Ambient Intell. Humaniz. Comput.*, 10, 2, 477–489, 7, 109555–109565. 2019.
23. Wang, T., Guan, X., Wan, X., Shen, H., & Zhu, X. A spectrum-aware clustering algorithm based on weighted clustering metric in cognitive radio sensor networks. *IEEE Access,* 7, 109555–109565, 2019.
24. Shah, S.B., Chen, Z., Yin, F., Khan, I.U., Ahmad, N., "Energy and interoperable aware routing for throughput optimization in clustered IoT-wireless sensor networks". *Future Gener. Comp. Sy.*, 81, 372–381, 2018.
25. El Fissaoui, M., Beni-Hssane, A., Saadi, M., "Energy efficient and fault tolerant distributed algorithm for data aggregation in wireless sensor networks". *J. Ambient Intell. Humaniz. Comput.*, 10, 2, 569–578, 2019.
26. Carie, A., Li, M., Marapelli, B., Reddy, P., Dino, H., Gohar, M., Cognitive radio assisted WSN with interference aware AODV routing protocol. *J. Ambient Intell. Humaniz. Comput.*, 10, 10, 4033–4042, 2019.
27. Raymond, J.W., Olwal, T.O., Kurien, A.M., "Cooperative communications in machine to machine (M2M): solutions, challenges and future work". *IEEE Access*, 6, 9750–976, 2018.
28. Tyson, B. M. A Trust-Based Relay Selection Approach to the Multi-Hop Network Formation Problem in Cognitive Radio Networks, 2015. https://www.semanticscholar.org/paper/A-Trust-Based-Relay-Selection-Approach-to-the-in-Tyson/bbcdf0a664a0b56b70922a65b34f0d940e407012
29. Nadikattu, R.R. *et al.*, "Novel Economical Social Distancing Smart Device for Covid19". *Int. J. Electr. Eng. Technol.*, 11, 4, 204–217, 2020.
30. Nadikattu, R. R., "Information Technologies: Rebooting the World ActivitiesduringCOVID-19", June 9, 2020. https://papers.ssrn.com/sol3/papers.cfm?abstract_id=3622733

31. Whig, P. and Ahmad, S.N., "Simulation of Linear Dynamic Macro Model of Photo Catalytic Sensor in SPICE", in: *Compel, The International Journal of Computation and Mathematics in Electrical and Electronic Engineering*, vol. 33, 2014.
32. Bhatia, V. and Whig, P., "A secured dual tune multi frequency based smart elevator control system,". *Int. J. Res. Eng. Advanced Technol.*, 4, 1, 2319–1163, 2013.
33. Whig, P. and Ahmad, S.N., A Novel Pseudo NMOS Integrated ISFET device for water quality monitoring. *Active Passive Components*, Hindawi article i.d 258970. 1, 1, 1–14, 2013(Scopus).
34. Bhatia, V. and Whig, P., "Modeling and Simulation of Electrical Load Control System Using RF Technology". *Int. J. Multidisp. Sci. Engineer.*, 4, 2, 44–47, 2013.
35. Whig, P. and Ahmad, S.N., "Development of Economical ASIC For PCS For Water Quality Monitoring". *J. Circuit Syst. Comput.*, 23, 6, 1–13, 2014.
36. Shaikh, F.K. and Zeadally, S., "Energy harvesting in wireless sensor networks: A comprehensive review". *Renew. Sust. Energ. Rev.*, 55, 1041–54, 2016 Mar 1.
37. Raza, M., Aslam, N., Le-Minh, H., Hussain, S., Cao, Y., Khan, N.M., "A critical analysis of research potential, challenges, and future directives in industrial wireless sensor networks". *IEEE Commun. Surv. Tut.*, 20, 1, 39–95, 2017 Oct 4.
38. Görgü, L., Kroon, B., O'Grady, M.J., Yılmaz, Ö., O'Hare, G.M., "Sensor discovery in ambient IoT ecosystems". *J. Ambient Intell. Humaniz. Comput.*, 9, 447–458, 2018.
39. Carie, A., Li, M., Marapelli, B., Redd, P., Dino, H., Gohar, M., "Cognitive radio assisted WSN with interference aware AODV routing protocol". *J. Ambient Intell. Humaniz. Comput.*, 3, 1–10, 2019.
40. Akan, O.B., Karli, O.B., Ergul, O., "Cognitive radio sensor networks". *IEEE Netw.*, 23, 4, 34–40, 2009 Aug 4.
41. Ali, A. and Hamouda, W., "Advances on spectrum sensing for cognitive radio networks: Theory and applications". *IEEE Commun. Surv. Tut.*, 19, 2, 1277–304, 2016 Nov 18.
42. Darsena, D., Gelli, G., Verde, F., "An opportunistic spectrum access scheme for multicarrier cognitive sensornetworks". *IEEE Sens. J.*, 17, 8, 2596–606, 2017 Apr 15.
43. Mohjazi, L., Dianati, M., Karagiannidis, G.K., Muhaidat, S., AlQutayri, M., "RF-powered cognitive radio networks: Technical challenges and limitations". *IEEE Commun. Mag.*, 53, 94–100, April 2015.
44. Mikeka, C. and Arai, H., "Design issues in radio frequency energy harvesting system", in: *Sustainable Energy Harvesting TechnologiesPast, Present and Future*, pp. 235–256, InTech, 2011. https://cdn.intechopen.com/pdfs/25376/InTech-Design_issues_in_radio_frequency_energy_harvesting_system.pdf
45. Sudevalayam, S. and Kulkarni, P., "Energy harvesting sensor nodes: Survey and implications". *IEEE Commun. Surv. Tut.*, 13, 443–461, July 2010.

46. Lu, X., Wang, P., Niyato, D., Kim, D., II, Han, Z., "Wireless networks with RF energy harvesting: A contemporary survey". *IEEE Commun. Surv. Tut.*, 1, 757–789, November 2014.
47. Singla, J., Mahajan, R., Bagai, D., A Survey on Energy Harvesting Cognitive Radio Networks, in: *2018 6th Edition of International Conference on Wireless Networks & Embedded Systems (WECON)*, IEEE, pp. 6–10, 2018, November.
48. Bhowmick, A., Roy, S., Kundu, S., "Throughput of a cognitive radio network with energy-harvesting based on primary user signal". *IEEE Wirel. Commun. Lett.*, 5, 2, 136–139, Apr. 2016.
49. Gao, Y., He, H., Deng, Z., Zhang, X., Cognitive radio network with energy-harvesting based on primary and secondary user signals. *IEEE Access, 6*, 9081–9090, 2018.
50. Shafie, A.E., Ashour, M., Khattab, T., Mohamed, A., "On spectrum sharing between energy harvesting cognitive radio users and primary users". in: *Proc. Int. Conf. Comput., Netw. Commun*, Garden Grove, CA, USA, pp. 214–220, 2015.
51. Nguyen, V.T., Villain, F., Guillou, Y.L., "Cognitive Radio RF: Overview and Challenges", in: *VLSI Design*, vol. 2012, ArticleID 716476, p. 13 pages, 2012, https://doi.org/10.1155/2012/716476.

13

Fingerprint Image Identification System: An Asset for Security of Bank Lockers

Mahendra, Apoorva, Shyam, Pavan and Harpreet Bedi*

SEEE, Lovely Professional University, Punjab, India

Abstract

In the discipline of biometric authentication, fingerprints are the most widely prescribed biometric feature for individual identification and verification. The implementation of a based method to fingerprint recognition and verification of the fingerprint image collected at the bank is presented in this chapter. *The fingerprint-based bank locker system is a step forward from the traditional key-operated bank locker system. Thefts who are aware of this can now quickly copy and make keys. Furthermore, the keys must be handled with care and may be misplaced due to carelessness. A fingerprint-based bank locker scheme, on the other hand, is here to solve these problems.*

***Keywords*:** Biometric fingerprint sensor, bank locker security system

13.1 Introduction

Security is a major concern, and in today's hectic and competitive environment, people are unable to notice ways to manually secure their sensitive personal belongings. Instead, one discovers an alternative that can provide maximum protection while remaining globalized.

Individuals may readily access their information at any time in today's global network society [1], and from any place, there is also the possibility that others may be able to access similar information at the same

**Corresponding author*: harpreet.17377@lpu.co.in

Anita Gehlot, Rajesh Singh, Jaskaran Singh and Neeta Raj Sharma (eds.) Digital Forensics and Internet of Things: Impact and Challenges, (227–236) © 2022 Scrivener Publishing LLC

time and from the same location. This technology, which can differentiate between existing users and fraudsters, is now catching everyone's attention due to the possibility of personal identity being exposed. The fingerprint-based bank locker system is safe as well as simple to use and maintain. You will not have to deal with keys, and you would not have to worry about losing them [2]. The machine reads the person's fingerprints with a fingerprint sensor and then stores the recorded fingerprints against bank locker records or in a separate record or cloud dedicated to fingerprints. If current prints match, then microcontroller receives a signal which displays the data on the LCD monitor. For approved customers, the controller also tells the motor driver to open the bank locker door. Customers who are not allowed to open locker doors will be denied access [3].

Passwords, which are four-digit PIN numbers and identification cards, are currently used for private authentication. Identities and data filled are frequently estimated, whereas cards are frequently stolen. Biometric identification technology, which recognizes individuals based on their specific biological details, is gaining traction as a solution to these issues [4].

Biometrics is described as the process of recognizing and identifying a physiological or behavioral characteristic that is unique to an individual. Biometric identification entails storing a database of the microcontroller receives a signal from the account holder's physical characteristics or actions (habits) and comparing them to someone Others may attempt to somehow get access to the account to evaluate if the request is real [5]. Fujitsu has specialized in biometric recognition technology such as fingerprints, ears, and voiceprints.

Many methods are still in the development and estimation stages. Among the available biometric characteristics, fingerprints prove to be one of the simplest, with a low mismatch ratio, high security accuracy, and dependability [6]. This scenario for working in a bank locker involves locks and keys (Figure 13.1). We cannot say that we are providing adequate protection for our lockers because of this. We are using two separate technologies, embedded systems, and biometrics, to provide perfect protection and make our work easier [7]. Microcontrollers or optical signal processors are used as computing cores in embedded systems (DSP). The most important trait, though, is being committed to completing a particular mission.

Fingerprints are one-of-a-kind and unlike everyone else and using them will increase security. This protection system can be used by people who are illiterate. The user spends less time operating this tool.

For engineering purposes, Arduino is very common these days. Arduino can also be used for coding work because it allows us to add software programming and run our programs.

The motor that is used which allows to rotate or precise angular or linear position, speed, and acceleration control.

A 16 × 2 LCD is a liquid crystal display module that produces a visible display. It shows 16 characters per line, and there are two lines in total, so it shows 32 characters at once.

For the power supply, we used a Step-Down Transformer that has been controlled to 12 V.

Block Diagram

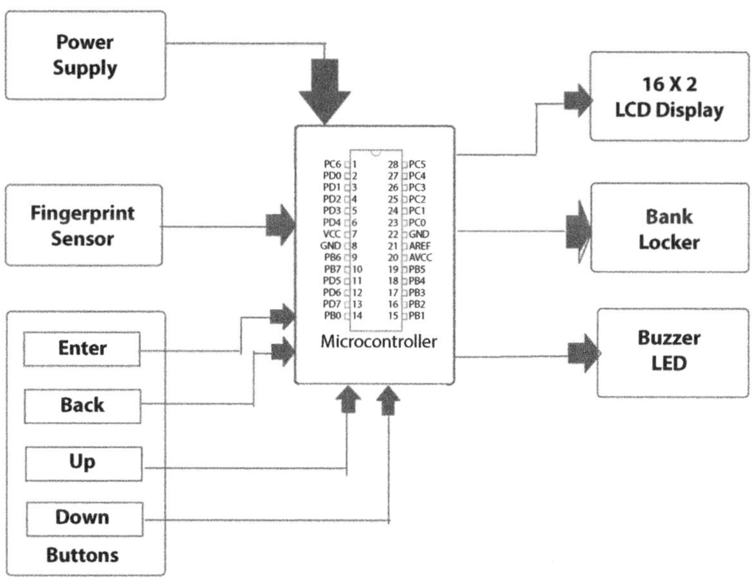

Figure 13.1 Block diagram.

13.1.1 Design Analysis

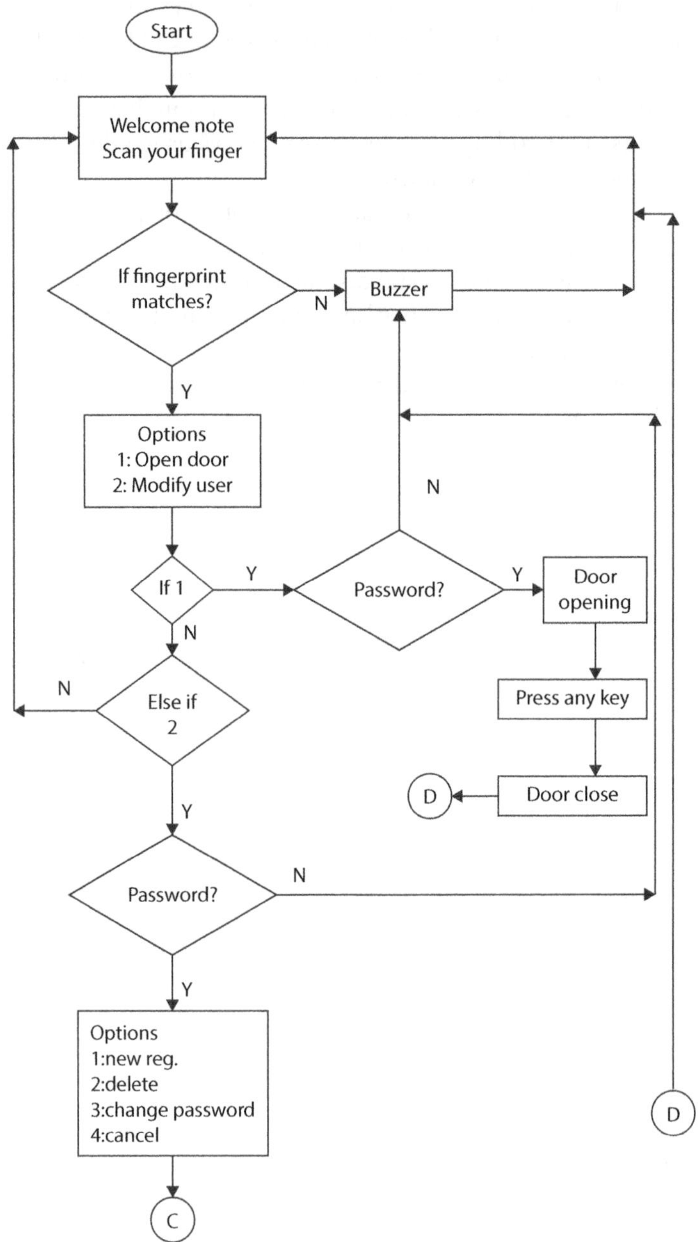

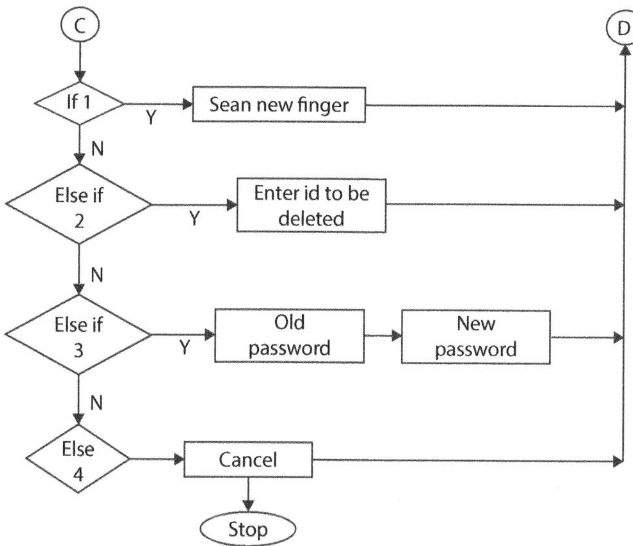

In an automated fingerprint recognition scheme, image enhancement and minutiae matching are two crucial stages (Figure 13.2). Fingerprint identification depends on the impression left by minute ridge formations or patterns on the fingertips to identify people. Nobody's ridge pattern composition is the same, and no one's pattern varies over time [8].

Feature extraction for a high-quality fingerprint is much faster, more precise, and reliable than for a lower-quality fingerprint [9]. Skin conditions (e.g., damp or dry, cuts, and bruises), sensor noise, non-uniform contact with the sensor surface, and generally poor-quality fingerprint images all degrade fingerprint quality (e.g., those of the elderly and laborers).

Isolated areas of distinct and continuous ridge detail may appear in a single finger impression, but there is insufficient detail to make an exclusion or identity inference, as shown in Table 13.1. If the areas between these areas can be clarified in a way that maintains the ridges' continuity, then a significant opinion that would not have been possible otherwise can be created.

13.2 Result and Discussion

A false match occurs when images from two different fingers match, and a false non-match occurs when images from the same finger do not match. As a result, a successful fingerprint matching system's main goal is to reduce each of these errors as shown in Figure 13.3. However, since both

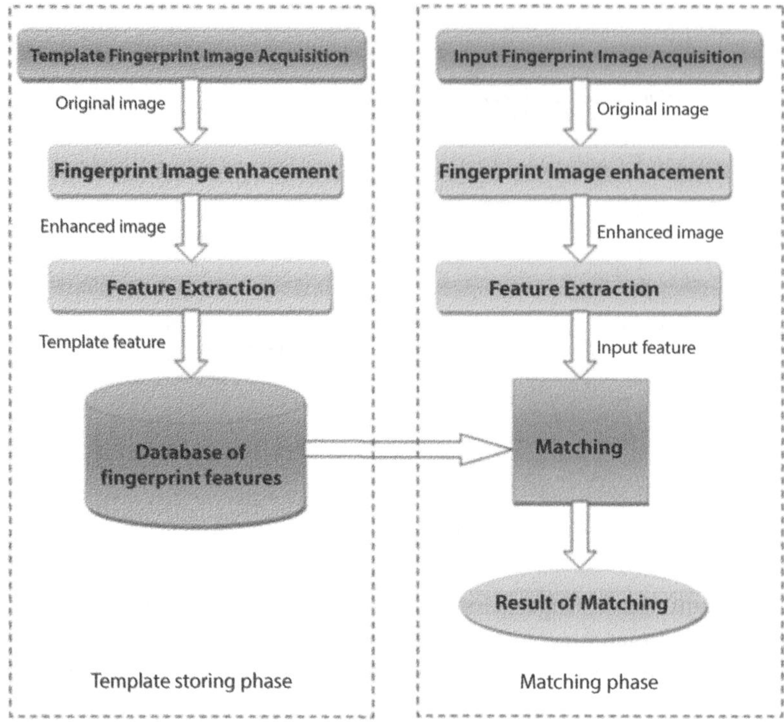

Figure 13.2 Fingerprint pattern recognition.

error rates are inversely related, they cannot be minimized at the same time. Another significant design consideration is the fingerprint recognition system's protection, as well as the fingerprint template database security. Unauthorized access to or disclosure of fingerprint template data from such databases poses a significant security and privacy risk, as shown in Figure 13.4. This biometric bank locker system has many advantages over conventional locking systems, making it indispensable. This locker device is very user-friendly.

13.3 Conclusion

Authentication of fingerprints has been practiced for over a century. However, thanks to the advancement of automated fingerprint recognition systems, its use has only recently become widespread and mainstream. We have developed a biometric-based locker that provides a high level of protection. The locker will be inaccessible to any registered person.

Table 13.1 The physical state, liveness detection, and resolution of current fingerprint sensors.

Technology	Outer physics	Flexible physics	Liveness detection	Resolution [R]	Limitations
Optical	Solid	No	No	R < −600 dpi and 1,000 dpi possible	Optical focusing and alignment mechanism size
Capacitive	Solid	No	No	R < 600 dpi	ESD protection, poor performance for damaged and dry skin
Thermal	Solid	No	No	R < 600 dpi	Environment-dependent, need training, more power consumption
Pressure (piezo electric)	Solid	No	No	R < 600 dpi	Less sensitive, protective layer reduces the quality of images
Radio frequency	Solid	No	Possible	R < 600 dpi	Low accuracy with dry fingers
Ultrasonic	Solid	No	Possible	R < 600 dpi	large size, cost, more time, 10 acquire images
Micro-Electro-Mechanical Systems	Solid	Possible	No	R < 600 dpi	Not particularly for fingerprint sensing

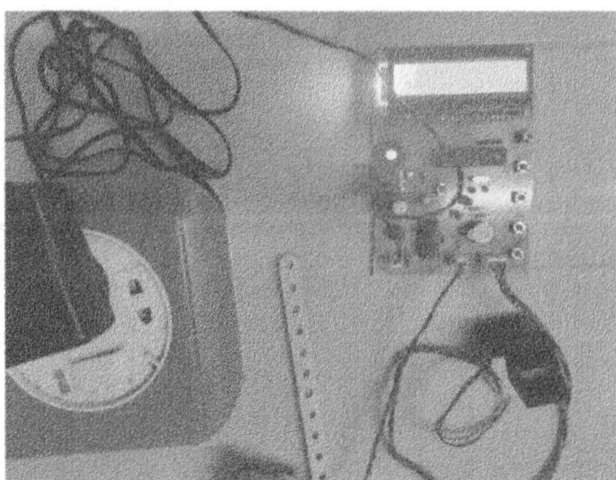

Figure 13.3 Working of the circuit.

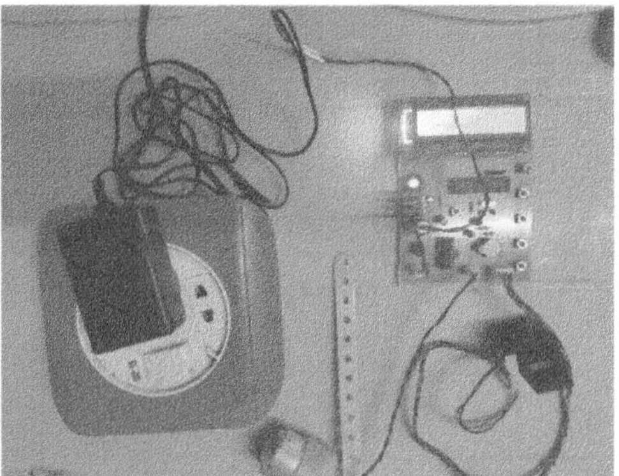

Figure 13.4 Finger print do not matched.

We use fingerprints because replication of a fingerprint is impossible to verify. The system is reasonable and straightforward to use. This technique is often mounted anywhere, where you would like high degree of security. This locker system is extremely reliable and safe. The paper also provides a description of the various steps involved in developing fingerprint-based individual identification.

13.4 Future Scope

For well over a century, people have been researching fingerprint authentication. Due to the advancement of automated fingerprint recognition systems, its use has only recently become widespread and popular. Biometric systems will be used in bikes for antitheft systems; this biometric system can be used in bike locking and to start the bike's engine to provide an improvement in car biometric systems are often implemented, which is a great idea for starting the car and running it so that only the car's owner can drive it. Retina scanners are often used in place of fingerprint scanners.

References

1. Takeda, M. and Uchida, S., *Finger Image Identification Method for Personal Verification*, IEEE, CH2898-5/90/0000/0761$01, 1990.
2. Afsar, F.A., Arif, M., Hussain, M., Fingerprint Identification and Verification System using Minutiae Matching. *National Conference on Emerging Technologies*, 2004.
3. Ratha, N.K., Karu, K., Chen, S., Jain, A.K., "A real-time matching system for large fingerprint databases,". *IEEE Trans. Pattern Anal. Mach. Intell.*, 18, 8, 779–813, Aug.1996.
4. Jain, A.K. and Hong, L., "Online fingerprint verification,". *IEEE Trans. Pattern Anal. Mach. Intell.*, 19, 4, 302–341, Apr.1997.
5. Kumar, A. and Zhang, D., "Combining fingerprint, palmprint and hand-shape for user authentication", in: *Pattern Recognition, ICPR 2006. 18th International Conference on*, vol. 4, IEEE, pp. 549–552, 2006.
6. Zhao, F. and Tang, X., Preprocessing and post processing for skeleton-based fingerprint minutiae extraction. *Pattern Recognit.*, 40, 2007, 1270–1281, 2007.
7. Ruili, J. and Jing, F., "VC5509 A Based Fingerprint Identification Preprocessing System,". *International Conference on Signal Processing*, pp. 2859–2863, 2008.
8. Yun, E.K. and Cho, S.B., "Adaptive Fingerprint Image Enhancement with Fingerprint Image Quality Analysis,". *International Conference of Image and Vision Computing*, pp. 101–110, 2006.
9. Dhameliy, M. D., and Chaudhar, J. P., A Multimodal Biometric Recognition System Based on Fusion of Palmprint and Fingerprint. *International Journal of Engineering Trends and Technology (IJETT).* V4(5):1908–1911, May 2013.

14

IoT Forensics: Interconnection and Sensing Frameworks

Nidhi Sagarwal

Lovely Professional University, Jalandhar - Delhi, Grand Trunk Rd, Phagwara, Punjab, India

Abstract

This chapter begins by talking briefly about the history and vast application of Internet of Things devices in various fields such as medicine, agriculture, hotel industry, surveillance, and military.

The chapter then sheds light on various investigative models, frameworks, and protocols used by digital forensic investigators (DFIs) around the world. The field of IoT forensics is dynamic and developing every day. But most DFIs lack the required technical knowledge to deal with the cases when such need arises. Also, the manufacturing standards of the IoT devices vary from manufacturer to manufacturer. Therefore, researchers and experts are constantly working together to come up with an investigative framework that could be used as a standard of operation. Some of those frameworks have been discussed further in the chapter.

Keywords: Internet of Things (IoT), framework, investigation, protocols, forensics

14.1 Introduction

In the past decade, IoT devices have become a common household name due to their affordability and features. They have made our lives easier by assisting us in performing a variety of tasks ranging from simpler tasks to seemingly complex tasks. Ever since the term was popularized by Gartner's IT Hype Cycle in 2011 [1], the number of IoT devices across the globe has

Email: nidhi.11816304@lpu.in

Anita Gehlot, Rajesh Singh, Jaskaran Singh and Neeta Raj Sharma (eds.) Digital Forensics and Internet of Things: Impact and Challenges, (237–254) © 2022 Scrivener Publishing LLC

increased from 800 million in 2010 to 11.7 billion in 2020 [2]. As per the updated forecasts by IoT Analytics, it is expected to cross the 30bn mark by 2025 [2]. A market survey report by Mordor Intelligence estimates the global IoT market to grow by a CAGR of 10.5% during 2021-26 [3].

The Internet of Things (IoT) as a term did not exist until 1999 when Kevin Ashton coined the expression to describe a network that serves as a connecting link between physical world and digital world [4]. However, the idea that led to IoT dates back to the 1970s when it was called "embedded internet" [5]. The term gained popularity around 2011 after Gartner report listed the IoT as one of the new emerging technologies [1]. Next year, IoT became the theme for one of the prestigious internet conferences in Europe—the LeWeb. But it was not until January 2014 that the market gain mass awareness about IoT when Google bought Nest [5].

Many experts and researchers have tried to explain and define IoT based on their understanding. Atzori *et al.* [6] defined the IoT as a paradigm which emanates by the union of three viewpoints. These were *things-oriented* visions such as RFID and UID; *internet-oriented* visions such as IP for smart objects (IPSO), internet, and web of things; and *semantic-oriented* visions such as semantic technologies and smart semantic middleware. Gubbi *et al.* [7] attempted to give a more user-centric definition by not limiting it to any standard communication protocol and defined IoT as follows:

"Interconnection of sensing and actuating devices providing the ability to share information across platforms through a unified framework, developing a common operating picture for enabling innovative applications [7]."

An IEEE project on IoT, IEEE P2413, considers IoT architecture as a three-layered structure containing application layer, networking and data communication layer, and sensing layer [8].

According to McKinsey report, IoT is a system of interconnected sensors and actuators which often communicate through the same Internet Protocol [9]. Similarly, the Gartner report, 2017 defines IoT as a network of specialized physical items that include embedded technology to communicate, perceive, or interact with their internal states or the external environment [1].

Therefore, a simplistic definition of the IoT could be that it is a system of physical devices connected through the internet that use sensors, software, and other related technologies to connect to or transmit data to another device or network. Sometimes, it is entirely automated, while some other times, it is conditional.

Some common examples of IoT devices include *wearable devices* such as smartwatches and fitness trackers; *smart appliances* such as Google Home,

Amazon Echo, Smart LEDs, and Smoke and CO detectors; *digital assistants* such as Siri, Alexa, and Google assistant; and *home assistants* [10–12].

The International Telecommunication Union (ITU) has classified IoT devices into four categories based on their functionality. These are general device, data storage device, data capturing device, and sensing and actuating device [13].

Based on their application in various fields, IoT devices can be classified into following categories [14]:

- Consumer IoT includes IoT devices most commonly used for consumer usage such as smartphones, smart appliances, wearables and hearables, fitness trackers, voice assistant, and smart lighting [10, 11].
- Industrial IoT (IIoT), on the other hand, includes IoT devices used for manufacturing, supply chain monitoring, and management systems such as smart grid, smart city, smart agriculture, robotics, smart communication, and smart power [14, 15].
- Commercial IoT includes smart pacemakers, medical sensors, health monitoring systems, and smart cars [14].
- Infrastructure IoT includes smart cities, management systems, and security systems.
- Internet of Military Things (IoMT) includes application of IoT in military and warfare. It offers services such as surveillance devices, biometric cybersecurity scanners, and secure information exchange between units [16, 17].

IoT devices have tons of applications in a vast majority of fields. IoT devices are not meant to be a replacement for medical diagnosis but they have surely made people stay alert and aware of their health. The wearable IoT devices collect and record data that such as sleep pattern, heart activity, O_2 level, stress level, calories spent, and fitness activity. It was only last year in October 2020, when the ECG feature of Apple watch saved a man's life by sending him alerts for irregular heart activity [18]. In healthcare industry, IoT devices help in monitoring patient health remotely, tracking treatment progress, and helping doctors with diagnosing medical condition by transmitting any such user data directly to them that is deviation from norm.

Some other applications of IoT include health monitoring, traffic management, automated irrigation system, crop health, soil temperature and pH monitoring in agriculture, grid management and energy saving, automated check-in and check-out, room services, and digital room keys, in hospitality industry [19, 20].

A close look at the history and growth of IoT reveals that it has huge potential in the forthcoming years as well. While IoT devices gained popularity among the masses due to simplicity of their use and manufacturers quickly responded the demands of the market, attacks saw an easy way in to steal the information from their potential targets. Since the devices are connected to a common Wi-Fi network, the amount of data at risk is huge. According to an estimate by Cybersecurity Ventures [21], there will be approximately 200 zettabytes data on the internet by 2025. It includes data stored in private and public infrastructure, private and public clouds, personal devices along with data stored on IoT. Therefore, it is crucial for the digital crime investigator to understand the challenges of the field and thereby plan and execute the investigation in such a way that the criminal can be arrested and brought to justice.

14.2 The Need for IoT Forensics

The market for IoT devices is huge. There is no doubt that IoT devices have made human lives easier. It has made life changing contribution to various fields such as lifestyle, medicine, agriculture, smart home systems, management systems, business models, military and security, and defense. While it has increased productivity of individuals and businesses as well, it also has some cons such as privacy and security issues, loss of jobs, and over-reliance on technology [22, 23]. While all these features strive to offer best experience to the user on one hand, they also open a can of worms for the investigator to deal with. There is no uniformity in IoT devices at architectural level. Due to this reason and lack of standardized definition and protocols in place, IoT forensics is a problematic issue. If these diverse issues can be addressed, data stored in IoT devices could be a rich source of evidence [24].

There are several options available from different brands based on usage, functionality, and budget. IoT devices generally constitute of four components: sensors or actuators, connectivity component, data processing/storage component, and user interface. While the basic components of IoT devices remain the same, different companies use their own dedicated operating systems, software, data sharing and storage system, and encryption system integrated with hardware.

Based on their usage, functionality, and design, IoT devices have different hardware and software configuration. The way in which an IoT connects to and shares data with the hardware, whether to cloud or to device memory, has significant bearing in the type of forensic data which is generated. Each company uses a software well-integrated to its hardware. They use various technologies to store and protect data generated by IoT device. Traces recovered from IoT devices include location, temperature, movement, step count, distance walked, calories spent, device configuration settings, camera configuration settings, time-stamped logs of events when camera turned on in case of a motion sensing camera, network log, event log, and Wi-Fi passwords [25, 26].

The evidence in digital forensics investigation is sensitive. One misstep and the evidentiary value is lost. Therefore, digital evidence needs to be acquired and analysed in such a way that its integrity is not lost. Some of the common issues involve the vast amount of information that IoT devices generate. Since they are always online, they are constantly generating and updating data which in some cases they periodically sync to the cloud. This results in a huge amount of data, which makes it difficult for the investigator to find information relevant to his investigation. The investigative process is complex and requires specialized knowledge. Some of this data acquired by the investigator require dedicated plugins with the script written in Python to interpret the data [25, 27]. It only complicates the job of an investigator because to carry on the investigation, he must be able to understand and be able to code in Python. Some other issues include legal issues and jurisdictional problems. An assortment of IoT devices is available to consumers, and he can choose based on his requirements and the features being offered. But the problem here is that the manufacturers are compromising on the device and data security and focusing only on giving more and more features. It becomes especially challenging considering the vast application of IoT devices in public and private sectors, government and private offices and offices and our homes. End-to-end encryption is one of the solutions against IoT breaches. Some other solutions include traditional measures such as firewall, antivirus, malware protection, two-factor authentication (2FA), digital certificates, encryption using cryptographic algorithms, and secured companion apps for IoT devices [28, 29]. The ultimate challenge in IoT forensics is to choose between the success of the investigation or the privacy of the user.

Because of the diverse nature of the digital devices, there cannot be a "*one size fits all*" approach. However, a forensic investigative framework has some basic requirements, which are as follows:

- The framework should be structured.
- The standard operating procedures (SOPs) should take practical problems into consideration. Ideally, they should

be made by a group of individuals who have experience in dealing with diverse nature of cases encountered [30].

- The evidence should be extracted and collected for further analysis in a forensically sound manner and its integrity must be maintained.
- Blockchain-based solutions may be employed to maintain evidence integrity and prevent any accidental mishaps which may result in losing the data, making changes to it or compromising the evidence in some manner [31–35].
- The forensic process should not compromise on user's security.

14.3 Various Types of Evidences Encountered

Cloud: Database generated by IoT companion application, login credentials, etc. [25, 27, 37].

Device: File system images, memory dump, factory settings, user configuration, system logs, etc., can be recovered from device. The device memory and file system may be accessed using serial connections such as UART and JTAG [25]. Apart from this, IoT companion application may save data such as configuration files, cached images, and data based on device locally. Additionally, login credentials may be recovered from app and may be used to acquire data from cloud. However, a legal authorization is required to access that data beforehand [36, 37].

Network: IoT devices generate data when they communicate with the network such as login requests and time when sensors were activated or disabled. It contains all the log data and network logs [25, 27, 37].

14.4 Protocols and Frameworks in IoT Forensics

Digital forensics is the branch of forensic science concerned with recovery and analysis of digital device. Digital forensics is based on digital data obtained by scientifically accepted methods of data acquisition and validated tools. The principal aim of digital forensics is to effectively convict criminals by providing forensically sound evidence before the court.

EC Council defines digital forensics as "*the process of identifying, preserving, analyzing, and documenting digital evidence*" [38]. While NIST SP 800-86 document [39] goes further and specifies that the integrity of data should be preserved and strict chain of custody should be maintained through the entire process.

In digital forensic investigations, there is certain number of steps that should be performed in the specified order from the original incident till the reporting of findings [40]. These steps are based on recognized scientific principles and well-established forensic practices. The entire process is called a digital forensic process. The increasing number of cases, the complexity of the cases encountered, vast variety of devices available, cloud storage, encrypted devices, etc., have made it mandatory to have standardized framework which can serve as a guide for digital forensics investigation and expedite the entire process. The following two models are predominantly used in digital forensics investigation and help in developing a better understanding of the digital forensic process.

McKemmish's model: McKemmish described digital forensics as "*the process of identifying, preserving, analyzing, and presenting digital evidence in a manner that is legally acceptable*" [27, 41]. There were four stages to the digital forensic model proposed by McKemmish, which were *identification* (related to identifying the location of evidence), *preservation* (preserving the integrity of the evidence), *analysis* (associated with extraction, processing, and interpretation of digital evidence), and *presentation* (process how evidence was gathered and the final report with the findings) [27, 41].

Kent *et al.* The digital forensic model proposed by Kent *et al.* [42] also had four stages which were collection (associated with identification, preservation, and acquisition of evidence), examination (manual and automated tools to extract data relevant to case), analysis (findings based on data previously extracted), and reporting (associated with preparation of report and presenting the findings) [27].

14.5 IoT Forensics Process Model

Researchers have previously proposed that IoT forensics take place with specialized frameworks in which the traces are retrieved efficiently and effectively from devices and the network in which incident took place must be available for analysis [43].

To address the challenges faced by investigators in IoT forensics, the research community has proposed few conceptual models and frameworks. Some of these models are just theoretical in nature and require focused research.

1. Next Best Thing (NBT) Triage Model
The Next Best Thing (NBT) triage model [44] was proposed by Oriwoh *et al.* It is based on the 1-2-3 zones of digital forensic process model. Evidence extraction can be done either in a zone-specific manner or in isolation depending on the nature of investigation. Since IoT devices, data stored on them, or accessible through them may be compromised or become unavailable, it is crucial for an investigator to be able to identify those elements of data which are of evidentiary value. The NBT triage model helps the investigator during identification phase to determine potential sources of evidence.
2. Building Information Modeling
The National BIM Standards [45] suggested a potential solution to identification of data. The integration of IoT device data with Building Information Modeling (2013) helped with identification of relevant evidence. It used the information about the IoT capabilities (physical and functional) of a structure and answer questions as to origin of data, how it is stored and location where it is stored. This, in turn, helped in narrowing down the scope of investigation by weeding out the data which was not relevant to the scope [27].
3. Forensics Edge Management System
Oriwoh and Sant [46] proposed a four-stage *Forensics Edge Management System* that was used to automate security and conduct preliminary forensic services in home-based IoT. In FEMS, the researchers suggested a three-level system architecture approach consisting of perception, network, and application layer. The FEMS security services include features such as standard network monitoring, intrusion detection and deterrence, data categorization and creation of threshold. The FEMS system would temporarily collect and store the data for a specified time. If any data passing from the FEMS system triggers an event, then the FEMS system goes into forensic mode and makes a note of the occurrence. Any data after that point would be relevant to the investigation. The FEMS forensic services include data compression and parsing, creating timeline of relevant events, alerting, preparation and presentation of results, and storage.
4. Forensics-Aware IoT (FAIoT) Model
Zawaod and Hassan were first to give a working definition of IoT forensics [47]. They identified IoT forensics as a specialized branch of digital forensics comprising of network forensics, device level forensics, and cloud forensics. They defined IoT forensics as a collective process of identification, collection, organization, and presentation dealing with IoT infrastructures to gather information about an IoT related crime.

They proposed forensics-aware IoT model to assist the investigators to conduct forensically sound investigations in an IoT environment. FAIoT model had a centralized evidence repository combined with evidence preservation module and provenance module. The researchers proposed the use of Hadoop Distributed File System (HDFS) which made the centralized evidence repository even more secure. This evidence repository could be accessed by the investigator only through a read-only API [47]. This study laid the groundwork for the IoT forensic area and a distinguished investigative model for procuring artefacts that may prove useful as evidence.

5. Digital Forensic Investigation Framework for the Internet of Things (DFIF-IoT)

Kebande and Ray in 2016 proposed Digital Forensic Investigation Framework for the Internet of Things (DFIF-IoT) [48, 49]. This framework was in compliance with ISO/IEC 27043:2015 [50] for IT, security approaches, and the concepts and procedures for incident investigation. It contains three modules: proactive processes, IoT forensics, and reactive processes. It was later found to be too generic, and hence, its effectiveness could not be tested [48, 49].

6. Privacy-Aware IoT Model (PRoFIT)

The Privacy-Aware IoT model (PRoFIT) was put forward by Nieto, Rios, and Lopez in 2017 [51]. It followed the privacy framework laid under ISO/IEC 29100:2011 [52]. This model uses various privacy principles and allows the IoT user to be control of their sensitive information while collaborating with the investigator. This work was later combined with digital witness, an e-evidence management device, to advance IoT forensics while the user remained in control of their personal data.

7. Forensic State Acquisition from Internet of Things (FSAIoT)

The FSAIoT model was proposed by Meffert *et al.* [53]. It has a centralized Forensic State Acquisition Controller (FSAC). This model allowed the acquisition of device memory without physically accessing it and suggested that a change in device state might be of forensic importance.

8. Application-Specific Investigative Model for Internet of Things Environments

The model proposed by Zia *et al.* [54] was specific to IoT applications. It has three components: application specific forensics, digital forensics, and forensics process. The type of application under investigation determines the flow of information between these components. The data would be processed in the "Application-Specific Forensics" component and then be fed into "Digital Forensics" component. The *forensics process* generates the results which then may be used by the investigator [54].

Shin et al. focused on reactive process after the event has occurred and used digital forensic methods to collect data from IoT devices. Their approach was limited to certain devices and communication protocols [55].

10. IoTDots: A Digital Forensics Frameworks for Smart Environments

The IoTDots framework [56] was proposed by Babun *et al.* It is meant for smart environments such as mobile application which control IoT devices. It analyzes and modifies the smart applications to identify forensically relevant data generated by the apps. The framework has *modifier* and *analyzer* components. The relevant information is then transmitted to secure database by the modifier. Then, using data processing and machine learning, forensically relevant information is identified from that data.

11. Last-on-Scene (LoS) Algorithm

Harbawi and Varol [57] combined NBT approach and 1-2-3 zone approach and developed an enhanced model for acquisition of digital evidence from IoT. According to their LoS algorithm, "*the device that represents the last node in the communication chain must be the first one investigated*" [57]. The algorithm helps with limiting the scope of investigation and thereby saving valuable time and resources.

12. Top-Down Forensic Methodology

The four-level model used for investigating the IoT was proposed by Perumal *et al.* [58]. It was based on the work of Oriwoh *et al.* [44] and 1-2-3 Zones model [44]. This model covers all the stages ranging from approval of investigators to evidence archival on completion of investigation and thereby serving as a comprehensive tool. Further studies revealed that the model failed to address digital forensic preparedness plan.

13. Holistic Forensic Model for Internet of Things by Sadineni, Pilli, and Battula

The holistic forensic model for IoT [59] proposed by Sadineni, Pilli, and Battula was one of the first few investigative models to follow international standards. This model was founded on the standards laid down under ISO/IEC 27043 [50]. There are three stages in this model: proactive stage, incident stage, and reactive stage.

The *proactive stage* deals with collection and preservation of digital evidence related to IoT environment. It limits the scope of investigation and thereby saves time, money, and efforts. This phase has difference modules:

a. Readiness configuration: In this module, security experts and administrators provide instructions to identify forensically relevant events, collection, and preservation of evidence.

b. Scenario definition: It defines events that forensically sensitive to IoT applications such as unrecognized activities, failed login attempts, and login from a new device.
c. Device setup: It keeps log of all the devices being connected to or removed from an IoT environment. It also saved forensic properties of device before it starts operating.
d. Event detection: Based on scenarios defined in second module, this module identifies forensically sensitive events.
e. Evidence collection: It discusses the process of collecting potential evidence from IoT devices and environment.
f. Evidence preservation: It deals with preserving the evidence securely, for future investigations.

The *forensic initialization* or the incident phase has three modules which are as follows:

a. Incident detection: Appropriate tools and techniques are used to continuously monitor an environment for malicious behavior.
b. First response: It deals with transmission of alerts to user or investigator in case of an incident.
c. Investigation preparation: A detailed plan is prepared to help with the specifics of investigative process. Incident response team is prepared and offered technical and operational support. The details of plan are shared with the team during training stage. The entire process is documented and reviewed so that necessary modifications can be made in the plan if required.

Forensic investigation or reactive phase helps in reconstruction of events by implementing investigative plan prepared during incident phase. This is done by analyzing the potential evidence collected during readiness phase.

a. Evidence acquisition: Evidence related to reported events are acquired from storage.
b. Evidence examination and analysis: The acquired evidence and logs are formatted and made suitable for analysis.
c. Incident reconstruction: Based on the evidence recovered, the sequence of events is reconstructed.

d. Evidence preparation: Evidence is presented as per the requirements of legal system.
e. Investigation closure: It deals with post-investigation activities such as archiving the evidence and records.

14. NIST Interagency Reports and Guidance Document
Keeping in mind the vulnerabilities of IoT devices and considering the nature of data that is at stake in federal government databases, the U.S. government has taken one of the first among many steps. Recently, IoT Cybersecurity Improvement Act of 2020 [60] was introduced which directs the National Institute of Standards and Technology (NIST) to issue standards and guidelines for use of IoT devices in federal government in addition to already existing documents NIST IR 8259 [61] and NIST IR 8259A [62]. In response to that, NIST has issued four documents: three Interagency Reports (NISTIRs) 8259B [63], 8259C [64], and 8259D [65] and a guidance document titled "IoT Device Cybersecurity Guidance for the Federal Government" [66] which elaborately discuss specifications to be followed by for manufacturers supplying to federal government and process to be followed when federal government acquires these devices. The NIST Interagency Reports 8259, 8259A, 8259B, 8259C, and 8259D contain specifications of IoT device specifications for manufacturers supplying to federal government and process to be followed when federal government acquires these devices [63–67].
15. Digital Forensic Investigation Process Model (DFIPM)
The *Digital Forensic Investigation Process Model (DFIPM)* [68] was proposed by I. Mitchell *et al.* It allows the DFIs to recover IoT artefacts from the three categories: device, network, and cloud. It then tries to determine the root cause of incident based on IoT levels of relevance.
16. Holistic Digital Forensic Readiness Framework
In 2020, Kebande *et al.* [69] have proposed a Holistic Digital Forensic Readiness Framework for IoT enabled organizations. It closely aligns with the DFIF-IoT model proposed by Kebande and Ray in 2016. It is ISO/IEC 27043 [50] compliant. This model has more of a proactive approach.

14.6 Suggestive Solutions

- The IoT device manufacturers should maintain production standards [61] and should assist investigating agencies.
- A fog-based IoT forensics framework was put forward by Al-Masri *et al.* [70]. This framework could identify and

mitigate cyber-attacks on IoT devices in early stages. It was based on DFRWS investigative model. This framework is still in early stages and needs to be further explored.
- Comprehensive decision model [71] by Fernandez-Carames and Fraga-Lamas checks if any blockchain-based solution is applicable to the incident (2018).
- DFIs can employ blockchain technology for maintaining evidence integrity by time-stamping digital evidence and offering a secured storage to evidence collected from IoT devices [72–74].

14.7 Conclusion

It is evident that researchers and experts are dedicatedly working on improving methods and investigative frameworks for IoT forensics. It is crucial to address these issues as early as possible because not doing so would result in incorrectly performing a forensic process and thereby compromising the evidence. If the investigator is not able to identify digital evidence relevant to his investigation, then the criminal might go scot-free.

While researchers are working to have a standardized, structured, comprehensive and investigative framework, the investigators may follow a traditional approach and follow standardized protocols that follow international standards. Meanwhile, manufacturers may be instructed to follow product standards more strictly and improve security at device level as well.

References

1. Gartner, "Hype Cycle for Emerging Technologies, 2011,", 19, 2011. [Online]. Available: https://www.gartner.com/en/documents/1754719/hype-cycle-for-emerging-technologies-2011. [Accessed: 24-Mar-2021].
2. IoT Analytics, "State of the IoT 2020: 12 billion IoT connections, surpassing non-IoT for the first time,", 19-Nov-2020. [Online]. Available: https://iot-analytics.com/state-of-the-iot-2020-12-billion-iot-connections-surpassing-non-iot-for-the-first-time/. [Accessed: 24-Mar-2021].
3. *"Internet of Things (IoT) Market - Growth, Trends, Forecasts (2021 - 2026),"*, 2021, Mordorintelligence.com.
4. Kramp, T., Van Kranenburg, R., Lange, S., Introduction to the Internet of Things, in: *Enabling Things to Talk*, A. Bassi, (Eds.), Springer, Berlin, Heidelberg, 2013, https://doi.org/10.1007/978-3-642-40403-0_1.

5. IoT Analytics, "Why the Internet of Things is called Internet of Things: Definition, history, disambiguation.", 19-Dec-2014. [Online]. Available: https://iot-analytics.com/internet-of-things-definition/. [Accessed: 24-Mar-2021].
6. Atzori, L. *et al.*, The Internet of Things: A survey. *Comput. Netw.*, 54, 2787–2805, 2010.
7. Gubbi, J., Buyya, R., Marusic, S., Palaniswami, M., "Internet of Things (IoT): A vision, architectural elements, and future directions,". *Future Gener. Comp. Sy.*, 29, 7, 1645–1660, Sep. 2013.
8. Minerva, R., Biru, A., Rotondi, D., *"Towards a definition of the Internet of Things (IoT),"*, IEEE, Dartmouth, USA, May 2015, [Online]. Available: https://iot.ieee.org/images/files/pdf/IEEE_IoT_Towards_Definition_Internet_of_Things_Revision1_27MAY15.pdf
9. McKinsey & Company, "The Internet of Things,", 2010. [Online]. Available: https://www.mckinsey.com/industries/technology-media-and-telecommunications/our-insights/the-internet-of-things. [Accessed: 24-Mar-2021].
10. Reply, "Internet of thing IoT trends 2018: consumer IoT evolution.", 2018. Reply.com,. [Online]. Available: https://www.reply.com/en/topics/internet-of-things/the-evolution-of-the-consumer-internet-of-things. [Accessed: 24-Mar-2021].
11. DataFlair, "6 Important IoT Consumer Applications - DataFlair,", 04-Jun-2018. [Online]. Available: https://data-flair.training/blogs/iot-consumer-applications/. [Accessed: 24-Mar-2021].
12. Meola, A., Business Insider, 27-Jan-2021, [Online]. Available: https://www.businessinsider.com/internet-of-things-devices-examples?IR=T. [Accessed: 24-Mar-2021].
13. International Telecommunication Union, *Recommendation ITU-TY.2060: Overview of the Internet of Things*, International Telecommunication Union, 2012.
14. "The IoT Rundown For 2020: Stats, Risks, and Solutions – Security Today,". *Secur. Today*, 2020. [Online]. Available: https://securitytoday.com/Articles/2020/01/13/The-IoT-Rundown-for-2020.aspx?Page=1. [Accessed: 24-Mar-2021].
15. Taylor, K., *"10 Examples of Industrial Internet of Things (IIoT) in Detail,"*, HitechNectar, 24-Apr-2020, [Online]. Available: https://www.hitechnectar.com/blogs/examples-industrial-internet-of-things/. [Accessed: 24-Mar-2021].
16. Computer.org, *"IoT Meets the Military | IEEE Computer Society,"*, 2019, [Online]. Available: https://www.computer.org/publications/tech-news/research/internet-of-military-battlefield-things-iomt-iobt. [Accessed: 24-Mar-2021].
17. Gotarane, V. and Raskar, S., "IoT Practices in Military Applications,". *2019 3rd International Conference on Trends in Electronics and Informatics (ICOEI)*, Tirunelveli, India, pp. 891–894, 2019.
18. IANS, *"ECG feature on Apple Watch saves man's life in India,"*, National Herald, 20-Oct-2020, [Online]. Available: https://www.nationalheraldindia.com/national/ecg-feature-on-apple-watch-saves-mans-life-in-india. [Accessed: 24-Mar-2021].

19. "Iot Transforming the Future of Agriculture". *IOT Solutions World Congress*, Barcelona, 5-7 October 2021, 22-Apr-2019.
20. Wipro, *"IoT in Healthcare Industry | IoT Applications in Healthcare"*, 2021, Wipro.com, [Online]. Available: https://www.wipro.com/business-process/what-can-iot-do-for-healthcare-/. [Accessed: 24-Mar-2021].
21. "The World Will Store 200 Zettabytes Of Data By 2025,". *Cybercrime Magazine*, 03-Jun-2020. [Online]. Available: https://cybersecurityventures.com/the-world-will-store-200-zettabytes-of-data-by-2025/. [Accessed: 24-Mar-2021].
22. Bhagat, V., *"What are Pros and Cons of Internet of Things? Let's check out!"*, PixelCrayons, 23-Jun-2019, [Online]. Available: https://www.pixelcrayons.com/blog/what-are-pros-and-cons-of-internet-of-things/. [Accessed: 24-Mar-2021].
23. *"Internet of Things (IoT): Pros and Cons - KeyInfo,"*, KeyInfo, 30-Sep-2016, [Online]. Available: https://www.keyinfo.com/pros-and-cons-of-the-internet-of-things-iot/. [Accessed: 24-Mar-2021].
24. Stoyanova, M., Nikoloudakis, Y., Panagiotakis, S., Pallis, E., Markakis, E.K., "A Survey on the Internet of Things (IoT) Forensics: Challenges, Approaches, and Open Issues,". *IEEE Commun. Surv. Tut.*, 22, 2, 1191–1221, 2020.
25. Servida, F. and Casey, E., "IoT forensic challenges and opportunities for digital traces,". *Digit. Investig.*, 28, S22–S29, Apr. 2019.
26. Rahman, K.M.S., Bishop, M., Holt, A., "Internet of Things Mobility Forensics,". *Information Security Research and Education (INSuRE) Conference*, 2016.
27. Hegarty, R., Lamb, D., Attwood, A., *"Digital evidence challenges in the Internet of Things,"*, usir.salford.ac.uk, 01-Jul-2014, [Online]. Available: http://usir.salford.ac.uk/id/eprint/56335/. [Accessed: 15-Mar-2021].
28. Rapyder Cloud Solutions, *"Rapyder Cloud Solutions - AWS Partner Full Stack Cloud Services,"*, 02-May-2019, [Online]. Available: https://www.rapyder.com/blogs/top-10-iot-security-solutions-for-common-iot-security-issues/. [Accessed: 24-Mar-2021].
29. Crinon, G., *"IoT Security: Real Problems and Solutions,"*, Avnet.com, 08-Mar-2017, [Online]. Available: https://www.avnet.com/wps/portal/us/resources/article/iot-security-real-problems-and-solutions/. [Accessed: 24-Mar-2021].
30. Wu, T., Breitinger, F., Baggili, I., "IoT Ignorance is Digital Forensics Research Bliss,". *Proceedings of the 14th International Conference on Availability, Reliability and Security - ARES '19*, 2019, [Online]. Available: https://dl.acm.org/citation.cfm?id=3340504. [Accessed: 27-Sep-2019].
31. Atlam, H.F., Wills, G.B., Alenezi, A., Alassafi, M.O., "Blockchain with Internet of Things: Benefits, challenges, and future directions,". *Int. J. Intell. Syst. Appl.*, 10, 6, 40–48, 2018.
32. Tian, Z., Li, M., Qiu, M., Sun, Y., Su, S., "Block-DEF: A secure digital evidence framework using blockchain,". *Inf. Sci.*, 491, 151–165, Jul. 2019.
33. Singh, S., Ra, I.H., Meng, W., Kaur, M., Cho, G.H., "SH-BlockCC: A secure and efficient Internet of Things smart home architecture based on cloud computing and blockchain technology,". *Int. J. Distrib. Sens. Netw.*, 15, 4, 1–18, 2019.

34. Banerjee, M., Lee, J., Choo, K.-K.R., "A blockchain future for Internet-of-Things security: A position paper,". *Digit. Commun. Netw.*, 4, 3, 149–160, 2017.
35. Cebe, M., Erdin, E., Akkaya, K., Aksu, H., Uluagac, S., "Block4Forensic: An integrated lightweight blockchain framework for forensics applications of connected vehicles,". *IEEE Commun. Mag.*, 56, 10, 50–57, Oct. 2018.
36. James, J., II and Jang, Y., Practical and legal challenges of cloud investigations. *J. Inst. Internet, Broadcast. Commun.*, 14 6, 33-39, 2015. https://doi.org/10.7236/JIIBC.2014.14.6.33.
37. Chernyshev, M., Zeadally, S., Baig, Z., Woodward, A., "Internet of Things Forensics: The Need, Process Models, and Open Issues,". *IT Prof.*, 20, 3, 40–49, May./Jun. 2018.
38. EC-Council, *"What is Digital Forensics | Phases of Digital Forensics | EC-Council,"*, 2021, [Online]. Available: https://www.eccouncil.org/what-is-digital-forensics/. [Accessed: 24-Mar-2021].
39. Content Editor, C.S.R.C., *"Digital forensics - Glossary | CSRC,"*, Nist.gov, 2015, [Online]. Available: https://csrc.nist.gov/glossary/term/digital_forensics. [Accessed: 24-Mar-2021].
40. Casey, E. and Dunne, R., *Digital evidence and computer crime: forensic science, computers and the Internet*, Elsevier Academic Press, Amsterdam; Boston, 2004.
41. McKemmish, R., *What is forensic computing? Trends & issues in crime and criminal justice no. 118*, Australian Institute of Criminology, Canberra, 1999, https://www.aic.gov.au/publications/tandi/tandi118.
42. Kent, K., Chevalier, S., Grance, T., Dang, H., *"Special Publication 800-86 Guide to Integrating Forensic Techniques into Incident Response Recommendations of the National Institute of Standards and Technology,"*, NIST, Gaithersburg, MD, Aug. 2006, [Online]. Available: https://nvlpubs.nist.gov/nistpubs/Legacy/SP/nistspecialpublication800-86.pdf.
43. Cognixia, *"IoT in digital forensics "*, 22-Jan-2020, [Online]. Available: https://www.cognixia.com/blog/how-can-iot-help-digital-forensics. [Accessed: 24-Mar-2021].
44. Oriwoh, E. *et al.*, "Internet of Things Forensics: Challenges and Approaches,". *9th IEEE Int'l Conf. Collaborative Computing: Networking, Applications and Worksharing (Collaboratecom)*, pp. 608–615, 2013.
45. Nationalbimstandard.org, *"Frequently Asked Questions About the National BIM Standard-United StatesTM"*, National BIM Standard - United States, 2021, [Online]. Available: https://www.nationalbimstandard.org/faqsfaq1. [Accessed: 24-Mar-2021].
46. Oriwoh, E. and Sant, P., "The Forensics Edge Management System: A Concept and Design,". *2013 IEEE 10th International Conference on Ubiquitous Intelligence and Computing and 2013 IEEE 10th International Conference on Autonomic and Trusted Computing*, Vietri sul Mare, Italy, pp. 544–550, 2013.

47. Zawoad, S. and Hasan, R., FAIoT: Towards building a forensics aware ecosystem for the Internet of Things. *Proceedings of the IEEE International Conference on Services Computing*, pp. 279–284, 2015.
48. Kebande, V.R. and Ray, I., A generic digital forensic investigation framework for internet of things (iot), in: *2016 IEEE 4th International Conference on Future Internet of Things and Cloud (FiCloud)*, IEEE, pp. 356–362, 2016.
49. Kebande, V.R. and Venter, H.S., Novel digital forensic readiness technique in the cloud environment, in: *Australian Journal of Forensic Sciences*, vol. 50, p. 552, 2018.
50. ISO/IEC 27043:2015, *Information Technology - Security Techniques – Incident Investigation Principles and Processes*, International Organization for Standardization, Geneva, Switzerland, 2015.
51. "IoT-Forensics Meets Privacy: Towards Cooperative Digital Investigations,". *Sensors*, 18, 2, 492, Feb. 2018.
52. *ISO. Information Technology—Security Techniques—Privacy Framework; ISO/IEC 29100:2011 Standard*, International Organization for Standardization (ISO, Geneva, Switzerland, 2011.
53. Meffert, C., Clark, D., Baggili, I., Breitinger, F., Forensic state acquisition from Internet of Things (FSAIoT): A general framework and practical approach for IoT forensics through IoT device state acquisition. *Proceedings of the Twelfth International Conference on Availability, Reliability and Security*, article no. 65, 2017.
54. Zia, T., Liu, P., Han, W., Application-specific digital forensics investigative model in Internet of Things (IoT). *Proceedings of the Twelfth International Conference on Availability, Reliability and Security*, article no. 55, 2017.
55. Shin, C., Chandok, P., Liu, R., Nielson, S.J., Leschke, T.R., "Potential Forensic Analysis of IoT Data: An Overview of the State-of-the-Art and Future Possibilities,". *2017 IEEE International Conference on Internet of Things (iThings) and IEEE Green Computing and Communications (GreenCom) and IEEE Cyber, Physical and Social Computing (CPSCom) and IEEE Smart Data (SmartData)*, Exeter, UK, pp. 705–710, 2017.
56. Babun, L., Sikder, A.K., Acar, A., Uluagac, A.S., *'A digital forensics framework for smart settings'*, pp. 332–333, 2019.
57. Harbawi, M. and Varol, A., An improved digital evidence acquisition model for Internet of Things forensics I: A theoretical framework. *Proceedings of the Fifth International Symposium on Digital Forensics and Security*, 2017.
58. Perumal, S., Norwawi, N., Raman, V., Internet of Things (IoT) digital forensic investigation model: Top-down forensic approach methodology. *Proceedings of the Fifth International Conference on Digital Information Processing and Communications*, pp. 19–23, 2015.
59. Sadineni, L., Pilli, E., Battula, R.B., "A Holistic Forensic Model for the Internet of Things,". *Advances in Digital Forensics XV*, pp. 3–18, 2019, https://link.springer.com/chapter/10.1007/978-3-030-28752-8_1.

60. Congress.gov., *"H.R.1668 - 116th Congress (2019-2020): IoT Cybersecurity Improvement Act of 2020,"*, 2019, [Online]. Available: https://www.congress.gov/bill/116th-congress/house-bill/1668/text. [Accessed: 15-Mar-2021.
61. Fagan, M., Megas, K.N., Scarfone, K., Smith, M., *"Foundational cybersecurity activities for IoT device manufacturers,"*, NIST, Gaithersburg, MD, May 2020, https://nvlpubs.nist.gov/nistpubs/ir/2020/NIST.IR.8259.pdf.
62. Fagan, M., Megas, K.N., Scarfone, K., Smith, M., *"IoT device cybersecurity capability core baseline,"*, May 2020, https://nvlpubs.nist.gov/nistpubs/ir/2020/NIST.IR.8259A.pdf.
63. Fagan, M., *"Profile of the IoT Core Baseline for the Federal Government,"*, NIST, Gaithersburg, MD, Oct. 2020.
64. Fagan, M., Marron, J., Brady, K., Cuthill, B., Megas, K., Herold, R., *"Draft NISTIR 8259C Creating a Profile Using the IoT Core Baseline and Non-Technical Baseline 4 5,"*, NIST, Gaithersburg, MD, 2019, https://nvlpubs.nist.gov/nistpubs/ir/2020/NIST.IR.8259c-draft.pdf. [Accessed: 15-Mar-2021].
65. *"Foundational Cybersecurity Activities for IoT Device Manufacturers D,"*, NIST, Gaithersburg, MD, Dec. 2020.
66. Fagan, M., *"IoT Device Cybersecurity Guidance for the Federal Government"*, NIST, Gaithersburg, MD, Oct. 2020.
67. *"7 Critical GitHub Security Controls,"*, Security Boulevard, 16-Oct-2020, https://securityboulevard.com/2020/10/the-good-and-not-so-good-of-the-iot-cybersecurity-improvement-act-of-2020/. [Accessed: 24-Mar-2021].
68. Mitchell, I., Hara, S., Jimenez, J., II, Jahankhani, H., Montasari, R., "IoT and Cloud Forensic Investigation Guidelines,", in: *Policing in the Era of AI and Smart Societies*, H. Jahankhani, B. Akhgar, P. Cochrane, M. Dastbaz, (Eds.), pp. 119–138, Springer, Switzerland AG, 2020.
69. Kebande, V.R., Mudau, P.P., Ikuesan, R.A., Venter, H.S., Choo, K.-K.R., "Holistic digital forensic readiness framework for IoT-enabled organizations,". *Forensic Sci. Int. Rep.*, 2, 100117, Dec. 2020.
70. Al-Masri, E., Bai, Y., Li, J., A fog-based digital forensics investigation framework for IoT systems. *Proceedings of the Third IEEE International Conference on Smart Cloud*, pp. 196–201, 2018.
71. Fernandez-Carames, T. and Fraga-Lamas, P., A review of the use of blockchain for the Internet of Things. *IEEE Access*, 6, 32979–33001, 2018.
72. Banerjee, M., Lee, J., Choo, K., A blockchain future for Internet of Things security: A position paper. *Digit. Commun. Netw.*, 4, 3, 149–160, 2018.
73. Jesus, E.F., Chicarino, V.R.L., de Albuquerque, C.V.N., de A. Rocha, A.A., "A Survey of How to Use Blockchain to Secure Internet of Things and the Stalker Attack,". *Secur. Commun. Netw.*, 2018, 1–27, Apr. 2018.
74. Ali, M.S., Vecchio, M., Pincheira, M., Dolui, K., Antonelli, F., Rehmani, M.H., "Applications of Blockchains in the Internet of Things: A Comprehensive Survey,". *IEEE Commun. Surv. Tut.*, 21, 2, 1676–1717, 2019.

15

IoT Forensics: A Pernicious Repercussions

Gift Chimkonda Chichele

Lovely Professional University, Jalandhar - Delhi, Phagwara, Punjab, India

Abstract

The rapid increase of Internet of Thing (IoT) devices across the globe has added countless benefits in several aspects like health, sports, homes, market, and cities. Heterogeneous devices can be located and recognized using inexpensive sensors which collect big data on the environment they are in and share it across the internet via wired or wireless connections. Cybercriminals have taken advantage of this development as they are aware of the security breaches on IoT devices and cloud servers and the complications of investigation as well. They are aware of the huge amount of raw data that IoT devices generate in an IoT environment and how difficult it makes the investigators job. The IoT technology has even increased a burden in the digital forensics field as the investigator's find more challenges in performing data acquisition from these devices. This chapter will present the challenges in IoT forensics and suggests the solutions in dealing with those challenges.

***Keywords*:** Internet of Things (IoT), Heterogeneous devices, sensors, cybercriminals, digital forensics

15.1 Introduction: Challenges in IoT Forensics

The rising prevalence of IoT devices in our communities seemingly brought relief to forensic investigators as it meant an increased opportunity for sources of digital evidence. As reported by Stoyanova *et al.* [1], the IoT environment contains a rich set of artefacts that could benefit investigations. However, instead of being helpful to investigators, they have posed so many forensic challenges, and some of which have been discussed below.

Email: gift.11919465@lpu.in

Anita Gehlot, Rajesh Singh, Jaskaran Singh and Neeta Raj Sharma (eds.) Digital Forensics and Internet of Things: Impact and Challenges, (255–262) © 2022 Scrivener Publishing LLC

15.2 Scope of the Compromise and Crime Scene Reconstruction

In conventional forensics, investigators can identify the scene of a crime, gather physical evidence, and probably have a list of suspects. Similarly, in digital forensics, the investigators can gather physical evidence in form of digital devices or analysis reports. In most cases, they have some way to physically link the attacker to the digital scene of crime [1]. But with Internet of Things (IoT) devices, it is quite difficult to reconstruct the scene of crime as well as identifying the scope of damage due to ever increasing changing nature of data transfer as the devices are wirelessly connected to various nodes and information is always in real time which moves very fast from one node to another. In some instances, advanced cyber criminals use virtual machines to perform their malicious activities. These machines keep information so long as the machine power is turned on. Once the virtual machine is switched off, all information that is forensically important like registries is gone and can hardly be traced and retrieved. So, IoT devices pose a great challenge to crime scene reconstruction [2].

15.3 Device and Data Proliferation

The IoT devices are increasing day by day, resulting in an increase in data transferred over the network. The International Data Corporation (IDC) predicted that, by 2020, data transmitted on the network was expected to reach an estimate of 40,000 Exabyte [2]. As per the updated estimates done by Cybersecurity Ventures, there will be approximately 200 zettabytes of data on the internet by 2025 [3]. With this tremendous increase of data, there is a need to develop new forensic tools that can be able to analyze such big data with the capability to discard irrelevant data and concentrate only on relevant data in order to save time.

15.4 Multiple Data Location and Jurisdiction Challenges

Some IoT devices can easily be moved from one physical location to the other, causing data to be stored across different locations which can be out of the user's control. For instance, fitness trackers, smartwatches, or larger movable objects, such as cars, bikes, and drones, move between different wide area networks (WANs). Due to this, data is not stored in one dedicated host. Consequently, it is spread across different cloud resources, third party locations, attached storage units, online social networks, etc. [4]. This multiple storage of data gives digital forensic professionals tough time to locate the exact place storing relevant data for investigations. They may even fail to identify the physical device which is alleged to be a source of evidence that is being looked for to help to reconstruct the scene of a crime. Sometimes, when the location of evidence is known, it even becomes so hard to acquire the system as it would affect the customers from accessing its services.

In some instances, the data location might be subjected to more than one jurisdiction which might have different regulations on data protection policies that may also be contradictory in nature. In such instances, investigations might be hampered by the opposing legislation in the location the resource is located [1].

15.5 Device Type

IoT devices come in different sizes and shapes and have various degrees of battery life.

If very small IoT devices have been involved in criminal activities, then forensic professionals may find it harder to locate them. If those with short battery life have been involved in cybercriminal activities, then they can hardly be detected once they run out of power. Some have their shapes designed in a way that is so difficult to distinguish from the traditional appliances like dishwashers, refrigerators, baby monitors, and pressing irons. Forensic professionals find it difficult to locate or identify such devices when they are used or involved in criminal activities [5].

15.6 Lack of Training and Weak Knowledge Management

As data in IoT devices is periodically synced to secondary storage usually cloud servers, most first responders cannot do much for the investigation because neither they are trained to deal with such scenarios nor they have the expertise. This makes data acquisition in IoT devices unsuccessful. In some cases, the data relevant to investigations is lost because evidence acquisition from devices was delayed [6].

15.7 Data Encryption

As data in IoT devices travel from node to node over the cloud servers, it is highly protected with encryption keys to ensure there are no data breaches in between. The encryption algorithm allows the user to encode the data before being transmitted to the cloud and decode it before it gets back to the system [1]. Most IoT devices users are capable of using these cryptographic tools, and this has made the number of encrypted files in cloud computing increased. During the investigations, the vendor is required to obtain a decryption key from the user for him to be able to process that data needed by the investigating officers or forensic professionals. This puts the vendors in an uncomfortable position as they try to find a balance between the lawmakers and the privacy of their customers.

15.8 Heterogeneous Software and/or Hardware Specifications

Manufactures of IoT devices on the market are enormous and each manufacturer adopts different hardware and software systems which may also have different communication protocols like ZigBee, Wi-Fi, and Bluetooth. This has flooded the market with devices that have different hardware specifications running on different system wares. To successfully handle an IoT crime, an investigating officer should have a great amount of knowledge related to various IoT systems and hardware standards [7].

15.9 Privacy and Ethical Considerations by Accessing Personal Data

Privacy is another area that ought to be taken into account when extracting data from IoT devices. Some IoT devices like fitness tracker or remote health monitoring systems do possess very sensitive personal data such as users' medical records, prescription, or current health status. Cloud service providers cannot share user data with law enforcement agencies without proper permissions and court orders because doing so would be a violation of user privacy. It might also be difficult to do data imaging without violating ethical considerations since it is difficult to weed out personal data irrelevant to investigation [7].

15.10 Lack of a Common Forensic Model in IoT Devices

Data extraction in IoT devices has no specific standard procedure that is generally accepted. Every investigating body uses its own model depending on the nature of crime and location of evidence. Such methodologies can be challenged in court due to some areas that might not have been followed during data acquisition. In cross border crimes, problems might arise to bring together the standard operating procedure if no part has one. As a result, data extraction in such cases may face hassles and hurdles [8].

15.11 Securing the Chain of Custody

In IoT forensics, it is expected that evidentiary data may be extracted from more than one cloud servers due to their fast transmission of data as it moves from one node to another as well as having different manufacturers and service providers. This situation brings about difficulties in maintaining a proper chain of custody. Furthermore, the format of data that is collected in the IoT devices might not be the same as that from remote cloud server. As a result, investigating officers find it difficult to have a well-documented chain of custody [9].

15.12 Lifespan Limitation

Most IoT devices have limited memory space. As a result, data is easily overwritten in those small memories because IoT devices run continuously. This might result in the possibility of missing the data that can be of evidential value. Other IoT devices do not store data because they use a real-time operating system, thus posing forensic challenges when an illegal activity has occurred [9].

15.13 The Cloud Forensic Problem

Cloud services have got many security standards as it comprises of different technologies such as networks, virtualization, database, operating system, resource scheduling, and transaction management [10]. Each of these technologies has got some vulnerabilities offering malicious users a wide range of possibilities to enter into the system and manipulate the data stored in the remote server. This therefore renders the data less valuable forensically.

15.14 The Minimum or Maximum Period in Which Data is Stored in the Cloud

The length of period to store data in the cloud is mostly determined by service providers. However, some countries put across policies of a period for cloud service providers to keep data. For instance, in European Union countries, the period in which data can be stored varies from half a year to almost 10 years depending on the significance of data. While in United States of America, the period is determined by individuals. However, some countries have no legal provisions of period in which data can be stored. Such scenarios create more room for criminals and forensic investigation is quite hard as data may have been deleted more often [1].

15.15 Evidence Analysis and Correlation

A good number of IoT nodes do not store any metadata and temporal files. The absences of these create correlation problems especially when evidentiary data has been corrected from the different nodes [11].

15.16 Conclusion

Different studies have proposed solutions to mitigate challenges faced by a digital forensic expert when dealing with evidential data from IoT devices and their associated infrastructure. Some of these are listed as follows:

1. Toward standardization and certification in IoT forensics
   Digital forensics in IoT devices involves a number of devices with heterogeneous formats and manufacturers. Establishing a forensic standard in such ever-increasing technologies with huge and different groups of stakeholders cannot be a simple task. Different standard bodies and security laboratories have been there to provide infrastructure for forensic science by addressing quality issues.

Since 1998 till date, several digital forensics investigations standards have been developed and implemented in Europe and worldwide. Some notable standards include the following:

ISO/IEC TR 20547-2 Information technology – Big data reference architecture; Part 2: Use cases and derived requirements [12].

ISO 22320 – Security and resilience – Emergency management – Guidelines for incident management [1].

A good number of these standards were developed for traditional forensics. But with the prolific use of IoT devices nowadays, these standards do not suffice. Thus, there is a need for a revised and standardized methodology for evidence acquisition in IoT devices.

2. Data processing via high-performance computing

   IoT devices have increased the data stored in cloud servers. As such, there is a need to have high performing forensic work stations to be at pace with the increased data needed for analysis. This would reduce processing time and produce efficient results.

3. Need for IoT devices forensics tools

   Digital forensic experts are currently using the traditional toolkits in data acquisition when a crime is reported. They spend a lot of time completing the task due to the huge volume of data they work with within IoT devices. Mostly, their acquisition does not yield successful results as the tools used do not match the complexity of the devices as well as the volume of the data to be analysed. In order to sort out this problem, there is a need to develop digital forensic tools specifically for IoT devices that can also have the capacity to analyze big data stored in cloud servers.

4. The need to build a dedicated central server for tracking the location of IoT device

   The issue of data location can simply be overcome by building a centralized server of IoT devices that may contain information related to an IoT based cybercrime. This server must be programmed in a way that could allow an automatic update whenever there is a change of the IoT topology. Additionally, countries should make agreements to build a chain of location-based servers that can be distributed over different countries.

References

1. Stoyanova, M., Nikoloudakis, Y., Panagiotakis, S., Pallis, E., Markakis, E.K., A Survey on the Internet of Things (IoT) Forensics: Challenges, Approaches and Open Issues. *IEEE Commun. Surv. Tut.*, 1–1, 2020.
2. Yakubu, O., Adjei, O., Babu, N., A review of prospects and challenges of Internet of Things. *Int. J. Comput. Appl.*, 139, 10, 33–39, 2016.
3. "The World Will Store 200 Zettabytes of Data By 2025". *Cybercrime Magazine*, 03-Jun-2020. [Online]. Available: https://cybersecurityventures.com/the-world-will-store-200-zettabytes-of-data-by-2025/. [Accessed: 24-Mar-2021].
4. Montasari, R., Jahankhani, H., Hill, R., Parkinson, S. (Eds.), *Digital Forensic Investigation of Internet of Things (IoT) Devices*, Springer International Publishing, Cham, 2021.
5. Hameed, S., Khan, F., II, Hameed, B., "Understanding Security Requirements and Challenges in Internet of Things (IoT): A Review". *J. Comput. Netw. Commun.*, 2019, 1–14, Jan. 2019.
6. Hou, J., Li, Y., Yu, J., Shi, W., "A Survey on Digital Forensics in Internet of Things". *IEEE Internet Things J.*, 1–1, 2019. doi: 10.1109/jiot.2019.2940713.
7. Tawalbeh, L., Muheidat, F., Tawalbeh, M., Quwaider, M., "IoT Privacy and Security: Challenges and Solutions". *Appl. Sci.*, 10, 12, 4102, Jun. 2020.
8. Tavana, M., Hajipour, V., Oveisi, S., "IoT-based Enterprise Resource Planning: Challenges, Open Issues, Applications, Architecture, and Future Research Directions". *Internet Things*, 11, 100262, Jul. 2020.
9. Hossain, Md. M., Fotouhi, M., Hasan, R., "Towards an Analysis of Security Issues, Challenges, and Open Problems in the Internet of Things". *2015 IEEE World Congress on Services*, Jun. 2015.
10. Ahmed, R. and Ali, M.L., "Minimization of security issues in cloud computing". *J. Inf. Commun. Technol. Robot. Appl.*, 3, 1, 1–39, 2017.
11. Yaqoob, I., Hashem, I.A.T., Ahmed, A., Kazmi, S.M.A., Hong, C.S., "Internet of things forensics: Recent advances, taxonomy, requirements, and open challenges". *Future Gener. Comp. Sy.*, 92, 265–275, Mar. 2019.
12. Krivchenkov, A., Misnevs, B., Pavlyuk, D., *Intelligent Methods in Digital Forensics: State of the Art*, vol. 1, Springer Int., Cham, Switzerland, 2019.

About the Editors

Prof.(Dr.) Anita Gehlot is currently associated with Uttaranchal University as Professor & Head (R&I) with more than Fourteen years of experience in academics. She has been featured among top ten inventors for ten years 2010-2020, by Clarivate Analytics in "India's Innovation Synopsis" in March 2021 for filing two hundred and sixty three patents. She has forty four patents grant (39 Australian and 5 Indian patents), 5 PCT and published more than hundered research papers in SCI/Scopus journals.

She has published thirty five books in the area of Embedded Systems and Internet of Things with reputed international publishers. She has been awarded with "Gandhian Young Technological Innovation (GYTI) Award", as Mentor to "On Board Diagnostic Data Analysis System-OBDAS", Appreciated under "Cutting Edge Innovation" during Festival of Innovation and Entrepreneurship at Rashtrapati Bahawan, India in 2018. She has been honored with "Certificate of Excellence" from 3rd faculty branding awards-15, Organized by EET CRS research wing for excellence in professional education and Industry, for the category "Young Researcher", 2015.

Prof.(Dr.) Dr. Rajesh Singh, is currently associated with Uttaranchal University as Professor & Director (R&I) with more than seventeen years of experience in academics. He has been featured among top ten inventors for ten years 2010-2020, by Clarivate Analytics in "India's Innovation Synopsis" in March 2021 for filing Three hundred and fifty eight patents. He has forty four patents grant (39 Australian and 4 Indian patents), 5 PCT and published more than hundred research papers in SCI/Scopus journals.

He has published thirty six books in the area of Embedded Systems and Internet of Things with reputed international publishers.

He has been awarded with "Gandhian Young Technological Innovation (GYTI) Award", as Mentor to "On Board Diagnostic Data Analysis System-OBDAS", Appreciated under "Cutting Edge Innovation" during Festival of Innovation and Entrepreneurship at Rashtrapati Bahawan, India in 2018. He has been honored with "Certificate of Excellence" from 3rd faculty branding awards-15, Organized by EET CRS research wing for excellence in professional education and Industry, for the category "Award for Excellence in Research", 2015 and young investigator award at the International Conference on Science and Information in 2012.

Dr. Jaskaran Singh (Gold Medalist), Ph.D. in Forensic Sciences from Amity University Noida, serves as faculty in Sharda University, India. He has more than 14 research publications, 13 patents, 3 copyrights and one edited book to his credit. He has collaborated with multidisciplinary and transdisciplinary experts of other branches of sciences and engineering in the Forensic field, both nationally and internationally. Dr. Singh also serves as guest trainer for international and national police officers. He is an executive member of Indo-Pacific Academy of Forensic Odontology, and has been a guest speaker for various conference across the globe. He has been conferred with various prestigious awards and fellowships notably, INSPIRE fellowship (DST), Ministry of Science and Technology, Govt. of India, CSIR travel grants for International conferences, Shri. Baljit Shastri award for Best in Human Values and Ethics. He has served as referee for a number of International and National journals.

Dr. Neeta Raj Sharma, Ph.D. in Biochemistry from Jiwaji University Gwalior, leading the School of Bioengineering and Biosciences as Additional Dean in Lovely Professional University, Phagwara, Punjab. She is visiting professor of Birmingham City University, UK and working in association of University of British Columbia, McGill University; Laval University and University of Victoria in Canada. Her versatile multidisciplinary experience includes applied bio-chemistry and biotechnology to develop diagnostic tools and exploration of bioanalytical instrumentation in diagnosis in forensic science and other applied areas. Dr. Sharma is the fellow member of Association of Biotechnology and Pharmacy and also having membership of societies such as Indian Science Congress, Association of Indian Science Congress (Elected Member for North Region ISC106; Association of Microbiologists of India, Indo-US Collaboration of Engineering Education 2013, Fellow Member International Science Congress Association, Life membership of association for promotion of DNA Finger Printing and other DNA Technologies. She has published above 55 publications, 20 patents, 04 copyrights, 2 edited books, articles in reputed magazines.

Index

Printed and bound by CPI Group (UK) Ltd, Croydon, CR0 4YY

27/10/2024

14580469-0002